FROM PRISON TO PARLIAMENT

BY

FRANK HOWARD

Printed in Victoria, Canada.

FIRST EDITION

National Library of Canada Cataloguing in Publication Data

Howard, Frank, 1925-
      From prison to Parliament / Frank Howard.
Includes index.
ISBN 1-55369-045-1
      1. Howard, Frank, 1925-. 2. Canada. Parliament.
House of Commons—Biography. 3. Legislators—British
Columbia—Biography. 4. Politicians—British Columbia—
Biography. 5. Orphans—British Columbia—Biography. I.
Title.
FC3828.1.H69A3 2003   971.1'104'092   C2001-903623-X
F1089.S5H69 2003

TRAFFORD

This book was published *on-demand* in cooperation with Trafford Publishing.
On-demand publishing is a unique process and service of making a book available for retail sale to the public taking advantage of on-demand manufacturing and Internet marketing.
On-demand publishing includes promotions, retail sales, manufacturing, order fulfilment, accounting and collecting royalties on behalf of the author.

Suite 6E, 2333 Government St., Victoria, B.C. V8T 4P4, CANADA
Phone   250-383-6864   Toll-free   1-888-232-4444 (Canada & US)
Fax   250-383-6804   E-mail   sales@trafford.com
Web site   www.trafford.com   TRAFFORD PUBLISHING IS A DIVISION OF TRAFFORD HOLDINGS LTD.
Trafford Catalogue #01-0447   www.trafford.com/robots/01-0447.html

10   9   8   7   6   5

Dedicated to Anthony and Danielle,
two adorable step-children;
and to the loving memory of their Mother.

The Moving Finger writes; and, having writ,
Moves on: nor all your Piety nor Wit
Shall lure it back to cancel half a Line,
Nor all your Tears wash out a Word of it.

Rubaiyat of OMAR KHAYYAM
Fifth edition
Rendered into English
by
Edward Fitzgerald

ACKNOWLEDGMENTS

Alma Said-Peters is a long-time friend who thoughtfully reviewed a couple of chapters covering events with which she was familiar. Her opinions and information were most helpful. I thank her also for visiting the National Archives in Ottawa on my behalf and for locating material which I have incorporated.

Bill Knight was the M.P. for the Saskatchewan Riding of Assiniboia and gave me his thoughts and opinions about matters in which he and I were involved. He refreshed my memory and confirmed some of the information in this account.

My thanks go to the employees at the National Archives in Ottawa and at the Provincial Archives in Victoria for their help in allowing me to examine their historical records.

Employees of the Library of Parliament in Ottawa generously gave me access to House of Commons and Senate of Canada documents.

Ms. Joan Barton, Director of the Legislative Library in Victoria, and Library employees were also helpful in providing that extra assistance which allowed me more readily to locate and examine material in their possession.

My thanks also to employees in the Langley office of Elections B.C. who set aside for me statistics relating to provincial elections.

My appreciation to Ms. Kate Braid who took the time to read a portion of the manuscript (all that was available) and give me invaluable advice about structure, organization, and composition.

Bill Piket, a High-School English teacher, assiduously examined the manuscript and suggested worthwhile changes in grammar and punctuation. To Bill I extend my thanks.

I thank Barbara Cruikshank for her sound and sage advice.

My final and unstinting gratitude is offered to J.J. McColl, a playwright, broadcaster, and songwriter. J.J. edited and teased the manuscript into greater coherency. Her suggestions confounded me at times, but, in the words of Stephen King, "The editor is always right."

Contents

FOREWORD
by
THE RT. HON. JOHN N. TURNER, P.C., C.C., Q.C.
FORMER PRIME MINISTER OF CANADA

Even though Frank Howard and I sat in Canada's House of Commons at the same time, I knew very little about his background; his upbringing; his early-day influences. That was not unusual because M.P.s were much more concerned about the events of the day than they were about personal historical matters.

In his autobiography Howard relates to us details of his life which must have produced, as he was setting them down, some emotional trauma for him. He tells us of his loneliness, his fears, and of his anguish at having a chaotic and unstable pre-pubescent and teen-age existence. He tells us of his psychological instability. I believe he reveals more about himself than most other people would about themselves.

My thoughts are not so much opinions about Frank Howard per se. They are not about politics nor partisanship. They are simply an acknowledgment that a person can increase the possibility of self-improvement by taking responsibility for the actions and behavioural patterns in one's life.

There are a lot of kids today who live on the street. They come from broken homes and from homes where family abuse, in one form or another, has occurred. The message which Howard gives us, and gives those kids, is that they can turn their backs on the past. They can live a better life. The can improve their lot. It may take a great deal of effort, but it can be done.

I had the greatest respect for Frank Howard when we were both Members of Parliament. And I liked the guy.

Now that I know more about him, my admiration for him has doubled.

INTRODUCTION

Autobiographies are notoriously self-serving. Written in the first person, by the first person, and about the first person they tend to become glossy accounts of one's life; a portrait which so easily can obscure or ignore objectivity. In the back of the author's mind there is usually the hope that the reader will conclude: well, the writer wasn't such a bad guy after all.

These memoirs developed in response to the curiosity of my two step-children, Danielle and Anthony Peacock. Their mother and I met in 1969 and subsequently married. Danielle and Anthony were then in their early teens and naturally wondered about this stranger who had entered their lives. On different occasions we talked about where I was born, how far I went in school, who my parents were and so on. I guess my life was intriguing to them for they wanted to know more and have it set down in writing, preferably in chronological order.

I wasn't interested in merely reciting facts and events; self-examination and self-communion had to take hold. Why had I behaved in a particular way? Was the influence genetic? Was it environmental? Was it a mix of both? Was it something else? My life, up to the time I was about twenty, was chaotic. I was filled with anger; emotionally disturbed. A couple of times I considered taking the easy way out by short circuiting the flow of nature's juices; by blowing the fuses.

During the writing of this book I was able to examine my behaviour using the hindsight which comes with age, but which so often eludes us. I will probably never know "who I am." Who does? Life is a mystery so why shouldn't we be a mystery to ourselves?

Trying to answer the questions about self brought more of an understanding about myself than I had ever had before. That's a benefit worth all the tears and anguish of introspection.

I struggled with the question: Is our behaviour the result of genetic or environmental influences? I have to conclude that opting for either is an excuse, a cop-out. I'm stuck with my own character. It's my own fate. It's what determined my behaviour. It's easy to blame others, to pile the responsibility on them. For me to blame myself was difficult. Perhaps that difficulty helps to prove the contention that, when faced with choices involving moral obligations, choosing the most difficult one is the correct one.

I've tried to capture that very elusive creature called truth, but I was only able to come to an understanding of some aspects of myself. One which I accept without condition is: I have never met anyone who has caused me more difficulty and trouble than I have. I never will.

This late-found understanding of me is more valuable than my rattling around in my head looking for truth. I recognize understanding, but truth is an arguable matter. I may not be able to change my character, but understanding it, and thereby accepting it, helped me to change my behaviour.

In this account I've tried to keep in mind that I've done some stupid things, some bad things, some good things. I hope I have provided a journal which is more revealing and admitting than concealing and denying.

I have isolated recollections of childhood, snap-shots with the supporting memory not always fully reliable. Conversations in which I was involved are necessarily based on remembrances and have been constructed. Those conversations, though, reflect the sense of what was said.

Am I proud of my life? Not fully. I'm ashamed of having committed illegal acts in my youth. On the other hand, I'm proud of having been able to move from breaking laws to making them. If this chronicle can lead others to take a miserable life style and change it into one more honourable and respectful, it will have served a good purpose. I will be pleased with that.

1

AN OVEREXPOSED FILM

I was six when Mom told me it was O.K. to lie if money was involved. She didn't put it that bluntly, but I got the message. She didn't intend to injure me emotionally or to influence me to be a bad kid; it was just her way. It was easy for me to accept her comments and extend them.

Dad, a blacksmith, also without design, left me with the idea that it was acceptable to steal things. He worked for the Consolidated Mining and Smelting Company (C.M.&S.)—now Cominco. In his lunch bucket he would often bring home toilet paper, soap, a hand cleaner called Snap, nails, screws, nuts and bolts and the like. Stuffed into the legs of his pants would sometimes be pieces of twisted iron which he'd made at work. He would bolt these pieces of iron together, for gates, fences, and grave-side ornaments—custom-made for sale to certain friends. At times he would barter for a bottle of rum or whisky.

Opening his lunch bucket and pulling out a sheaf of toilet paper he'd say something like: "Now, we can wipe our asses on the C.M.&S," or, "They bloody well can afford it. Stealing from them buggers is hunky-dory. They steal from everyone else." He didn't rob banks or embezzle money. He only stole little things from his employer. But, so did many other people who worked for the mining company in Kimberley, B.C., the town where I was born.

Those whom I called Mom and Dad were foster parents. Their

family name was Woodd. They came to Canada from England some-time after World War 1. I lived with them from about the age of six months (so said Mom) to the time I was twelve years old. They were parents in all but blood-line, and I still think of them that way.

They didn't hide from me the fact that I was not their child. They told me the names of my putative parents and what kind of people they were. He was Rollie (Rowlat). She was Dot (Dorothy). His family name was Steeves. Mom and Dad always classified Rollie and Dot as being unmarried, no-good, rotten sons of bitches. They were strangers to me. I'll refer to them as mother and father. With this arms-length designation they will remain strangers.

Some socially-accepted businesses in Kimberley when I was a kid were called "hook shops" or "sporting houses" (whore houses). There were a couple of them at McGinty Hill, just outside of town. Someone developed a parody of the first two lines from Sir Walter Scott's "Lady Of The Lake":

"The stag at eve had drunk his fill,

And staggered up McGinty Hill."

We kids would recite this whenever we went to the McGinty Hill hook shops to cadge or steal beer bottles. Beer bottles were our form of currency—they could be sold for one cent each. Breweries refilled them.

My mother was an inmate of one of the houses, but that meant nothing to me for I remember nothing about her or my father. They'd agreed to pay the Woodds to care for me, but had left Kimberley shortly afterwards.

Mom and Dad kept saying how much they'd like to know where those buggers went so they could get the police to bring them back to Kimberley and pay up. I had the impression that I was a kind of stranger in the Woodd's house, a transient who should have been somewhere else. I kept expecting Steeves to show up and take me away with him.

There is doubt about my parentage. Mom and Dad said my date of birth was April 25, 1926 and that I was the first baby a Doctor Davis delivered when he came to Kimberley to practice. I used the name Woodd in my earlier years. At about the age of seventeen I needed a birth certificate so went to see Doctor Davis. He confirmed that I was what he called "his first baby." He told me, "Look up the records at the hospital and the first baby I delivered will be you."

One of those black-covered school scribblers was used to record births. In it the first baby delivered by Doctor Davis was born on April 26, 1925 (a transposition of dates). I got a birth certificate which gave the date of birth as April 27, 1925 and the name of the baby as Frank Robert Howard. The father's name was Roland William Howard; the mother's was Dorothy Janet Naas.

The family name Steeves is wide-spread in New Brunswick and there are extensive records of the family dating back some ten or twelve generations. William Henry Steeves, who could be a forebear of mine, was one of the Fathers of Confederation. According to those records, which I recently obtained, my father was Rowlat Widlake Steeves and my mother was Dorothy Naas. Dorothy Naas gave birth to a son on April 20, 1926. His name is given as Frank Robert Steeves. So, here I am with two different surnames and four different birth dates. Who the hell am I?

I was probably receptive to negative and injurious influences because I always knew I had the inherited tendencies and same vulgarities as Rollie and Dot. If I got into any trouble or even a mild mischief I was told it was because my mother was a whore and my father was a pimp.

Inside my head it was like a sheet of black and white film able to receive images, but no colours. Colours such as family love and family acceptance were not picked up.

Mom was 100% British with an inculcated snobbery and an attitude of racial superiority over anyone who was not British. I don't blame her for that. Britannia-rules-the-waves was the theme song of her generation.

Our next door neighbours were from central Europe; to Mom they were "bohunks." Two doors away was an Italian family, "dagos" to her.

The only people in Kimberley who were ever in our home were those with British names. Still, all us kids, regardless of name, played together in relative harmony.

Dad wasn't much better. He taught me a little ditty:
"Chinky, chinky Chinaman
Sittin' on a fence,
Tryin' to make a dollar
Out of fifty cents."

Mom had given birth to a son, Tom, before coming to Canada. Tom stayed in England and, in 1929, was killed in an airplane accident near Lahore, India. He was in the British Royal Air Force engaged, as Mom put it, "In bombing them bloody Indian rebels out of their mountain caves."

Tom's death was a severe blow to her. She told the events surrounding his death to anyone who would listen and to many who were not interested. I'd come into the house many times and hear her talking to Tom and cursing those whom she called Indians. To her, rebels and non-rebels were all alike. They killed her son. "If is wasn't for them black-assed bastards my Tom would be alive today."

Mom went back to England and took me with her. Alf, her nephew, stayed in Kimberley with Dad. Alf and I always considered that Mom and Dad were his true parents and it wasn't until years later that we discovered otherwise. To me, Alf was always my brother. His nickname was Woodie, mine was Young Woodie. I was six years old when I went to England; Alf was fifteen.

Years later Mom told me that she'd heard from Rollie's relatives in New Brunswick that they wanted me to live with them. She took me to England to prevent that from happening. But, why didn't they pursue it when we returned?

We travelled by The Canadian Pacific Railway (CPR) to Halifax using the day coach and then by ship to England. Each time a new train crew boarded the train and checked tickets I was warned by Mom to say nothing about my age. If asked by the conductor, or anyone else, how old I was, my reply was to say that I was five years old.

I asked, "Why?"

"Frankie, if you say you're only five I won't have to buy a ticket for you. You can travel for nothing."

I didn't like being called Frankie.

"Yes, them CPR buggers make enough money off us as it is. When you can get something from them for nothing you take it."

I was proud to be six, but lied about my age so many times that it became second nature to say that I was five.

2

JACK WAS NIMBLE, JACK WAS QUICK

In England we stayed with Mom's brother and his wife in the same house where Mom had been born. We visited Mom's relatives, one of whom was her sister whose husband was a retired naval officer. They had a daughter about my age. One day we were in the parlour innocently playing with some toys when a couple of other relatives came to visit. They went out in the garden leaving us in the house. Uncle Jack was one of the new visitors, although I don't think he was truly our uncle.

I remember Uncle Jack being in the parlour at one point and sitting in a chair. He just sat there and didn't say anything while we kept on playing.

Then he spoke "Margaret, Frank." We looked up. "Did you ever see each other's wee wees?"

I think we probably giggled.

"Did you ever see a man's puddin'?" He pulled his out of his pants and began stroking it. Margaret and I couldn't keep our eyes off that huge thing. Then he put a handkerchief over it, got up and nimbly left the parlour.

Margaret and I were probably lucky. In me there was a mixture of anxiety and fascination. It must have been the same for Margaret. We were both intrigued by Uncle Jack's first question which our fertile minds changed into a suggestion.

So there we were; two six-year old kids looking at our differences, touching ourselves and touching each other. I think neither of us had a clue that this would all be revealed to us sometime in the future.

Uncle Jack's action must have seemed innocuous, or harmless, or maybe even shameful because we didn't tell anyone about it. If he had touched us we probably would have kept that to ourselves also.

Neither Mom nor Dad told me anything about sexual matters. None of the kids I chummed around with seemed to have been told anything by their parents either. There were older brothers and sisters, though, who passed on the rudimentary information, thus permitting us to know more than our parents thought we knew.

It also resulted in our knowing a great deal less than we should have known. I believe a child should learn about sexual matters at home from parents who talk about such things in a loving and respectful way.

All parents, though, are not loving and respectful. The formality of the school class room is the next best forum for explaining such matters. There are too many antediluvian mentalities out there who oppose the use of schools to teach children about some basic facts of life.

If kids don't learn about sex in the home and can't learn about it in the formality of school they will learn about it on the street. This results in unwanted pregnancies, the spread of diseases, the lack of responsibility by males, sexually aberrant behaviour, sexual brutalities, street-level prostitution by both males and females, and in personal emotional problems.

Not only was sex not discussed at home, it was treated as something dark and forbidding. Masturbation, for example, caused hideous, unmentionable things to happen, blindness being one of them. We had a family medical book in the house, kept in a locked trunk so we couldn't see the pictures.

In Kimberley the Yale Cafe was run by a Chinese man. Mom,

Dad, and others referred to him as the Chinaman at the Yale. Dad called him a Chink. We kids called him Charlie.

Charlie sold us tailor-made cigarettes for one cent each. He would break open a ten-cent package if necessary, but he usually had loose cigarettes lying around. We took what he gave us. None of your favourite brand stuff here.

There was another guy, Charlie Fellows, who hung around the Yale Cafe. He was an older white guy who lived in a shack down the alley from the Yale. Mom and Dad said his real name was Charlie Bennett which meant nothing to me. My name was Woodd, but it was also Steeves.

On the way home from school one day I went into the Yale Cafe with one of those big pennies in my hand to buy one cigarette. It was to be shared with two others kids who waited outside the Cafe.

A garage was at the other end of the alley from the Yale Cafe. Behind the garage were wrecks of old cars. We would climb into one of these cars, puff away at the lone cigarette while we rattled our fictitious way along dusty roads pretending we were John Dillinger and his gang escaping from some bank robbery.

Charlie Fellows was in the Cafe, leaning on the counter talking to Charlie, the owner.

"Hello Frankie, buying cigarettes today?

"Uhh." No answer came out because we were not supposed to smoke. It would stunt our growth and, worse still, we'd probably get switched if our parents found out.

"It's all right, Frankie. I know you kids smoke. Nothing wrong with that and I'm not going to tell on you."

He put his hand on my shoulder, "Put your money in your pocket, Frankie. Come with me. I'll give you one of mine."

He led me into the kitchen and over to a table. He sat in a chair, moved me around in front of him and took a pack of cigarettes from his pocket. The other Charlie had followed us and was standing in the doorway.

"How old are you, Frankie?"

I wished he would stop calling me that. "I'm eleven, Mr. Fellows."

"Do you play with yourself?" And then his hand was on the crotch of my pants squeezing and rubbing.

I mumbled something like, "Don't. No, don't."

"Why not, Frankie, doesn't it feel nice?"

I think I was more embarrassed than frightened. I turned to go, but he grabbed my arm with his unoccupied hand and held me standing there. I tried to twist away from him and just then the front door of the cafe opened.

Charlie, the cafe owner, turned from the doorway. Charlie Fellows removed his hands. I ran out into the cafe and saw that the two kids who were waiting for me had come in to see why it was taking me so long to get a lousy cigarette.

Outside I told the two other kids what had happened. One of the kids, Sonny Sampson, said that his older brother, Benny, had told him about Charlie Fellows.

We knew that boys and girls were made differently. We knew that these differences were to be rubbed together or touched together and that the boy would be able to slip his difference inside the girl. We knew all the appropriate Anglo-Saxon words and used them any time we talked among ourselves about these mysteries.

We knew about cornholing, and that it was a bad and unclean thing to do. Not only unclean, but it could tear you inside. We knew it was wrong for men to touch or handle or fondle young kids the way Charlie Fellows did to me. We were not old dogs or worldly-wise about such matters: we just knew it was wrong.

3

ALMOST INVISIBLE

We were in England for about a year. Mom didn't enroll me in school, saying that I would not learn anything in England that would be of use to me when we got back home. She said they taught different things in England than they did in Kimberley.

While in England I acquired a "limey" accent. When we returned to Kimberley I went into Grade two, taking my accent with me; it generated ridicule and bleeding noses. What I needed was the Grade one preparation. I did miserably in Grade two. By some stroke of fate, probably age, I moved on to Grade three.

Neither my Mom nor Dad seemed to care about what was happening to me in school. I can recall no interest being shown in whether I had homework. I can recall no conversation about progress in school or lack of it. I can recall no attempts by anyone to sit with me and go over any school matters.

I brought those precious blue report cards home, got them signed and took them back again. The presenting of report cards, and the signing of them, was ritualistic. The fact that the marks on the card dealt with a human being seemed so unimportant.

Someone in the school system in Kimberley goofed, because I skipped the sixth grade. I had passed out of Grade five and upon returning to school in the fall of 1936 found myself in Grade seven. At home they thought that was great, but no one bothered to look any further. Grade seven was an absolute disaster.

I was mired in a jungle of nouns and participles and iambic pentameters and litmus paper. A few of us stole some litmus paper and pissed on it. I don't remember if it turned colour. That was not important; it was not an experiment, it was a lark. We gave some of the paper to girls in our class, telling them what we had just done. They didn't report back.

The easiest way to deal with the strangeness of Grade seven was to avoid it. In good weather hookey became the order of the day. I was off to school in the morning, but wandering around town in the day. One of my favourite activities was to take some kid's bike from the school yard and ride all over town. No one saw me. Here was this school-age kid riding around town during school hours. The invisible man.

1937 was the year I "lost" my report card a couple of times. It was the year I got back to school late one day and was seen returning a bike I had "borrowed." It was the year the policeman came to our house more than once. It was the year playing hookey was discovered. It was the year age didn't come to my rescue. I failed Grade seven.

Partly because of the nine-year age difference, Alf and I had very little in common except that we lived in the same house. I knew he was not, as Mom put it, "your real brother." He was their son. I was someone else's son.

One activity in the mining game is to grind or mill the ore into a slurry and, using chemicals, separate the minerals from the rock. The plant for such an operation is called a concentrator or a mill. Alf made an announcement one day saying that he was going to quit school and go to work on what was called the Bull Gang at the mill.

"Well, if that's what you want," was Mom's only response.

Dad's reply related to the work. "Stone is a tough bugger to work for. You'd be better off inside the mill." Stone was the Bull Gang foreman. The Bull Gang did all the pick-and-shovel and clean-up work around the mill.

Only in later years did I realize that Mom and Dad had a restricted focus about education. Dad apprenticed as a blacksmith in the south of Scotland when he was fourteen years of age. He went into the British Army as a blacksmith. He came to Kimberley in 1922 and worked as a blacksmith. When he retired, after about 25 years of working for the C.M.&S., he and Mom moved to the lower mainland of B.C. In Surrey he set up a blacksmith shop on his own. When he entered the trade, apprenticeship was education and he was well trained.

Mom stopped going to school at ten years of age. She got a scullery maid's job in some resort hotel. Her first marriage was to a British Army Corporal by the name of Cook. She travelled with him to Ireland, Malta, and India. His chief occupation, according to her, was drunkenness. Mom was a housewife all of her married years. Her perception of education, life, and social relationships was simply reflective of her experiences.

To both Mom and Dad a formal education might be nice to have, but it was not necessary. If I could survive to the age of 16 or 17 I could also get a job with the C.M.&S. Alf did this, as did many of his peers. They reached that certain age and then went to work.

Mom was proudly British; she came to Canada, but her heart stayed in England. Her adoration for things British was an embarrassment. She wanted to have me look upon her as a model and absorb her perception of life.

In addition to bringing back an accent, I had to wear short pants and knee socks because that is what kids in England wore. She said they were more comfortable. Every other kid in Kimberley wore long pants; I stood out as something different.

On May 24th our house was decked out with British flags, ribbons, and banners, plus pictures of England's King and Queen. It was unique, the only decorated house in town. It brought on additional ridicule.

I always felt that Alf was their favourite and I was just there for the meals and the clothes. I was told that Dad didn't have the money to get me a bike. How was I to know whether he did or didn't? He said he didn't have it. But, in 1936, he bought a brand new Dodge.

I had to ask for a nickel if I wanted an ice-cream cone. I learned that money doesn't bloody well grow on trees. It was easier to steal beer bottles and sell them for a cent each. That way it was my own money.

I stole other things. I sneaked into homes when no one was there. I stole from unlocked cars. Mom and Dad discovered what I had been doing and said that my behaviour was inherited. Why did I steal? I didn't know why. I didn't think about it then.

Punishment was mild and ineffective; harsh words and condemnation mostly. Dad never hit me, but Mom kept a limber branch from a bush beside the kitchen stove and would sting me across the ass with it when she felt I needed it or when she lost her temper. I was also denied the opportunity to go outside to play with other kids, but that was a short-lived denial.

4

WHAT'S IN THAT BOX?

As a kid in Kimberley I don't recall getting any guidance about honour and respect. If I did I must have had a mental block about heeding it. I was able to wander along the pathways of life uninhibited by any formal family guidance except negative responses to unacceptable behaviour. My fellow travellers were my mentors, as I was theirs. We were enticed by our own boldness and experimentation. A few kids having a hell-of-a-good time. Fishing for trout, trapping gophers, sneaking into the Catholic Church to light the candles and crawling through a back window of Walkley's Butcher Shop after hours to look for loose change in the till were all in the same category.

Our house was one in a row of four; our back yards fenced in by the wooden wall of a building supply company, referred to simply as Fabro's. Across the street was another lumber yard called Cranbrook Sash and Door. After business hours and on Sundays these lumber yards were our playgrounds. Fabro's was also the trysting-place for pubescent explorers, whose giggling could be heard from our back yard.

If we wanted a piece of wood to make arrows for our home-made bows or to make simulated guns or hoop sticks we crawled under the gates of the lumber yards and helped ourselves. At home no questions were ever asked about where we got the wood.

The Cranbrook Sash and Door yard was operated by a man named

14

Morrison who lived on the premises. His living quarters were easily entered. Often I'd get into his place and take what few pennies or nickels I could find. On one of these break and enter escapades I picked up a five dollar bill. Wow, I was a millionaire.

I treated other kids to ice creams and the picture show, trying to buy friendship I guess. Even though we played together I felt isolated from other kids. Was that the result of Mom's denigrating comments about non-British families? Was it the result of being told that I was different from other kids; that I was an orphan, that my mother was a prostitute?

There was one general store in town, The Mark Creek Store. Stealing fly-hooks and other items from the Mark Creek Store was not only standard, it was almost obligatory. Increased stature with one's twelve-year-old compatriots was enhanced by a collection of Black Gnats and Silver Doctors, not to mention cigarette lighters, pen knives, and other pocket-sized items. At home it might be, "Where did you get all those fish hooks?"

"Oh, they're not mine. Billy lent 'em to me."

"Where did he get them?"

"I don't know. I think maybe they're his brother's."

The stolen fish hooks had a special quality. They were far better at hooking trout than were the bought kind.

Like motion-picture Indians sneaking up on cowboys we would wiggle our way over rocks and through bushes to steal beer bottles from the sheds behind the McGinty Hill whore houses. As a bonus we might glimpse one of the ladies.

We sold the beer bottles to a guy in town who kept his purchases in a wood shed. Our greatest success was to sell him some of his own bottles which we had stolen out of his wood shed the night before. No worries. Just a few kids with runny noses living with our own misguided honour and immature pride.

The McGinty Hill forays flipped open the lid of the memory box in my head. So my mother had been here behind those doors, curtains, and drawn shades doing whatever it was that whores did. So what? It meant nothing to me. So my father had moved around in there doing whatever it was that pimps did. So what? It meant nothing to me. They were not real, live people. They were fictionalized characters, somewhat like the weird and sordid villains in the Doc Savage magazines.

I didn't know them, only about them. I had a stained, scratched-up, out-of-focus picture of them, developed for me by Mom and Dad, and then plunked down into that tightly-lidded memory box. Keep them in the darkness; they are at home there.

No matter how long the lid of the memory box was open, it was murky inside with the contents shrouded in darkness.

I don't recall having a birthday party to which other kids were invited. One of my playmates just a few houses from our place had such a party and I went, obviously by invitation.

Mom made sure I was properly dressed and clean. She put a small present in my hands and away I went.

The CPR connected Kimberley to Cranbrook and the outside world. It also took the ore from the mine to the concentrator, a distance of about two miles. The rail tracks were next to Fabro's lumber yard which was right behind our house.

On railway sidings freight cars were parked. At the back of the birthday party house was such a place.

I gave my little present and left the party to play by myself among the box cars, some of which contained coal. I must have felt that I didn't belong with the other kids. I only know that I didn't want to be there.

When I got home, with blackened hands and coal dust on my clothes, I was bawled out by Mom. I don't recall feeling any remorse or sorrow. There must have been something attractive about being dirty and unkempt.

5

THE BUTTERSCOTCH PIE CAPER

When I was ten or eleven years old I had heroes with fanciful and bewitching names. When we kids played "cops and robbers" I always wanted to be one of the "robbers." I was "Pretty-boy Floyd", or "Machine-gun Kelly", or "Baby-face Nelson." I didn't know much about them, only what was filtered through radio broadcasts. Why were these guys my heroes? Was it because I had been told so many times that I had inherited the traits of Rollie and Dot?

On October 15, 1937 I was taken to Kimberley's police station and stood up before a judge. I was afraid and bewildered. I didn't know why I was there, except that I had obviously done something wrong. Maybe it was that butterscotch pie. Three of us kids stole a butterscotch pie from the kitchen window of the Sullivan Hotel. I was the one who removed the pie from the window sill. I was recognized. Later that evening a policeman came to our house.

In response to questions I told him that I took the pie, that I was alone, and that I ate it all.

Years later I looked up the records of that 1937 Court appearance. The pie wasn't the only factor. I was also there so the judge, James Arthur Arnold from Cranbrook, could determine if I was a neglected child. The records show that this was his conclusion.

The only people who spoke were the judge and some woman whom

I later learned was a child welfare worker. Mom and Dad were not allowed to speak. The child welfare worker had talked to them earlier when she had come to our house.

On October 8, 1937 this child welfare worker had prepared a report which was presented to Judge Arnold. It said, in part:

"Mr. Willis, Presbyterian Minister, Mr. Stafford, school principal, and others have expressed the idea that Frank has so often had thrown at him by other kids the notion that his parents were bad that he thinks he cannot be anything but bad and is trying to live up to his reputation."

Judge Arnold must have found me guilty of something for he sentenced me to six years in the care of the Children's Aid Society.

I returned home in shock and tears. Mom was in tears and Dad was cursing the judge, the police and "that welfare bitch."

Every kid I knew, including my older brother Alf, had done the same things I'd done. They all got visits from the police. They got bawled out. They got confined to their homes for awhile. They had to be in by a certain hour. They got a few whacks across the ass with a switch or a belt.

I got sent away for six years. I hated the judge. I hated the police. I hated "that welfare bitch." I hated my brother. I hated myself. I hated the whole goddamn world.

6

WHICH WAY IS INSANITY?

1937 seemed a good year at the beginning, but was a wretched one at the end. On October 19th two provincial policemen took me to Cranbrook. Two wooden soldiers, in dull, brown uniforms, transporting the captured enemy to some offensive reform school operated by a hateful, and probably a cruel group called The Children's Aid Society.

Leaving Mom and Dad, home, and my dog, Mac, was tearful for all of us. Even Mac sensed the grief. The policemen put me in the front seat of the car, with one of them on each side of me. We drove out of Kimberley, past Chapman Camp, past Marysville, past the near-ghost town of Wycliffe. It was good-bye to these communities as well. I was twelve years of age, and six years was not a long time. It was forever.

One policeman took the car back to Kimberley, the other stayed with me. We were to board a train the following morning which would take us to Vancouver.

I couldn't eat supper that night. I was a scared twelve-year old kid, sitting in a miserable restaurant across from a miserable wooden-soldier policeman. I was quarantined by my own fright and resentment; withdrawn into my fear.

We stayed overnight in a hotel, the policemen and I sharing a double bed. I cried that night, as silently as I could, lying on my side at the edge of the bed, my back to the policeman. He spoke to me a couple of times, but I couldn't answer. The silence and the darkness were as a soothing poultice to my wounds. The only sounds I could hear were my own laboured breathing and snuffling, but those sounds were added to by the creaking of the bed as the policeman rolled over towards me. He put his hand upon my arm, then down to my wrist. He tugged my hand towards him, and placed it on his rigidity.

I screamed and shrieked something, leaped out of bed, and stumbled to some corner of the room. I have vivid memories of being in a corner, of shaking and sobbing uncontrollably, and of huddling down on the floor. I was in a catatonic state and, except for the involuntary shaking, I couldn't move. My whole body was quivering yet was stiff as a poker. My joints were glued together and my throat was gripped by terror.

I awoke in the morning still in the corner, but with a blanket over me. To me the wooden soldier had turned into a pillaging conqueror. The conqueror spoke. "You better get up and get dressed."

I didn't utter a word. I was struck dumb by the memory of his hand on my wrist. Home was so far away and I would never see it again. Mom and Dad and Alf and Mac were gone forever. Kimberley was no longer in existence; it was just a memory.

In late February of 1936 a man and a woman lived together in Kimberley. The story is that she wanted to break off the relationship, but he didn't. He ended it about a block away from where we lived. One night we heard this tremendous bang and wondered what it was. We soon found out. Some neighbours came to our house and told Mom and Dad that someone had just blown himself up using dynamite. The story was all over town the following morning. It was the only item of childhood gossip.

It seems the man had taken some sticks of dynamite, a blasting cap, and a short length of fuse home in his lunch bucket. He probably hugged her to him and lit the short fuse.

The next morning we kids walked along the creek-side path, the locale of the blast. We gawked at the blood all over the snow, at the visceral parts dangling from trees, and at what was left of someone's ribs.

This dramatic event taught us a new word—suicide. We incorporated this drama into our play-time games. We took turns "blowing one another up."

In Cranbrook that morning I was a scared young kid with a cop who frightened me even more. I had no place to hide, no chance to run, no one to complain to, no one to plead with, no hope.

But, there was suicide. I would be out of my misery and the cop would be at fault. I could get back at him, at that ancient judge, and at that "welfare bitch." I didn't have any dynamite; nothing else came to mind, and I was stuck with just the idea.

My only defence and protection was to hide inside myself, keep a shell on the outside so no one could notice the jelly on the inside. The cop towed me around with him. He ate breakfast while I looked everywhere but at him. He towed me to the train. He towed me onto the train. He towed me to our seats.

He spoke to me. I didn't reply. I just shook or nodded my head, or grunted. I wanted nothing from him. He was a foul, defiling intrusion. I was scared of him. It would be pleasant if I was dead. I was a sad, lonely, abandoned kid who couldn't go home.

Sure, I developed a dislike of cops. Because of that one event I painted them all with the same brush. The police may be a part of the justice system, but they don't dispense justice. They are trained to be suspicious, to invade and violate one's privacy, to watch for the furtive glance. I wouldn't want one for a neighbour.

Religion was not of any importance in our home. Mom and Dad didn't attend church and even though I was not encouraged to go to Sunday School I went anyway. I attended the Presbyterian Sunday School because one of my school chums went there.

As I remember Sunday School, it dealt with memorizing and reciting parts of the Bible. I got many lovely little gold stars for memorizing passages such as The Ten Commandments and The Beatitudes.

I even committed the order of the Books of the Bible and lots of other stuff to memory.

I was so good at memorizing that I got a Bible from Mr. Willis, the Presbyterian Minister. He put an inscription in it,

"It's not how we die, but how we live,

Not what we take, but what we give,

Not what we reap from life and zest,

But how we stand and meet each test."

I don't recall that moral or ethical instruction was a part of Sunday School. We were told that God existed and that He was good and helpful.

God was not in that wretched hotel room. He was not even in the hotel. He was not on the train. He was not anywhere that I could see. He did not stand and meet the test. He did not exist.

7

WAREHOUSE GOODS

A Miss Colgrove from the Children's Aid Society met the policeman and me at Coquitlam. She drove into Vancouver and deposited me in the Alexandra Children's Home. It was on Seventh Avenue between Pine and Burrard Streets. I later learned that the other kids in the Home called it an orphanage.

This Home was built in 1891 as a hospital for women and children. In 1894 it became the Alexandra Non-sectarian Children's and Orphan's Home. While the words "Non-sectarian" and "Orphan's" had disappeared by 1937, it still housed non-sectarians and orphans, along with troubled kids.

It was a hulking two-storey, wood-frame building. The entrance was centred between two identical extensions or wings. Time and the weather had camouflaged the painted exterior to produce muddy-brown blotches with the look of decaying leaves.

The worst activity in that institution was washing socks. Every Saturday morning after breakfast we trooped up the stairs and lined up in front of the beds on one side of the dormitory. The person in charge, nicknamed "Inches", assigned the chores.

I don't remember his real name. He got tagged "Inches" because of his display in our communal wash room. There was more than one shower stall, so a number of kids would be showering at the same time.

"Inches" would point to our genitals, undo the fly of his pants and wave his penis at us. He would say that when we had as many inches as he had, we could call ourselves men. As far as I know, he didn't go any further.

"You six kids at this end. The floor is your job today," ordered Inches. "You three here, you do the washroom. And you four will do the dusting. You two wash socks and you two wash the underwear. The rest of you come downstairs with me."

Washing socks meant bending over a tub containing a week's accumulation of wet, sweat-soaked, dirt-smeared, reeking wool.

I would be almost sick during the whole laundering process.

"Jesus, I hate this," I said to my fellow sock washer one Saturday morning.

"Why don't you get sick, then?" was his response.

"Get sick? What do you mean?"

"Go and drink a lot of water. Then come back and stick your finger down your throat. That'll make you puke."

That earned me the morning in the sick room and a visit from the nurse. She took my temperature, felt my pulse, pressed my stomach, and asked me if I had a headache.

Something must have clicked somewhere for that was the end of my sock-washing.

Relationships with the staff of the orphanage were all formal; names were prefixed by Mr., Mrs., or Miss. The staff used the same form of address to one another, a solemnity which emphasized that a familial atmosphere couldn't exist.

This was a place where no cats purred; where the smell of a wet dog would never twitch the nostrils. The orphanage was not a home. It was a warehouse containing kids in institutional clothing, fully tested and ready for shipment. From this warehouse kids would be moved out to other, smaller warehouses called foster homes.

I went to one foster home in North Vancouver where the imitation parent insisted on being called Mrs. I don't recall her family name, but think it was Brown. No problem with calling her Mrs. Brown; I had learned my lines.

I arrived at Mrs. Brown's home on Halloween. That night I was permitted to stand on the front porch with a lighted candle as the flame for a packet of firecrackers. I dutifully lit each one and tossed it out onto the front lawn. My head, though, was in Kimberley where our Halloween dress-up game was to blacken our faces with a piece of burnt cork. Our cry at each house was not "Trick or treat"; it was "Halloween apples." Apples were available; candy was in short supply.

Mrs. Brown was a widow with three grown children, one of whom taught school in Hope, B.C. The evening family discussion involved her family; I was excluded, just a transient.

I believe the name of the school I attended was Ridgeway. One day one of the kids, who knew I lived with Mrs. Brown and her family, asked me if I was an orphan. Being in a foster home probably made me feel ashamed, so I told him I wasn't. I told Mrs. Brown about it and what I had replied. She said that it was alright to tell a white lie. I didn't know lies had colours, but all of mine were white ones after that.

One of Mrs. Brown's sons used to buy a magazine named *Liberty*. I got the bright idea of using this magazine as a ploy to get me into other people's homes. If someone came to the door when I knocked I offered to sell the magazine for five cents. I made no sales, but that wasn't the purpose.

If no one answered the door I went to the back of the house and knocked again. Still no answer, I'd try the door. If it was unlocked I'd sneak in to see if there was money I could steal. I was able to get into only two or three houses and had no luck. People didn't just leave it lying around.

I was in one house when someone (the occupants?) opened the front door. I scooted out the back door and across the yard into the lane. That ended my stupid break-and-enter career. In my haste I forgot the copy of *Liberty*. I wonder what the owners thought upon finding it.

I wasn't at Mrs. Brown's home for very long. I stole a bicycle one day and hid it in some bushes. A couple of weeks later I retrieved the bicycle and sold it to a second-hand store on Lonsdale Avenue. I planned on taking the ferry across to Vancouver. I'd actually boarded it, but just as it was getting ready to pull away from the dock a man came running towards it and leaped aboard. He was a policeman looking for me. The next day I was back at the orphanage.

The Children's Aid Society took me to doctors who poked long sticks up my nostrils; rapped my knees; scratched the soles of my feet; looked in my eyes, ears and mouth and decided that I needed to have my tonsils removed.

I went to a dentist who decided to pull two decaying molars and fill two decaying front teeth with porcelain. He also gave me my first instructions about brushing my teeth.

They took me to a doctor who had me put coloured blocks of wood into spaces set aside for them. He asked me to read some words, look at some pictures and tell him what they meant.

It started with Miss Colgrove who met me at the train. While driving me in her car from the train station in Coquitlam to the orphanage, she kept shooting a steady stream of questions at me. She asked me what I thought about my father, my mother, my brother, my school, the judge, the police, the Presbyterian Minister, even about my dog.

She went over the same subjects, and many more, during interviews with me at the offices of the Children's Aid Society. I'd imagine her careening along the streets of Vancouver, on her way home, chuckling and humming, telling herself how successful she'd been to get all those bits and pieces of me.

The inquisitions also took place at the orphanage with a Mr. Innes and one of the matrons; they explored my opinions, my attitudes, my fears, my hopes, my intentions, my everything. Do you love your mother? Do you love your father? Can you tell me what love means? Do you play with yourself? The worst experience was with the doctor who had me put the coloured blocks of wood into the correct holes. He was a psychologist or a psychiatrist. His questions were tricky; he would ask the same question more than once, but phrase it differently each time.

The questions were like hypodermic needles poking into me for blood. He asked me how I would feel if my dog died, if my mother died, if the judge who sentenced me died. I told him that I didn't want them to die. I told him how I would feel, but he kept coming back to the same theme, death. It was a numbing interrogation which left me confused and resentful, and which pushed me to respond repeatedly with, "I don't know."

That cop in the Cranbrook hotel room wanted more than a part of me; he wanted a brutalizing invasion which, if it had succeeded, would have given his sickness nourishment. He would have been able to feast on his memory that he had taken all of me.

They were all a bunch of bloodsuckers who wanted to leave me with a drained carcass to roam around in. They wanted to open up my head and peer inside, pointing at, and muttering about what was exposed to their inquisitive gaze.

The orphanage housed a number of kids who'd lived in different foster homes and had been returned. They told the rest of us about some of those foster parents, people who didn't seem to give a damn about the kids. There was scant attention given to food, clothing, and other needs, and, at the first sign of any difficulties, the foster parents shipped the kid back to the orphanage as unmanageable. Tell a kid a few times that he is unmanageable and he will become so.

It didn't matter if those stories were true. We had to believe them because all of us lived the same miseries. Our only source of comfort and solace was in our own circle; we were forced to find friendship from those in the same situation. We were the in-group. We wouldn't lie to one another—would we?

As a consequence I had suspicions about the motives of the foster parents. Did these people want kids because they really wanted a child in their home, or were they in it for the money?

An orphanage is an ideal school for kids to learn about suspicion. Its residents become wary of one another, and especially wary of adults in positions of authority. A warning light, handed down from prehistoric man and located in some remote chamber of the head, signalled me to be on guard when entering strange and unknown territory.

I learned it was not wise to extend trust. I had started collecting stamps in Kimberley, some of which I stole from the house of the Catholic priest. I brought this modest collection with me and kept it in a drawer in a bedside stand. Proud of it, I showed it to a couple of kids one day. The next time I opened the drawer the collection had vanished. I told a matron about it. She had the dormitory searched and the other kids questioned. No one knew anything about it. It wasn't found.

The orphanage forced me to be my own counsel. There were no family hugs; no sense of belonging; no love and, worse than that, not even the feeling that anyone gave a damn about me.

8

DAY DREAMING

Life in the orphanage was not totally restricted. We had certain freedoms, one of which was leaving the institution to walk to a public school. Another was the privilege to leave on a Saturday for a few hours in the afternoon, and, of course, return by a certain time.

Because I was a docile, quiet kid who caused the institution no trouble I was permitted to leave on Saturday afternoons. Where to go? What to do? I took to walking northwards on Burrard Street to go downtown, mostly to walk along Granville and gawk at the neon signs. Was I lonely? Yes, terribly so. Was I sad and depressed? Yes, terribly so. Was I able to communicate these feelings to anyone? No. All of the orphanage's administrative staff were of the enemy class.

Here I was, a twelve-year old kid, extracted from my home and plunked down in an orphanage. I was like an uprooted plant in a garden, just waiting to be transplanted. The mere fact that I was twelve, and not the most urbane kid in the world, almost demanded that I look at things in a simple way. Being lonely was something I could do nothing about. I had to live with the loneliness. Being sad was something I could do nothing about. Being depressed, although I didn't understand what depression was, was something I could do nothing about.

I could put these emotions into the background; hide them temporarily in some empty chamber in my head. Granville Street's neon signs helped. Merely watching the coloured lights was a replacement, as was looking into store windows. Standing on the Burrard Bridge and peering down into False Creek was a different kind of replacement. It offered permanency. No more pushing the sadness to one side so it could come back again, and again, and again. No more feeling lonely. The solution was in front of me.

All I had to do was climb over the bridge's railing and leap into False Creek. No more sadness; no more loneliness; no more weeping about my situation. Was I day dreaming or serious? I'm not sure, but I must have been dreaming for I didn't jump.

I was saved from the decision by a man and woman who stopped close to where I was standing. They were pointing to various parts of Vancouver and talking. They were a diversion, an intrusion into my fanciful thoughts. Truth is: I probably didn't have the guts to jump or I would have. I was simply feeling sorry for myself.

I was lonely, yes. But, I was also lonely a great deal of the time in Kimberley. I often felt like an outsider with the Woodds family. I was told many times that my parents had simply cast me aside.

9

I COULD RELATE TO TOBY

There was an iron foundry (The Western Foundry) in Vancouver near Renfrew Street and what was then the Grandview Highway. It was owned and operated by four brothers. One of those brothers and his wife became foster parents to me. In 1938 I went to live with George and Kay Crossley. Their house was on 41st Avenue near Ontario Street.

I had been in their home a couple of days when Mrs. Crossley asked me, "What name would you like to call me by?"

"I don't know," I replied.

"You can call me Kay; that's my name. You can call my husband George; that's his name."

"Sure," I said, "That'll be O.K."

"No, not O.K., just Kay, O.K.?" she said, laughing at the play on words.

"Come and sit down with me, Frank. I want to say a few things to you." We sat at the kitchen table.

"I know you've been in a lot of trouble. George and I hope you'll stay out of trouble while you're with us. We don't have any children ourselves, but, if we did we'd want them to grow up to be good people. I can't be your mother, and George can't be your father, but we want to think of you as our son, and if we can help you grow up to be a good man we will."

"We want you to like it here. We want you to talk with us about anything that troubles you." She paused and then said, "This must be too new for you, so, please think about what I've said. I'm not going to ask you anything now, but please think about it. We want you to trust us."

She continued to sit at the table, looking at me as if she wanted me to say something, but that made me feel confused. I didn't know what to say, so remained silent. I must have looked uncomfortable, because she got up finally, saying that she had a lot of things to do.

Kay was a plump, chatty, jolly woman. She had dark brown wavy hair cut rather short which, she said, made it easy to manage. She told me she had an eye problem, but didn't want to wear glasses because they made her look old. She scrunched up her eyes to bring objects into focus. She had a ready smile, a smile that was accentuated whenever she squinted.

She told me about her family. She was of Welsh descent, and had one brother and one sister. Her mother and brother lived in Giscome, B.C., her sister in Burns Lake, and her father was dead. She told me about George and his family. In addition to the four brothers there was one sister. His father and mother had a farm at Sumas Prairie, close to Abbotsford, but it was a losing proposition trying to farm what George called a stump ranch. The farm was sold and the family moved into Vancouver. Two of George's brothers got jobs at an iron foundry and, while working there, laid plans to start their own.

George, like Kay, had dark hair. He was muscular, with large, callused hands which, after years of working with iron, looked permanently dirty. He had thick, black eyebrows, a hawk-nose which gave him a look of severity, a furrowed brow, and eyes that shone like ripe blackberries. He was an easy-going, hard-working guy whose interests were confined to hunting and horse racing. He didn't seem too interested in me. Farm life had trained him to think that a woman's job was to raise the kids and keep the house.

The Crossleys lived in a four-room, stuccoed house with a lay-out similar to our home in Kimberley; the kitchen, front room, and the two bedrooms occupied the same locations within the house. The difference between the two related to the toilet: the Crossleys had an inside toilet with a bathtub. In Kimberley the toilet was outside; the bathtub did extra duty as a wash tub.

The Crossleys had a big, howling, black-as-a-raven Labrador named Toby, who was friendly and likeable. They had a tabby cat named Blotchy. When it rained Blotchy would sit in a puddle of water outside the back door, striking his paw at the rain drops splashing into the puddle. He never caught any.

The Crossleys' house was not home to me and probably could never have been. They had the same sanctions as we had at home about using the parlour only for special occasions like Christmas and about using the back door as the family entrance. It was a foster home on a first-name basis, complete with a cat and a dog.

10

TRUST? NOT TODAY

Kay Crossley told me nothing about the conversations she and George had with the Children's Aid Society. She was probably advised against such disclosure, but that did not hinder her from asking me a lot of questions. They were no doubt asked out of genuine interest but my caution light was on. I was suspicious about the Crossleys' motives. Was I there because of the money?

The kitchen became the interrogation room. One conversation related to my brother, Alf.

"Do you have any brothers or sisters, Frank?" she asked.

"Um. Yeh, I got one brother."

"What's his name?"

"Alf," I replied.

She asked many more questions about Alf, one of which was whether I liked him. I don't recall what I said.

But I do remember her telling me that young boys steal things because that's what older boys do. She said that if Alf ever stole things that might have influenced me to do the same.

I know she asked me to tell her whether Alf did steal things, and that maybe I did so because he did. I know I felt as if I was being forced to say something which I didn't want to say. Yes, I know Alf had stolen some things, but I couldn't tell Kay about that.

She got up from the table, went over to a cupboard, and came back with a bottle of Coca Cola. She shook it vigorously.

She asked me if I would then open the bottle. I told her no, that it would blow up.

"Exactly," she said, "and it will spray all over the table because there's pressure inside the bottle."

She told me that was the way it was with people, too. If you keep things bottled up inside your head, they'll just keeping building a pressure. She said that the pressure could get so strong that it could blow up something inside your head.

She smiled at me, reached across the table, and patted my arm. "We'll talk about it some other time, but think about what I just told you," she said. She removed her hand from my arm.

I could rationalize and say that I was too young to understand what she had just told me, but the reality is that I didn't want to understand. I had just completed six or seven months learning to be dumb and obstinate. The cop in Cranbrook, the orphanage, and that other foster home had squeezed the capacity to trust off into a closet. I didn't want to open the door.

Memories about Alf fizzed in my head, memories which had not had form for months, memories which bothered me until I went to bed, and bothered me further until I fell asleep.

Some events involving Alf were vivid enough to stay with me, and to be re-lived in the quiet of my bedroom at the Crossleys' house. Others had dream-like fringes, as if the memory was not good enough to bring the full picture into focus.

When Alf and his friends were going some place which, to me, seemed like an adventure trip, I'd try to follow him. But Alf didn't want me tagging along.

He would throw rocks at me to chase me back home. On one occasion a rock hit me on the forehead. I ran home with blood and tears streaming down my face and a huge lump developing. All I could say, over and over, was that Alf had hit me with a rock.

Yes, I disliked him for physically hurting me, for bouncing a boulder off my head, but what hurt more than the rock was being shunted out, being told I wasn't wanted. There was also an injury from Mom and Dad, because Alf wasn't punished for hitting me with that rock. Mom was sympathetic to me and bandaged up the wound, but she also bawled me out for trying to follow him and his friends when they did not want me to be with them. She said that they were too old for me.

We had a wooden side-walk in our back yard which went along the back of the house to our outdoor toilet.

I was pushing my scooter along the side-walk one day. Alf was sitting on the side-walk with his back to me. When I got to him I lifted the scooter, and hit him on the head with it. Then I ran up the stairs, yelling for Mom to come to my rescue.

Why did I crack him over the head with the scooter? I could not remember. Maybe it was getting even with him for the rock and the rejection. If it wasn't that, it was retaliation for some other real or perceived injury.

Kay's question: "Did Alf steal anything?", if answered, had to be answered with a "Yes." He was not different from most other kids of that age. I couldn't tell Kay anything about what Alf had done because the orphanage-induced suspicion was too strong. I could not trust her. I could not trust anyone. I probably could not trust myself.

He stole things and other kids in Kimberley stole things. Sometimes they got caught, but they didn't get sent away.

I did want to do the things Alf had done. He was earning money, and had bought a 1917 Ford touring car. It was black with a huge, swooping canvas top on it which could be folded back to allow a person to drive in the open air. There were side windows made of some flexible, translucent material which snapped into place to keep the elements out. Its coal-oil lamps gave out a feeble, yellow glow. It was a monstrously beautiful machine.

With pride he parked it in front of our house. I felt proud about it, just from living in the same house as the person who owned it. "Yehh, that's my brother's car, and he lets me drive it," I boasted.

He did let me try to drive it, but I could not reach the peddles with my feet, so he let me steer it while sitting next to him.

He took me fishing with him once, even though I didn't have a fishing rod. We went to Cherry Creek to fish for trout. He made a fishing pole for me from a bush, and tied a line with a hook to the end of it. He even let me use his fishing rod.

As soon as I got his rod in my hands I had a bite from a fish. Wow! I yanked on the rod as hard as I could, pulling the line, hook, and trout up over my head, and into the bushes behind me. Alf was not the least bit pleased with the tangle I caused, but he retrieved the fish and I proudly took it home.

In bed that night I couldn't stop thinking about that fish; it was the first I ever caught. It suddenly struck me that Alf had already hooked that trout, and had given me his rod so I could believe that I had caught it. I was resentful that Alf had tricked me yet pleased that he had wanted to make me feel good.

I was in a quandary after hearing Kay say that stealing results from copying others. I was told so often that I stole because Rollie and Dot were bad. I couldn't believe what Kay told me about young kids stealing because older kids do; that we are only copycats. I didn't try to find the answer. I didn't give a damn.

Kay was friendly, but I was still an abandoned boy with no understanding of who I was, or why I got where I was. How in hell could I have any vision about tomorrow when I had no idea about today? I was functioning on a day-to-day basis, using expediencies and lies; unable to think.

Jesus Christ, how many times did I have to go over the same stories? It seemed as if everyone wanted to bite a chunk off me and run into the bushes, nibbling away and acting like cannibals.

Kay, pleasant as she was, was doing the same thing. I wanted them to leave me alone.

Not long after Kay had given me the message using the Coca-Cola bottle and had told me that younger kids copy from their elders, we had another kitchen-table discussion. I had just come home from school. Kay gave me a glass of milk and a piece of something she called matrimonial cake.

She asked if I had thought about what she had said the other day. "Well, yeh, a little bit," I said.

"I've been thinking about it, too," said Kay. "George and I talked about it, and I... uh... shouldn't have asked you about Alf. It wasn't right for me to try to get you to say anything about him. I'm sorry for that. It's just that we want to help you get over your troubles and forget about them. Asking if Alf ever stole anything was not the right thing to do. It put you on the spot about him."

I didn't know what to say. I was probably both thankful and embarrassed, and found refuge in silence. I had enough of talking about subjects relating to me, to Mom and Dad, to Alf, and to things which happened in Kimberley.

She told me it was important to understand that younger children do the things they see others doing. She gave me a "for instance", telling me I ate with a knife and fork because my parents trained me to eat that way.

I had finished the milk and cake, and waited in silence. Did she have more to say? Was she going to ask me anything?

"Frank," she said, "these things are important, and it's important to talk about them. I get the feeling, though, that you don't want to talk about them."

I nodded my head.

"I'm sorry about that, Frank." She got up from the table, came over to me, put her arm around my shoulders, squeezed me, and told me everything was going to be all right.

Had anyone ever read me bedtime stories? Had anyone held me close and rocked me to sleep, or sang softly to me while cuddling me? Had any adult ever played games with me or made me feel loved and cared about? Not that I can remember.

My father and mother had a baby-disposal problem so they took me to the Woodd family. The Woodds accepted me on a temporary basis and gave more than adequate attention to my physical needs. Because I was a temporary deposit the emotional and psychological needs were not attended to. I have no memory of being loved as a baby or as a child.

Kay's show of affection made me feel more miserable and more lonely than ever. I did not know how to cope with affection, or with the simple act of friendliness.

I got up from the table, went outside to sit in a shed at the back of the house and burst into tears. Toby followed me.

11

NO LAUGHING MATTER

Kay enrolled me at the Van Horne School, the fourth school I had attended in six months, and it was my second year in Grade seven. Kay must have been told this by the Children's Aid Society for she goaded, pushed, and bullied me into paying attention to school work.

At Van Horne the teachers roamed the halls from classroom to classroom; the students stayed put. Our mathematics and science teacher was a Mr. Rustler. He was my favourite. We brightened up whenever he came into the room. He always had a story or an analogy or a joke available to make a point he was trying to get across. He was soft-spoken, genial, friendly, and helpful.

His classes were fun, but God help the student who became noisy, boisterous, or who didn't pay attention. There was never any doubt about who was in charge: Mr. Rustler with his heart of gold and his will of iron.

The grades at Van Horne stopped at eight. I moved from Grade seven to Grade eight with good marks. Kay continued to show interest in my Grade eight reports and marks, and was congratulatory where appropriate. However, her goading, pushing, and bullying eased off and finally stopped.

Often I would bring books home to do homework and take them back the next morning, unopened. If I had assignments to hand in, I sometimes did them while another subject was being taught. Grade eight was a breeze. I was carried through it by the momentum generated in Grade seven.

A world-famous pianist once related to a newspaper reporter that he spent six hours every day practising.

The reporter was somewhat astonished. "Six hours, every day?" he asked, "Do you ever miss a day?"

"If I miss one day, I'll notice it; two days, the orchestra will notice it. Three days and the world will notice."

The time span is much longer with school work and the student's world much smaller, but a lack of practice brings similar results.

I joined the Boy Scouts and earned a few proficiency badges which were sewn onto the upper portion of the sleeves of my shirt. I earned badges for cooking, mending shoes, first aid, knot tying, and laundering.

To earn the laundering badge I had to pass tests, one of which was to wash and iron a shirt and sew a button onto it.

The tests were conducted by a woman in the living room of her home near 36th Avenue and Main Street in Vancouver.

I was sitting on a sofa facing the front window, attempting to sew the button onto the shirt.

The woman walked to the window and I could see that she wore a flimsy dress which clearly outlined her legs.

She came over and sat beside me on the sofa, placed her hand under her dress and began to massage herself. I wanted to look, but was unable to. I dumbly sat still.

Suddenly she got up and left the room. What was I to do? All I can remember was staring at the needle and thread and the button and feeling dumb.

She came back into the living room and told me that everything was fine and that I could leave.

At the next Boy Scout meeting the Scout Master, Mr. de Pencier, called me to the front and handed me my laundering badge.

I returned to my place and the Scout next to me said, "Ah, I see you passed the test." He wore a laundering badge.

I still iron my own shirts and replace buttons.

During my school years George didn't seem interested in my scholastic progress, or lack of it. He was wrapped up with horse racing and with his foundry business, where cast-iron pipes and fittings for plumbing and sewage purposes were made.

The foundry worked six days a week and George would often go to work on Sundays as well. I started going to the foundry with George on Saturdays when I was in Grade eight. I helped with some of the minor and less arduous tasks. I became fascinated by the techniques of making sand moulds and pouring molten iron into them.

I think the Crossley brothers had been engaged in some illegal stunt not too long before I started spending some time at the foundry. They talked often, sometimes with amusement and laughter, about a fire which took place at the foundry.

It seems, from what I could pick up from the conversations, that their bookkeeping was not as carefully done as government would like. They knew that someone from the government was coming to check over their financial records which were kept in a small shed built onto the outside of the foundry. A few days before the government guy was scheduled to arrive a fire broke out in this office-type shed and all the records were destroyed. If it was arson, it seemed alright to me.

There is a story of two people who met on one of those luxury cruises to the Caribbean. They were lounging in deck chairs and got talking. One of them said that he was taking the cruise because his business had been destroyed by a fire and the insurance money paid for the cruise.

The other one said that, coincidentally, he too was using an insurance payment arising from a business he had which was destroyed in a flood.

The first person sat bolt upright in his deck chair and asked: "How do you start a flood?"

Moving out of Grade eight meant going to another school. I got no advice or guidance from Kay or George about which school to attend or which courses to take. It was purely my decision. I decided I would get the best of both worlds by enrolling in the Vancouver Technical School and taking the university entrance program. I could go to school and work in the foundry.

The foundry was located a few blocks from Vancouver Tech. I would ride in to school in the mornings with George and come home with him at night. We left the house about seven, getting to the foundry about eight. I would work around the foundry for about half an hour, then hike off to school. Sometimes I'd arrive at school with grimy and blackened hands. There were no washrooms or washing facilities at the foundry, only an outdoor toilet, poised over a soggy and swampy place named Still Creek.

I would be back at the foundry after school. The last hour or so of the work day involved drawing molten iron from the furnace, and carrying it in ladles to be poured into the moulds. This process was called casting.

Iron melts at a temperature of 1535°C. Casting was at least an hour of heat, sweat, and mist. Breaking up the moulds after the iron had set in them was more of the same, but with the addition of dust from the dried sand.

I had a set of old clothes at the foundry, as did everyone else, which were used for the cast. Washing after the cast was a simple process of rinsing off the sweat and sand with water warmed in a bucket for that purpose.

We would get home about six-thirty or seven. School and homework became secondary to foundry work. Books I borrowed from the school library all dealt with metallurgical matters.

I had chosen university entrance because I had this vague notion that higher education was the way to go. In the absence of guidance, or even conversation with George and Kay, I was easily influenced by my Grade eight contemporaries who were going the university entrance route. I also wanted to be a metallurgical engineer. Slogging my way through the grit and grime of the foundry floor would be ideal background experience.

George was pleased that I was interested in moulding and he enjoyed teaching me the tricks of the trade. On the way home from the foundry one day I told George of my metallurgical engineer dream.

George chuckled, saying, "That's quite an ambition." He wheeled the car along in silence. "Yeh, quite an ambition." He chuckled again. It was no laughing matter to me.

More silence, then. "Have you figured out how much that'll cost, and who's going to pay for it?"

"No, I don't know how much, but I'd save up for it."

"Think about the money. It costs a helluva lot to go to university. In a few years that Children's Society won't have anything more to do with you. They won't put you through university; you'll be on your own by that time, and you won't be living with us. You think on the money part of it."

More silence. We turned south onto Main Street. We were nearly home.

George broke into the silence, "You may find it'll cost too much money. Another thing to think on is this: you don't need a university education to get anywhere in this world. Look at me, I only got as far as Grade four."

I had discovered earlier that George would talk at great length about the foundry, playing the horses, and hunting. He gave scant consideration to other subjects. That, plus the fact he had never talked with me about school, prevented me from talking with him about it.

We turned west off Main Street onto Woodcock Avenue. We were two blocks from home and all I could think of saying, and I said it sarcastically, "I'm not asking you or anyone else for any money. If I do it, I'll do it on my own."

"Hey! hey! calm down," said George. "You'll learn the best way to do anything is to do it on your own."

I didn't mention university again. I took George's response to mean that he wasn't interested, and Kay's interest in my schooling had eased off to the point of non-existence.

While I was fascinated by foundry work I didn't want that to be a life-long vocation. Maybe that engineer bit was just day-dreaming, for I truthfully did not know what I wanted.

12

THE CITY BECKONS

In the summer between Grades nine and ten I worked at the foundry, making moulds and pouring the molten iron into them. Fifteen years of age and almost an iron moulder. Wow! My pride turned to arrogance; I became a crow, cawing at my neighbourhood friends. They were delivering newspapers or groceries; I was in a man's world, doing a man's job, earning real money—four dollars a week. I moved blindly along with my new-found stimulus of men's work and my own money.

There must have been some child-labour law which said that I shouldn't be employed in such work. One day John, George's older brother, told me to get out of sight because an inspector of some kind was coming to visit and I shouldn't be seen. I went into the bushed area on the other side of Still Creek and sat on a log for some time. The Crossleys were cheating in some way, and I thought it was great sport to agree with them. What was wrong with cheating? Nothing to me.

Everyone, and I think teenagers especially because they are still moving towards maturity, needs to succeed at something. My school work was not too successful, but my foundry work was.

The moulds I made were cubes of moistened and compressed sand. They needed to be constrained to ensure that the molten iron, when poured into them, would not force its way through the compressed sand.

We used two devices to keep the iron from pouring out through the moulds; one was a four-sided, form-fitting steel jacket which was pushed down around the mould to keep it intact. The other was a flat slab of iron called a weight which was placed on the top of the mould to keep the molten iron from pushing its way upward.

The molten iron was poured into the moulds though holes called sprues and the weight had holes in it to coincide with the location of the sprues. Some moulds were so large that it required three moulders simultaneously to pour the iron into three separate sprues.

When molten metal touches a wet, non-porous object such as the weight, the moisture evaporates and expands so quickly that a virtual explosion takes place. Such an explosion splatters gobs and drops of molten metal in all directions.

Three of us, John Crossley, Archie McLeod, and I were pouring iron into a mould when the accident happened. The molten iron being poured by Archie came into contact with a damp weight and splattered. Instantly, one of Archie's eyes was burned out.

Archie said later that he had felt no pain when the iron hit his eye; he only had the sensation of something like a grain of sand striking it. He continued pouring until the mould was filled, set his ladle down, put his hand to his eye, and said, "I've got something in my eye."

He was rushed to the hospital. It was the next day that we learned he had lost his eye. It could have been my eye, or both eyes.

On another occasion a gob of iron went down the front of my boot and burned a hole about the size of silver dollar on the top of my left foot. I was able to yank off my slip-on boot quickly enough so that the flesh burn was not too deep. George's only response was: "We'll make a man out of you yet."

I stayed at home for days while the burned foot healed. I began thinking that foundry work was not all glamour; there were a lot of disadvantages to it. The blossom had begun to fade.

Kay started waitressing in a downtown restaurant. Supervision of my activities stopped. I was my own guidance counsellor, operating a learn-by-yourself program, cheering myself on at any accomplishment.

St. Matthew had written, centuries ago, about blindly following guidance. He quoted Jesus as saying: "And if a blind man leads a blind man, both will fall into a pit." Neither Kay nor George attended church, and had no religious faith that evidenced itself. None of us knew anything about St. Matthew.

One youngster can be just as proud of his ability to steal cars as can another of his ability to construct model airplanes. Success seemed to be self-contained; it made no value judgements, no demands that any criteria be met. And, it fed on itself.

In the orphanage I learned the theory of "wiring a car" (getting it started without the use of an ignition key). In the late nineteen-thirties it was simply a matter of unhooking two wires underneath the dashboard and then of putting them together to make the connection.

Being in the house alone for about a week because of the burn got me thinking about running away and heading back to Kimberley. When the burned foot had healed sufficiently that's just what I did.

My running-away plan was to get as far away from Vancouver as quickly as I could. I took the train from Vancouver, arriving in Chilliwack at about nine in the evening with five dollars in my pocket. In Chilliwack I wired up a Chevrolet sedan parked outside a theatre, and drove from there to Yale. At Yale the toll road into the interior started. I didn't want to take the car through the toll station because it had probably been reported as stolen, and they might have the licence plate number. I abandoned the car and tried sleeping in some bushes alongside the Fraser River, shivering more than sleeping.

By hitch-hiking, riding freight trains, sleeping in second-hand cars in parking lots, and bumming meals I got to Kimberley in about four days.

The Provincial Police were expecting me; so were Mom and Dad. Kay and George had, of course, reported my absence, and the Children's Aid Society had alerted the police.

The Provincial Police Officer in Kimberley, Jack Kirkup, allowed me to stay home for about a week before shipping me back to Vancouver. Again it was a train ride with a policeman, but this time it felt as if it were voluntary.

I went back to live with Kay and George, who were forgiving. Kay told me that my running away had caused her a great deal of anguish because she didn't know if I had been hurt or killed or what. She said she was relieved when she heard that I was in Kimberley and that she understood why I had gone there.

It had been lovely being home with Mom and Dad for that week, but Kimberley was not Vancouver. It was exciting to see some of the kids in Kimberley, but I had been away for some two or three years and our experiences had little, if anything, in common.

Part of the song went: "How you gonna keep 'em down on the farm after they've seen Paree?" I wanted to return to Vancouver. It had many moving picture houses, any number of pool halls, street cars, a burlesque show on Hastings Street, beaches on the ocean. I had got used to it.

13

KA-BOOM

The first couple of years with the Crossleys went along fairly well. Kay was the communicative one; I felt accepted by her. George worked hard, was a moderate drinker, played the horses, and hunted ducks. He had a shotgun and a rifle. I don't recall that he read anything but racing sheets.

My interest in school diminished and I took to working on Saturdays at George's foundry. With no supervision and no guidance I brought homework from school, but seldom opened the books. I was, with a few limitations, free to do what I wanted.

One Saturday, at about age fifteen or sixteen and masked by the grime and dirt from the foundry, I obtained a liquor permit. I bought a mickey of rye whisky. We lived a short distance from Little Mountain. There were vacant lots close to the Crossley home, some of them heavily bushed and with trees.

After washing and having dinner, I went out of the house. No one asked me where I was going or what I was going to do. I had developed some friends in the neighbourhood from the Van Horne school days. It had become a common Saturday evening activity to visit back and forth and just roam the neighbourhood.

This particular Saturday was a drink-alone venture. The mickey and I went into the bushes. I sat on the ground with my back against a tree. The first gulp of raw whisky stung my mouth and throat, brought tears to my eyes, and was rejected by a gasping, spluttering, shortage-of-breath coughing and wheezing. I sat in my hide-away groping with the problem of what to do next.

Eventually, I took a small sip; it stung, but it stayed down. Then another small sip, and another.

I was lying in the tall grass outside my bedroom window when I awoke. It was dark. I was shivering and fuzzy-headed.

The back door of the house was locked. I must have tried it earlier, hence the awakening scene below the window. Eventually I got the window open, crawled through it and into bed.

When I awoke the second time, it was daylight, and there was still nobody else home. At the time I didn't know the word "blackout", but I must have had one. I still have no recollection of getting from my secret booze parlour to home; no recollection of anything beyond the first few sips.

I was relatively free to do what I wanted but, as a foster child, isolated and confined. Once again I had been abandoned. Misery and the rye-whisky aftermath were saying to me something like: "What the hell is the use? I'm free, but still locked up."

What to do about it? Run away and head back to Kimberley? But, I was like a fish on a line—to be reeled in by the police or some bored, indifferent social worker. A small, storage-type room next to my bedroom provided the answer. That's where I went. I got George's rifle and a box of shells from the closet.

Back into my bedroom. I put the barrel of the rifle in my mouth and found I could reach the trigger.

Move quickly so as not to have time interfere and turn me into a chicken. Out of the mouth, turn the rifle around, pull the lever down, put one of the shells in the chamber, snap the lever back into place. Not the usual click-clack of metal snapping against metal, but a teeth-rattling, heart-stopping KA-BOOM! The noise of the rifle deafened me temporarily, and sure as hell frightened me.

What I had done, whether by pure accident or a sub-conscious order, was pull the trigger as I closed the lever which jacked the shell into the barrel. The lead put a deep gouge in the iron bed post and buried itself in the wall behind the bed. I had effectively shot dead the idea of suicide. I was shaking so much I couldn't move the lever to eject the spent shell.

I told Kay and George what I had done, covering up with the statement that I was just playing with the rifle. Kay bawled me out; told me that it was dumb thing to do; that I could have hurt myself; and never to play with guns again.

George was furious. He also gave me hell, but complained that I might have damaged his gun. He went on in this manner for quite some time. Where did I get the knack to hear his words, but ignore his anger and his message about his rifle? Was I born with it? Did I learn it? Was it a mixture of both? I had no answer. I just knew that I was able to, and did, filter out his tirade so that it was as if he had not said a thing to me.

Yes, I did a dumb thing. But, it revealed that George considered me to be simply an object around the house, and his rifle was more important to him than I ever could be. My value to him was measured in dollars, those paid to him and Kay to house me.

14

HOME AGAIN

Sometime in 1939 or 1940 Kay started her own restaurant at Renfrew Street and the Grandview Highway, almost kitty-corner from George's foundry. It was a small hamburger/coffee-shop type of facility. Kay spent most of her time tending to her business, leaving me even more at my own mercy.

Kay's mother, Mrs. Owen, came from Giscome to live with us. I lost my bedroom and was given the small storage-type room with a cot. George had moved his guns. To me this room was more private and personal than the larger bedroom I had been used to. I had no doubt developed a warped personality which led me to be more secretive and less able to share my emotions. Maybe the smaller space somehow equated with my need to be left alone.

Another of Kay's relatives from Giscome also came to Vancouver. He had something to do with the Armed Forces. There was no space for him to live at the Crossley's home, so he had rented a small room pending being transferred. He made his own meals. I was warned not to touch any of his food, which was kept in a separate part of the refrigerator.

Mrs. Owen stayed pretty much to herself. Sometimes I made my own lunch to take to school; sometimes I made my own breakfast; sometimes I didn't eat breakfast.

I never could get interested in George's horse racing or duck shooting, and Kay's restaurant interfered with what limited communication I had with her.

In the interval between Grades nine and ten I decided, without advice from Kay or George, to change schools. There was probably some formal procedure involved, but I don't remember what it was. In the fall of 1940 I started Grade ten at John Oliver High School, which offered university-entrance courses and was only seven or eight blocks from the Crossley's house.

I was assigned an additional library period in place of physical education, giving me two library periods a week. I thought I was lucky because I didn't like running and jumping around anyway and could spend extra time reading and memorizing poetry such as Robert Service's *"The Cremation of Sam McGee."*

I worked in the foundry on Saturdays, and occasionally on a Sunday as a sort of watchman. All I had to do was hang around the place to make sure no one stole anything. A couple of times someone came and paid cash for certain fittings. I stuck the money in my own pocket. I started buying my own clothes. One of the items was a double-breasted, two-piece suit, an off-the-rack purchase which fitted me like a sack. But it was mine. I bought a tie which George classified as an old man's tie. I wore it anyway. I had become an arrogant teenager not particularly caring what others, especially George, thought.

There was a gasoline station near the foundry. The owner lived in a house behind the station. I would buy cigarettes there. One night I got the bright idea of breaking into the place for cigarettes. It was a smash and grab operation. I ran across the street with my loot and headed towards the foundry, hiding the cigarettes beneath some boards.

A couple of days later two policemen came to visit me and said that the gasoline station owner had recognized me while I was running across the street. The smashing of the glass had got his attention.

That got me lodged in Vancouver's Juvenile Detention Home, charged with breaking and entering.

This Juvenile Detention Home was just another institution like the orphanage except we were locked up and unable to go outside. The other kids were just like those I'd known earlier. I fitted right in. I was one of them.

We dusted furnishings, washed dishes, and helped serve the meals. Along with other breakfast food each kid got two pieces of toast and one pat of butter on a separate plate. That set-up allowed us to be sneaky and do things out of sight of the guards. We would slip two or three extra pats of butter between the slices of toast. We were getting away with something not sanctioned; in a sense it was "survival of the fittest."

We also washed the floors every day on our hands and knees. The first bit of advice I got from other kids was to stuff a wad of toilet paper in my underwear and behind my balls. Why?

I was told that one of the officers used a leather shoe lace as a sort of lash. He would sneak up on kids and try to flick the end of the lace against the asses of those washing the floors. He would laugh when he succeeded. The wad of toilet paper was protection. I got the tail end of the lace a couple of times. It stung.

Kay was furious with me, but told the court she would take responsibility for my future behaviour, and The Children's Aid Society approved. I think I got a suspended sentence. Kay went back to her restaurant.

In Grade ten I became less and less interested in school. Some days I would head downtown and just mosey around the big department stores like Woodward's and Spencer's, shoplifting small items.

I struck up a relationship with some older kids who lived in the Commercial Drive area of Vancouver. They, too, were petty thieves with more talk than action. One of them owned a car and was always looking for other cars from which gasoline could be siphoned. We mostly did a lot of hanging around a pool hall on Commercial Drive talking about potential escapades, but not doing anything about them.

I didn't finish Grade ten. I simply stopped attending John Oliver and went to work in a plywood mill along the Fraser River. Kay told me it was wrong for me to quit school, but didn't make any move to force me to return. She said that I would have to start paying her room and board. George said nothing. I think they'd both given up on me. I can't say that I blame them.

A couple of the Commercial Drive kids, including the one who owned the car, wanted to go to Trail. Trail was the location of the C.M. & S.'s smelter where all of the output from the mine in Kimberley was processed. I don't recall that there was a specific reason for going to Trail. I quit my plywood-mill job and went with them, leaving behind what few possessions I had. There were two girls and three boys, I being the extra and unattached one.

At Trail I left the others in order to return to Kimberley. By hitchhiking and riding a freight train from Nelson to Cranbrook I got home again with no mishaps. Kay and George must have reported my absence to the Children's Aid Society, but no one showed up to take me back to Vancouver. Maybe the Society had also given up on me.

About a mile from Kimberley was the community of Chapman Camp. Residents there worked at the C.M. & S.'s concentrator, the facility where ore was broken down into a concentrated form which was then taken to Trail.

There were bunkhouses for single employees and a cookhouse where they ate their meals. The cookhouse employed one cook, two waitresses, and one dishwasher.

I got the job as dishwasher and lived above the cookhouse. Work started every day at 5 A.M. and ended when everything was washed up after supper, usually about 6:30. We got a few hours off during the afternoon. I think I was paid a dollar a day plus room and board.

The sexual culture for us teenagers at the time was for the male to take the initiative, to pursue his quarry. The force of testosterone made every teen-aged girl a prospect. For me, and probably for many others, the major hurdle was inexperience.

I went one evening to visit a young girl whose parents wouldn't be home. This is it, I thought. All day I could think of nothing else but how to broach the subject. We sat on the wooden floor in her living room and played jacks. What to do? I thought the best way would be simply to put the question to her bluntly. At my next turn at scooping up the jacks I would say… Well, maybe I would do it at my next turn. The wooden floor stopped me; one scoop drove a sliver under one of my fingernails. Well, maybe another day.

The orphanage and the foster homes caused me to be withdrawn, shy if you wish. But, as a teenager I was also vain. I'd read in one of Mom's magazines that elbows could become soft and wrinkle proof by resting them in squeezed-out lemon halves. I tried that for awhile and finally gave up. It was too much trouble.

On Saturday afternoons I'd visit the barber, Joe, whose shop was in the pool hall. I'd have a shave and a facial and feel invigorated, handsome, and ready for the world. I was all of sixteen or seventeen at the time.

Another magazine told me that shyness could be overcome by embarrassing oneself. So, at dinner one evening in a friend's home I deliberately knocked over a glass of water. It got me attention alright, but I have no idea what it did for my shyness. Maybe it helped. More likely I just out grew it.

Alf married a girl named Borg who came from the Creston area. They lived in a small rented house. I'd visit them once in a while in the evenings. Another couple in Kimberley, also from the Creston area, knew both Alf and Borg, and also visited with them. The husband of this couple went to Vancouver to look for other work, leaving his wife behind. During his absence she made a play for me, her intentions quite clear.

She'd decided to go back to Creston and urged me to come with her to Cranbrook where she had to stay overnight. I was easily and readily persuaded; nervous, but eager. She boarded the bus in Kimberley in the afternoon and I joined her when the bus stopped at Chapman Camp. I neglected to tell anyone that I wouldn't be at work that evening or the next morning.

When I didn't show up for work the cook got in touch with Mom and Dad. They didn't know where I was. I was told later that someone reported seeing me board the bus. Dad took the next day off work and came to Cranbrook looking for me. By the time he got there I was headed back to Kimberley glowing with clear memories of the previous night's agreeable seduction. At the cookhouse I discovered that I had also lost my dishwasher's job.

Dad was angry and bawled me out for being what he called "stupid." He was also angry for having to take a day off work to try to find me. Mom had a cosmopolitan attitude, expressed to me when Dad was at work.

"Frankie", she said, "whenever you have the experience of discovering a lady's charms and favours you must keep that to yourself. It's no one else's business. Some men boast and brag about it. Don't you do that." I guess it wasn't Mom who kept the medical book locked away.

The McGinty Hill whore houses were part of Kimberley's texture when I was a kid. It was common knowledge that not all of the residents were transients. I always wanted to know whether my mother was a prostitute. Deep inside my head was probably the hope that she wasn't.

My desire to find out led me to talk with one local woman who'd worked there. Her family were neighbours; her youngest brother was a playmate of mine. I was sixteen or seventeen when I visited her. We needed no introduction. When she answered the door in response to my knock I simply said hello and asked if I could talk with her. She invited me into her two-room house. I recall her as being neat and tidy, as was her house.

I was distinctly cautious because in effect I was telling her that I knew she'd been a prostitute. She likewise was cautious because I was asking about my mother. The finality was that she confirmed what I'd been told by the Woodds.

I don't remember being disappointed. It was like hearing something about a stranger. That's what my mother was to me.

I got another job as a swamper on a truck with a cartage company. Most of the work was delivering coal and wood, and moving furniture. Sometimes I even got to drive the truck even though I didn't have a driver's licence. It was menial work, but all I was suited for. I thought of trying to go back to the C.M. & S. and apprenticing to a trade, maybe that of machinist. That didn't get beyond the thought stage. I was at loose ends; no plans and only vague thoughts about the future.

Maybe it was the earlier taste of the big-city life. Maybe it was the war in Europe. Whatever it was, I didn't want to spend the rest of my life in Kimberley. Other kids had gone off to war, others to the ship-yards in Vancouver.

Towards the end of 1942 I decided to join the Canadian Navy. Dad had been a Sergeant-Major in World War One. Mom, British, hated the Germans. They both thought my move to enter the Navy was a good one. Dad encouraged me to try the articifer branch, telling me that they repaired ships rather than sailing them. "That way," he said, "you'll stay on land and not be sunk at sea."

In January of 1943 I went back to Vancouver and took navy-entry tests at the H. M. C. S. Discovery in Stanley Park. The tests involved mathematical matters such as algebra and geometry, subjects I had failed to grasp in school. I failed the test.

I got a job in the shipyard at Prince Rupert. About two months of that and it was back to Vancouver. I re-established contact with my Commercial-Drive acquaintances and picked up where we had left off prior to taking that car trip to Trail.

15

A STONY ROMANCE

It isn't that experience is a slow teacher: the problem is a slow student. Some learn by their mistakes and others don't, or more precisely, won't.

As a teenager I believed my behaviour resulted from a genetic imprint; incorrigibility was my inheritance. I would not learn from my errors. I was one of the "had-no-chance", "it's-someone-else's-fault" types. My father's sperm and my mother's ovum were at fault for my shortfalls and problems. My mistakes didn't teach me anything for the simple reason that I was programmed and my mistakes not accepted for what they were. At the age of 18 I was a social belligerent with a lot of emotional baggage.

Sigmund Freud was a potent force amongst us teenagers; we talked a lot about him and his ideas. There was a great need for us to appear learned and knowledgeable in one another's presence; we had to boast. Each bit of new information was layered on top of the earlier stuff, making us profoundly brilliant—to ourselves.

Our conversations could move from Freud to what were the fashionable and acceptable measurements of a zoot suit. Each subject was approached with equal intensity.

We never got to such rare atmospheric heights as to whether or not there was a hereafter, or what is the meaning of life. The meaning of life was there with us, was right then. We were going to live forever.

The way I saw it, Freud was telling me that my subconscious was stuffed with inherited influences which could not be dug out, dusted off, placed under a sanitizing light and become a healthy transplant in the conscious part of my head. There was nothing that could be done about inherited personality disorders.

Both of my parents had been defined as dishonest and dishonourable specimens. They were, as Mom and Dad put it, bad bastards.

Whatever psychological quirks and convolutions my parents gave me were shut up in blackness, sealed off by a door which I couldn't open even if I wanted to.

On September 9, 1943, at the age of eighteen, my legs were shackled together by a three-foot long chain joined to a steel leg-cuff on each ankle. I was also in hand-cuffs. Walking was noisy and clanking; short steps with legs set apart.

I clanked my way from a security room in what was then Oakalla Prison Farm in Burnaby, B.C. into a police van and was taken to the B.C. Penitentiary (the B.C. Pen.) in New Westminster. There I was to serve a two-year prison sentence for a number of armed robberies.

My thoughts were ambivalent. I was not so much frightened as excited. There was certainly a chill at the prospect of living behind stone and steel for two years. There was anxiety about having no rights except the simple one of being kept alive by the prison officials pending my eventual departure. The thrill and excitement came from a perverse glamourization of prisons which stumbled around in the back and darkened rooms in my head. A romanticism existed which said, "Man, you have arrived. You have made it to the Big House. Amongst your peers you have hit the big time."

I think every kid who is moved through foster homes, detention homes, and orphanages comes to the conclusion that only his fellow travellers understand him. He is one of the in-group; one of those unique types who has had the same experiences, suffered the same miseries, knows the score. Everyone else is an outsider, an alien.

For me it wasn't much of a move from a detention home to a

prison. Both were in the same neighbourhood, had the same type of tenants, and the same type of landlords. Food, clothing, tobacco, and shelter were paid for by time, not by hard cash.

Prisons offer no threat to confirmed criminals. Going to jail is a home-coming. They experience the romantic and sensual anticipation of seeing old friends, of re-living past escapades, of planning for future joint ventures, and of guaranteeing to one another that next time it will be different. There is an element of excitement in being led to prison.

They look forward to involvement in jail politics; the smuggling in of dope, whisky, or whatever; fitting into the hierarchy; denouncing sex offenders; playing word games with prison psychologists; and working to "cure" their heterosexual behaviour.

The criminal is a gambler, a risk taker. I took risks. My first gamble wasn't really a gamble, it was a sure thing. My ingenuity was such that I knew for sure I wouldn't be caught. I also knew that the odds would eventually not be in my favour, but it would not be this time. I was too alert and too smart.

If a criminal is arrested he can gamble on being found not guilty or of getting a light sentence. If he is sentenced to prison he can gamble on a parole. To the criminal intellect the most exciting event in the world is to commit a crime and get away with it. The next most exciting event is to commit a crime and get caught.

There were no penologists in the prison system when I was in the B.C. Pen., but today they help the criminal with this parole gamble. The social scientists in the prison system love to play word games with convicts. Convicts love to play word games with psychologists. Who is conning whom?

Prison psychologists are too occupied with measuring responses and trying to fit the convict into a peculiar psychological bias. I don't think they grasp an important fact of prison life. The convict has one major goal: get out of jail. So, he tries to con the psychologist. If he succeeds, the Parole Board might get a favourable report.

The names of the cities or of the institutions don't matter. By car, train, plane or boat it is the same ride the world over. A prison is a prison. A convict is a convict. The names of the actors may change, but the play is always the same. The actors, as if in a Woody Allen film, are also the audience. They perform a kind of ritualistic fire dance for one another. They wear masks and disguises to prevent recognition of themselves and their own weird, befuddled, viperous personalities. I was one of them, but that was then.

16

A TWO-BIT LECTURE

Two massive doors, opening inwards, fronted the B.C. Pen. Trucks or cars gained access to the prison through them. People walked in through an ordinary-sized door to the left of the vehicle entrance. Passage through either was controlled by prison guards ("bulls") with keys. There are two classes of people in a prison; all convicts are of the keyless class. Wardens, shop instructors, guards, social workers, even preachers are all of the key class.

The doors were keyed open to permit the police van to enter. A jumping, clutch-grabbing start and the van's engine stalled. With a whir, a growl, and a snort the engine started again. This time the driver revved the engine too high and we virtually leaped into the prison across the border. "Dumb bastard," I thought, remembering my earlier experience with the cop at the Cranbrook Hotel. My memories were interrupted by a key clanking into the van's locked door.

"Out," said a tan uniform.

I clattered and clumsied my way out of the van, down one step and into the vestibule. The defense and response mechanisms learned in the orphanage and the Juvenile Detention Home came into play. Keep the mask on, wait for orders, do nothing overt. Do nothing voluntarily while in the presence or in sight of a prison guard. Keep the code; honour the class distinction.

The tan uniform unlocked the leg-irons and hand-cuffs. "Over there," it said, pointing to a door.

Another uniform unlocked the door. "Inside."

I looked around the room. I looked through the barred window to the outside; the outside that was inside. I saw grey, varying shades of it. The grey cement sidewalks led to grey cement steps and grey steel bars. The mottled grey walls of the main cell block were adorned with the figures "1914."

Grey: the colour of shrouds, of ghouls, and of rain-heavy clouds with no silver lining, a fool's grey. Richard Lovelace was too romantic when he wrote "Stone walls do not a prison make." He was from an extremely wealthy family and imprisoned because he supported the idea of restoring the British King's right to absolute authority. He was a political prisoner.

The key clunked into its slot, the door swung open, the same guard in the same tan uniform said, "Out."

"Over there," he said motioning me to a steel-barred gate leading from the administration section into the prison proper.

There was another tan-uniformed guard on the other side of the gate. The gate was unlocked and I was motioned through it.

"Come with me," said the second guard who was subsequently identified as Mawhinney.

I later learned that Mawhinney was considered by most convicts to be a decent sort of guy. He offered piano lessons to convicts, but I knew of no one who took him up on his offer. He used a piano which had no hammers, no strings. The keyboard was made of wood. It was a silent piano, in keeping with the silent system of the prison.

While walking up the hill towards the main cell block he initiated a conversation in lecture form.

"You look rather young. This your first time, huh?"

"Yeh."

"How long you doing?"

"Two years," I said, knowing that he knew that anyway.

"Hmmm," was the non-revealing preliminary to, "It may seem like a long time now, but it's the shortest bit you can do here. Anything less is done in Oakalla, but you know that."

No response from me. The silence was broken only by the click-clack of my heels on the cement.

"You can do your time here the easy way or you can do it the hard way. You want to do it the hard way? You'll find lots of guys in here who will help you. It's up to you. You want to do easy time, just do what you're told. Don't be a smart-alec or a big shot. It don't work."

"Yeh, I know all that."

"The thing ain't so much to know it, it's to remember it. Remember it and we'll all have it easier. I'm doing time also, except I get to go home at night."

Like the silent piano I made no sound, but thought: another two-bit lecture, like the one from that matron in the orphanage. As a child my vision was of leaving Kimberley when I got older and of returning with a fancy car and lots of money. People would guess how I got the money, but wouldn't be able to prove it. I would be a home-town hero.

On that morning of September 9th, I had the fleeting thought that maybe the dream wasn't going to be realized.

17

A DISINFECTED FISH

The security of a prison requires routine, orderliness, and following the book. Everyone's movements must be accounted for. Mawhinney's and mine were pre-determined and clicked along like a well oiled military operation.

When Mawhinney left the administration building with me in tow a guard phoned ahead to the main cell block to alert the guard there that we were on our way. The rifle-toting guards at the top of the stone wall had also received the message. We reached the building which housed the main cell block. Up a few steps to the entrance door. Mawhinney pushed a button alongside the door. A bell rang inside the building.

When the inside guard peered through the peep hole in the door he expected to see two people, Mawhinney and a "fish." I was the fish—the newly-entered convict.

Again the clank of key; the grate of metal; the toneless, order-issuing voice, punctuated by a sideways toss of the head, saying, "Inside."

Then: "Over there, against the wall."

Into the basement, to be processed somewhat like a fish in a cannery, except this was a different kind of can. Three convicts and four guards were in the basement. One guard was a porcine-jowled growler

with a sour face, ball bearing eyes, and a medicine-ball gut. He was the
Chief Keeper, Joe Goss, in charge of all guards. He instructed; others
obeyed. Cons had nick-named him The Pig.

"Off with your clothes. All of them," growled The Pig.

"Everything?"

He glowered at me, and growled some more, "When I say all of
them it means all of them. Get 'em off."

"Get in the chair," He said, pointing to a barber's chair.

With a sheet around my neck and nakedness I was given a thirty-
second haircut. A little short on the sides, Sir? Trim your eyebrows a
bit? Nothing like that. Just the simple use of clippers to reduce the
head to baldness. Like shearing sheep.

Next came a bath and a shower. Both a bath and a shower? "Over
here and get into the tub."

The liquid in the tub was a light amber colour as if a number of
people had used it for other than bathing. It was pungent and caustic.
I hesitated at the edge of the tub.

"Get in."

I got in and submerged myself to the neck as ordered.

"Close your eyes. Hold your breath."

A hand pushed my head downwards. That closed my eyes and
stopped my breathing. It closed my mouth, too.

When I came up spluttering Goss spit out: "We sterilize all vermin
in here. Get out and take a shower."

I was then ordered to bend over the back of a chair and place my
hands on the seat.

"Spread your legs apart. Come on, wider than that."

One of the convicts spread the cheeks of my ass apart and one of
the guards made a visual examination.

"Looks O.K. Chief," he said, speaking to Goss.

Then Goss placed one hand across the top of my hip bones and
made a painful jab at my anus with a finger. That brought me straight-
ening up and turning in anger.

Two of the guards grabbed me and I was held motionless.

Goss, wearing a rubber glove on his right hand, sneeringly said, "Don't like that, eh? We can do it the easy way or the hard way. The easy way is this way. Now, bend over."

This rectal search was for smuggled items such as drugs.

I was given a lump of ill-fitting and temporary prison garb. No belt, one button on the pants, no buttons on the coat, no shoelaces, no shoes. I slippered and slithered along the stone landings and up the steel stairs, holding my pants up with one hand and my coat around me with the other. A scarecrow with only the centre pole, a clump of shapeless blue unable to drive off sick crows, let alone vultures.

The fish tier was a group of ten cells, those at the top tier of the prison's east wing. I was segregated there for about a week while the prison administration decided where it was going to put me.

Meals were delivered to the fish tier by a guard and a fellow convict. The guard stood at the end of the tier and manipulated a device which allowed all cells to be opened or just selected ones. This allowed my fellow convict to open my cell door and, while standing about two feet away from the cell so as to be in full view of the guard, give me an aluminum tray of food. At the first such delivery he asked, in a very low voice, if I smoked. I gave him a "yes" nod.

Along the front of the cells was a walkway about four feet wide. A metal-tubing framework about three feet high ran along the outer edge of this walkway, a sort of safety-fence. The whole side of the east wing tier was also encased with wire-mesh something like chicken wire, but much thicker and stronger. The purpose was to keep those fish who might be suicidal from leaping over the metal-tubing framework to crash onto the cement floor some fifty feet below.

Directly in front of each cell this wire-mesh had a circular opening about a foot in diameter. Its purpose was to allow sheets and other bedding to be pushed through and dropped onto the main floor.

The faint hum of voices and the clatter of institutional equipment drifted up to the fish tier; background noise to a sort of peaceful privacy. The wire-mesh started to shake. Suddenly a convict's head and shoulders appeared above the floor of the tier. He pulled a lit cigarette from his mouth and tossed it through the circular opening towards me in the cell. His aim was perfect for it skipped through the bars and he was gone as quickly as he had appeared. He clambered up the wire-mesh two or three times. This was Doug R. and I was able to repay him with tobacco later on. Doug's eyes were always about half covered by his lower eyelids; a distinctive feature so unusual to me that I always remembered it.

The B.C. Pen was a massive composition of stone, brick, cement, and steel; an impersonal, heartless place. The only sanctuary was within oneself. It was not populated by realities, but by caricatured cardboard cut-outs, all dressed in the same type of clothes. Each cut-out was a number. Mine was Y5565 and it was stamped onto all my clothes. The "Y" indicated I was under the age of 21.

Convicts were counted many times during a day. 491 convicts locked in cells at night must result in 491 being let out the following morning. If the numbers don't add up to 491 everything stopped until the 491 were accounted for.

Some of these cut-outs lethargically shuffled about with pieces of emery paper to polish the steel bars; use moistened rags to remove the dust; pails and mops to swab the floors and wash the walls; brushes and brooms to sweep the debris. This cleansing, polishing, and shining is part of a hard-labour sentence. It keeps convicts busy.

18

TIME AND AGAIN

The prison was run by the warden and guards. They wore military-style uniforms embellished with the insignia of rank. Guards saluted the warden and snapped to attention in his presence. Convicts walked in straight lines and stood in the presence of the warden or other prison officials.

In the early 1940s there was no doubt about where a convict stood when he appeared before the warden. In Warden's Court, outlines of two feet were painted on the floor. The convict stood at attention with his feet inside the outlines. This put the convict about four feet in front of the warden's desk which was on a raised platform.

A convict can't be on the same level as a warden. The warden has to be looked up to. The warden can then look down on the convict-object. Kings and emperors did. Why not wardens?

It was Warden Meighen, brother of former Prime Minister Arthur Meighen, before whom all fish appeared for an interview.

A few days after being loaded onto the fish tier I was escorted by a guard to Warden's Court. It was an instructional session rather than an interview. The message was authority. That message came clearly from the Court and its fixtures and from Deputy Warden Douglass who was also there. Warden Meighen, in 1943, was sixty-four years old and had spent twenty-eight years of his life in the Penitentiary Service. He was a dumpy guy with a bland, round, expressionless face. His eyes were crumpled behind thick eye glasses. He didn't look like authority. Prison gossip said he was only counting the days until his retirement. He retired in 1946. Deputy Warden Douglass ran the prison.

Warden Meighen was reputed to have boasted that he was preordained to be a prison officer at the B.C. Penitentiary; that it was God's will. It was alleged that he based this claim on two coincidences: one was that he was born in 1878 which was the same year that the B.C. Pen. was built; and, two, he joined the Penitentiary Service as an accountant in 1914 which was the same year that the south wing of the B.C. Pen. was built.

Deputy Warden Douglass stood at the front of the raised platform; tall, militarily erect, hawk-nosed. His eyes were so dark it appeared as if iris and pupil had merged.

Meighen's glasses glimmered at me. "You have been given a copy of the rules of conduct. Have you read them?"

"Yes."

Douglass asked a question in a voice which gave an order. "Yes, what?"

"Yes, sir."

Douglass continued. "Those rules are to be obeyed. Disobey them and you'll be back here on charge."

Obeying prison rules earned the convict a reduction in his sentence. Officials called it remission; in prison parlance it was good time. Behave and one earns this good time. In earning good time one's sentence was reduced by a formula which, for example, saw a two-year sentence cut back to something like nineteen months. Break the rules and the Warden could "claw back" this good time.

The loss of good time, a bread and water diet in the hole (solitary confinement), and having your bared ass paddled or strapped were the punishments to reinforce discipline.

Was there any philosophic content to discipline? I doubt it. It was used to keep convicts in line and nourish the ego of the power structure. Discipline was not a rehabilitative tool.

In fact, rehabilitation was not a penological buzz word forty or fifty years ago. The practice was simple: barricade the convict from the rest of society. When he got out he and society were back on the same footing again. The barricade was down. The penitentiary with its blind imposition of discipline was intact, waiting for the return of those so recently released. Return they did and they still do.

That earlier prison system was not cluttered up with the theories of liberal-minded social scientists. It probably didn't cut down on recidivism, but it cost less.

Recidivism seemed to interest Warden Meighan. One of his questions dumbfounded me. "Many of the convicts in here have been in jail many times before. Time and again they keep coming back. Do you have any idea why they keep returning?"

My undernourished 18 year old brain couldn't contemplate such a puzzle. All I could think of was that the question was irrelevant. I was concerned with me and not with every other convict in the joint. I was number one. Screw everybody else for they would surely screw me at any opportunity.

Further questions asked for facts and intentions. I related that I left school before completing Grade ten and that I had worked in an iron foundry. I said that I was interested in mechanical matters and that working in one of the shops would be helpful. I was asked if I wanted to attend the prison school or take correspondence courses. "Yes, sir" to both. I was told to make a right turn and leave the room. A guard took me shuffling back to my fish-tier cell and the two pieces of reading material provided by the prison: the rules and the Bible.

19

THE DOME GANG

After the initial segregation of some four or five days the fish becomes an ordinary convict. He is dumped into one of the prison's working units (gangs), usually the dome gang.

The dome gang comprised the sweepers, washers, moppers, scrubbers, dusters, and bar shiners. It cleaned and scrubbed the central domed hall and the cell blocks. It was the underground message centre for the convict population.

The first chore of all who got assigned to the dome gang was to shine the steel cell bars by whisking emery paper around them. We didn't have to be speedy about it. There was no deadline to meet and we were not being paid at piece-work rates. There was enough work for everyone, forever.

Larry J. was my bar-shining tutor. He was a drug addict, a junky, a dope fiend—the handle changes from time to time. Today Larry would be a substance abuser, a euphemism which doesn't change a damned thing. We have this army of social scientists and helpers who dream up fancy words and phrases to describe age-old problems. New words won't provide a cure, but they will make it appear as if something new is taking place. When the new words lose their lustre, replacements will easily be developed, but the addict will still be there.

Any drug addict with an ounce of brains will admit that there are two ways to kick the habit. One is to stop taking drugs; the other is what is called the Chinese cure. Years ago a program existed in China under which opium dealers, opium-den operators, and addicts were shot.

Larry was off heroin only while in prison. The last time he was released he was met by other addicts who drove him into Vancouver. He got his first fix in the car as it was moving down the prison driveway. He said that he got one high from the heroin, and another from fixing "right under their goddamned noses." He was back in within two months.

He was a short, thin, black-haired guy who weighed less than a sack of cement. He had a two or three-inch jagged scar ranging from above his left eyebrow down across the outer edge of his eye to his cheek bone. His left eyelid drooped, covering the upper portion of his eye.

His eyes darted everywhere, always on the lookout for any movement by anybody. When he opened his eyes wide the left eyelid moved upward fractionally, giving him the appearance of something poisonous and unpredictable.

"We ain't never gonna get these bars the way them bulls want 'em, eh. So we gonna make it the best way we can, eh. The best way for us, eh." Larry spoke without moving his lips, an ability developed so guards couldn't guess what was being said by watching lip movement. His voice had a range of about four feet.

"O.K., how do we do that?" I asked.

"Keep your voice down, eh. We ain't paradin' up and down Granville Street. We don't want them bulls to hear nothin', eh." He proceeded to show me how the bar shining was done. It was simple, but, as with make-work projects the world over, elaborate attention had to be paid to details. The soft zzzz, zzzz was background noise helping to mask conversation.

"I'm gonna tell ya about tomorra mornin', eh. A guy in the kitchen says we gonna have johnny cake for breakfast tomorra. The word is...

"What's johnny cake?" I asked.

"What's johnny cake?" Larry repeated incredulously.

"Yeh, I don't know what it is."

"It ain't nothin' but bread made outta corn or somethin' like that, eh. But, the word is out. We don't eat it. We send it back and that'll tell 'em to stick it, eh."

"Why? What's wrong with it?" I asked.

"We had johnny cake twice this week awready and if it gets shoved back at 'em, maybe they'll back off, eh."

As soon as I said, "Do I have to?" I knew it was a dumb question and knew what the answer would be.

"Nah, you don't have ta. You don't have ta do nothin', eh. But, if you don't shove it back at 'em, someone might notice and ree-mem-ber."

Larry's eyes stopped scanning and bored directly into mine. His right eye glinted like the end of a steel rod. I nodded my head, said O.K., and went back to zzzzing the bars.

I got a break from the bar-shining drudgery by being assigned to school. The room was about thirty feet square. Desks and a blackboard marked it as a school class room, but it was the entire school.

Its eldest student was about sixty years old and had not got past Grade three; the youngest was eighteen. Our scholastic backgrounds varied, but none had got through high school.

Students were not lumped into particular grades. There were no grades. The teacher simply gave each student assistance with some subject of interest to the student. Some tried to learn arithmetic, some tried grammar. Some just tried to learn to read. No one graduated from this school.

It was located directly above the shoe shop. Incessant clattering and thumping of machines filled the school room. In the shoe shop they made and repaired shoes for the prison guards and for all convicts. The guards and the shoe-shop convicts got the best. Others got good quality shoes if they had an in with the shoe-shop workers.

My pre-prison attendance at school had always been casual. Sometimes I attended; sometimes I didn't. No one seemed to give a damn one way or the other. We had to do something while waiting for that magic age which would see us catapulted into a job.

So, here I was in prison; back in school along with a bunch of other society rejects. We were in a class by itself, the class without the keys. It wasn't that I had any long-range plans, any grand scheme for the future. The future was the day-to-day humdrum routine of prison life. I attended school partly to escape boredom and partly to learn. It was mostly something to do while filling in time.

Here I was again with the textbooks relating to the seventh grade. I finally got a grasp of the relationship of nouns to verbs, of adjectives to nouns, but dangling participles still dangled out of reach.

20

GOOD LUCK IN A BAD SCENE

The B.C. Pen. functioned under the silent system. Convicts were forbidden to speak to one another unless the conversation related to the work they were doing and at the time the work was being done. We were forbidden to speak to a prison guard unless spoken to first, or to make a request. Talking at other than the permitted times or for other than the permitted purposes was a punishable offence, but this rule was often overlooked.

When everyone was locked up for the night, each in his own individual cell, a period of time was assigned during which convicts could talk with one another. Talk is too gentle a word; it was more like conversational bedlam. Talking took place by shouting through the cell bars.

Talk time was bridge-playing time. One convict, not a player, would deal out bridge hands from his own deck of cards (perhaps for a dozen games at a time) and list each player's hand on separate sheets of paper, identifying each game numerically. Each player would be given the sheets for his hand. When bidding was completed, the dummy hand would be shouted out and each other player would make a list of the dummy hand.

When cribbage was introduced it caused some consternation among the bridge players, but this got sorted out by alternating bridge and cribbage nights.

Wagers were made in tobacco; that was the currency. Trust was a major factor and was honoured. I know of no instance when any of the players felt that information about the cards being held ever leaked out. Any breach of that trust would mean the end of the games, and he who breached the trust would suffer prison-level consequences.

The "Y" on our clothes made young convicts the butt for sexually oriented comments. Youths were referred to as "gunsels" by most older convicts. The "gunsel" tag could mean either the owner was not a seasoned crook, or he was an object for homosexual purposes. Compliance was not a prerequisite. The only requirement was any cavity, readily available or not, for an orgasm.

When not in use, the cleaning equipment for the dome gang's work was stored away in an open broom closet at the end of each tier of cells. I had been in the dome gang for about a month. One day I went into one of these storage compartments to get a scrubbing brush, but suddenly that was not important.

What was important was the appearance in the doorway of Mush W., a convict about whom Larry had warned me. Mush was a prison jock who sought out younger convicts; he would be their protector or "old man."

I don't know where he came from, for I had not seen him earlier. He stayed in the doorway. Showing all the charm of a coiled cobra he leered at me and then swerved his head towards the dome to see if guards were in sight. There were none, so the leer went back into place and he said, "You ever do time before?"

"No, this is my first bit."

"Whatcha need is someone ta look after you, ta protect you. There's lots of bad nuts in this joint and a young kid like you could get hurt. I can help. Uh, know what I mean?"

I knew what he meant. I had been in the Juvenile Detention Home for only a few days, but that was enough time for some of the east-end, street-wise kids to clue me into the fleshy and more coarse prison activities. They knew of such matters from older neighbourhood thugs or from older brothers.

"Yeh," I replied, "I know what you mean, but I don't want none of it."

"Listen, gunsel, some of the guys in here will have you doin' it both ways, and that ain't gonna be good for you. I can put out the word ta lay off, uh… and you won't be bothered by 'em. It'll just be you and me."

"I don't want nothing to do with that. I ain't a queer, and I don't want to become one." Brave words, but?

"Don't smart-ass with me, you gunsel punk. It don't matter ta me if you're queer or not."

With that he grabbed his crotch and juggled his hand toward me. "I got this for you and I'll ram it down your throat any time I want. And, I want ta right now. On your knees."

A stiff cock has no conscience, but when it belongs to an hedonistic psychotic there is extreme danger.

The situation called for a cold, rational plan from me. It's possible to deal with brutes by outwitting them, and surely I could outwit Mush. One course would be to grab one of the brooms, hold it by the brush-end, and spear Mush in the guts. Another would be to pretend to follow his order, but scuttle out between his legs or around them and gain entry to the safety of the dome. Still a third choice would be to pick up one of the buckets and attack him with that.

The truth is I was trapped. I didn't know what to do, but I had to fight back if he made any move towards me. He was prison-wise and stayed in the doorway to be able to see me and watch the dome at the same time.

I backed up further into the storage compartment and tripped over a bucket. The clanging racket broke the impasse. Mush quickly moved away from the doorway and walked towards the dome. As I was picking myself up a guard's voice shouted, "What's going on over there?"

The guard arrived on the run, repeating the question, "What's going on here? You," he said, pointing at Mush, "come back here."

"What were you doing?" he asked Mush.

"Nothin', Sir. I was just bringing back a broom."

"You," demanded the guard pointing at me, "what are you doing? What was that noise?"

"Nothing, Sir, I, uh, I just tripped and knocked this bucket over. I was looking for a scrub brush."

The guard's eyes looked at Mush, then looked back at me. His eyes said he didn't believe either of us.

"Both of you, get about your work."

That night I was brave and cool and rational. It was then that I had those visions of striking Mush over the head with the bucket I'd tripped over, or of beating him off with a broom handle, or of scuttling between his legs. It was easy for I was secure in 3-B-4, my one-to-a-convict cell.

The guard must have reported the incident along with whatever his suspicions were, for, within a few days, I was transferred to the machine shop.

A good feature of the Penitentiary Act of 1939 was Section 66 (4) which said that a convict shall be kept by himself in a cell at night. The re-enactment of that law would tend to reduce homosexual attacks in prisons. But who the hell cares? It would cost too much money.

Being confined by myself in a cell at night provided a refuge of sorts. The B.C. Pen. had a central radio system operated only at night and for a short period of time. The system's speakers hung from the cell-block wall, blaring noise at everyone. The choices were either to listen, or try to block out the sound.

When relative quiet did arrive, it was brought by the night-shift guards who, at a precise time, shut down the central radio. If peace and quiet can exist in a prison, it existed then.

The night-shift guards wore soft-soled shoes so as not to disturb our sleep, our thoughts, our misery, our despair, our peace and quiet. As soon as the radio and the lights went off we were back into silent time. Time for wide-awake type dreams, reminiscences, re-living the day's events, being apprehensive about the future, wondering what the hell it was all about. It was live-your-own-hell time; piss-on-the-world time; do-your-own-thing time, but don't get caught at it for that's a crime, too.

Here's how you do it. Tie a piece of thread securely around this rubber eraser. Tie the other end of the thread around those cigarettes which are wrapped in that toilet paper. Get down on your hands and knees. Take that 12 inch ruler and slip it through the bars. Place the eraser on the end of the ruler and push it out as far as you can. Keep the cigarette end of the thread inside in case retrieval is necessary. Here comes the tricky part. Flip the eraser in front of the cell next to yours. This will permit the guy next door to reach out, grab the eraser and pull in the cigarettes.

But, there are problems. This one had soft-soled shoes and tan-coloured, creased trousers. The guy wearing them had been standing just out of sight at the edge of my cell. When I flipped the eraser off the end of the ruler he moved into view.

"You'll be on the crime sheet for Warden's Court tomorrow," said the guard while looking up at my number above the cell door. He took the apparatus and cigarettes as evidence.

Infractions of prison rules result in the convict being charged "crimed", and having to appear in Warden's Court.

On the outside one is presumed innocent and it's up to the Court to decide otherwise. In Warden's Court the accused was presumed to be guilty. The foundation for this doctrine was that the prison guard was an honourable person, while the convict was a liar. The convict was not asked whether he pleaded guilty or not guilty, or how he pleaded. He was asked if he was guilty as charged which implied that guilt is presumed and that the convict had to prove his innocence.

"5565—in here—look smart," snapped the guard in attendance at Warden's Court. "Step forward. Halt. Right turn. Stand at attention." The Warden's Clerk chanted out something like: "Warden, Sir, convict 5565 is charged with attempting to give cigarettes to another convict contrary to the rule against such action with the attempt being made at approximately 10:15 last evening as reported by Officer Wimpson who was on duty at the time."

"Are you guilty as charged?" demanded the warden.

"Yes, Sir."

"Three days remission."

Right turn, step lively.

I would do three days more than I originally thought. Was it one day for each cigarette?

21

COMMITTING SIDEWAYS

A convict is usually pleased when moved from one part of a prison to another. It brings him into closer contact with other convicts. It breaks the monotony.

After a month or so on the dome gang I was moved to the machine shop. Changing from one gang to another was reason enough for me to welcome the move. An additional bonus was that, from working in Crossley's foundry, I knew something about working with metals and tools.

The move to the machine shop meant the end of school attendance, because convicts were locked in their places of work. Attending the prison's school was basically a relief from the monotony of sweeping, shining, dusting, and attempting to look busy. The one positive result of moving, though, was arranging to take correspondence courses. I signed up for three courses: English literature and algebra at the Grade-ten level, and mechanical drawing at the beginner's level.

In the machine shop we made and repaired items used by the penitentiary. The shop contained two lathes, a shaper, a milling machine, a power hack saw, a blacksmith's forge, a drill press, and an assortment of hand tools.

The machine shop was run by a machinist-instructor, a Mr. Chin. The machine shop didn't do a roaring business, the consequence being that we had a lot of idle time. Chin's only demands were that the work get done and that we stay out of sight when not working. He didn't want anyone to peer in the windows and see his charges lounging around.

When hands are idle, mischief results. In our spare time we made "trade goods"—items used by the convict population which couldn't be acquired otherwise. They were classified as contraband, and possession of them was a crime. It was common knowledge that we made such items. Chin's rule about making contraband items was simple: if you got caught, you got crimed.

The contraband items most in demand were belt buckles. We drew the line at making knives or any similar attack-type devices. Refusing requests to make knives was not an ideological decision, it was a practical one. The question was risk versus reward, and the risk was too high. Knives could kill and anyone could be on the receiving end.

There were five of us in the machine shop, two of whom had spent a lot of time in jails. They were the "old lags"; they were prison-level teachers. The other two and I constituted potential students.

Convicts enjoy boasting about their exploits and letting you in on the secrets of their specific professions. At that level the teaching is based on experience, interlaced with fiction.

One of the older convicts was a safecracker, a "pete man." He didn't use his given name but opted for the label of his profession. Pete was a short man, a few inches above five feet. He was stocky, wide-shouldered, wide-hipped, and slightly bow-legged. His sandy, greying hair fringed a bald head. His eyes were dull and lifeless, looking like boiled gooseberries peering through a flimsy grate of grey eyelashes. He had large, brilliantly white teeth set in a wide mouth, and, when he spoke, he sounded as if he was gargling. His voice got that way as the result of his being too close to a safe he was blowing. The explosion also deafened him in one ear.

He told us of the different safe-cracking techniques, describing the tools and materials in detail. I learned the theory of blowing safes, but would probably blow myself up if I ever tried it. It wasn't my game.

The other older convict earned the name Silver from his years as a con man. Silver was in his fifties, six feet tall with a full head of grey hair, grey eyebrows, and grey whiskers. (We were paraded into the barber shop once a week to be shaved. Safety razors were used—thought-provoking because one of the barbers was doing ten years for manslaughter. He killed a man by cutting his throat with a razor.) Silver was lean to the point of thinness, with a narrow face, hollowed cheeks, thin lips, and sparkling brown eyes. One of the characteristics, so said Silver, which gives a con man an aura of believability is that of looking straight into the eyes of the person being conned—the mark, the sucker.

Silver's voice matched his nickname and his line of work; it was gentle, well modulated, and so sincere. His diction was precise, almost professorial, and he used a lot of multi-syllable words. He refused to use jail-house language, saying he didn't want to get into the habit for fear it would intrude itself at the wrong moment outside.

Tank was the nickname affixed to the other young kid, so named because he moved like a tank, ponderously and in a straight line. Tank was a big kid. His neck was the same width as his head. His chest and stomach were barrel-shaped. His arms and legs were thick and solid. When he was standing his legs were spread apart and his arms angled outward from his shoulders, giving him a gorilla-like appearance. Tank was about 250 pounds of solid meat and bone.

Tank was psychologically uni-directional. Ideas became firmly fixed in his mind and he could not be persuaded that he was wrong about anything. With Tank, frustration produced aggression, but aggression didn't produce remorse. It was not wise to get into an argument with Tank; his response could so quickly be physical. He blew up at the slightest provocation, got it out of his system, went back to what was normal for him, and offered no apologies.

Silver nicknamed me Kid because I was the youngest person in the shop.

The convict doing ten years preferred to be called Bobby. He was in his early twenties, dark haired with a thin, pale face. His ten-year bit was for murder, but he didn't talk about it or much about himself.

Tank set his mattress on fire one night. The resulting smoke and the running, scurrying hustle of guards trying to douse the fire and get him out was the event of the evening. Apart from coughing, the rest of us in the area were absolutely silent. This was no time to get the attention of any guard. They were as on point as a cat at a mouse hole. Any undue noise from any of us would see us crimed for something.

Tank also slashed his wrists, apparently with a small piece of metal which he had smuggled out of the machine shop. He was band-aided for the cuts and lodged in the prison's hospital. Later, Warden's Court gave him time in the hole and took away a large chunk of his good time. He didn't return to the machine shop. He went to work on the Dome Gang where he would be under the constant surveillance of guards.

In the machine shop the next day we had something new to talk about. The common thread was that Tank was a "bug", so anything he did was not a total surprise. Pete's view was one of regret that Tank had not succeeded. Silver had a different view. He said that Tank was controlled by his emotions and the wrist-slashing, mattress-burning caper had simply been Tank's way of expressing his annoyance over some frustrating experience.

Silver said that Tank was not serious about suicide, for, if he had been, he would have been successful. He would have cut deeply into one of his arteries and bled to death, or taken the route of hanging himself. Slashing his wrist was a superficial act resulting in a scratch more than a cut. Silver also said that emotionally disturbed people often slashed their wrists to get attention. I couldn't help thinking of my efforts and concluding that I hadn't been serious either.

Prison-level jargon called suicide "committing sideways." One steps off the main path and takes a side road—a dead end.

During one of our lulls Bobby got to talking about tattoos. He said that we didn't need a tattoo parlour; just some india ink and a needle. All convicts were provided with a needle and some thread in case we needed to do some repair work at night. All convicts were not provided with india ink, but I was.

He sterilized the needle in the flame of a blow torch. He swabbed the inner part of my right forearm with gasoline, another sterilizing move. He drew the outline of a heart on my arm and placed a small amount of india ink over the outline. With quick, short jabs of the needle he forced the ink under my skin.

Somehow the system heard about it and I got crimed for malingering. Again I was in Warden's Court to answer the charge. Whoever tipped the authorities off was not called as a witness. Prison officials will not identify such people for it would place them in a vulnerable position.

I said I was not guilty as charged. Then the questions from the Warden.

"How did you get that tattoo?"

"I did it myself with a needle and some india ink, Sir."

"Where did you get the india ink?"

"I'm taking a course in mechanical drawing, Sir, and you authorized letting me have india ink for the course."

"Where did you do this tattooing?"

"In my cell at night, Sir."

I gloated because I figured I had them beat. Then Deputy Warden Douglass spoke up.

"Are you left handed?"

"No, Sir, but I thought it would be more difficult using my left hand."

That was it. The warden took away ten days good time. An expensive tattoo, but at least they didn't proceed against Bobby. Maybe one lesson was enough for all of us.

22

THEFT IS VOLUNTARY

Cell time was self-examination time. Was it the influence of Mom and Dad which taught me to lie and to steal? I came to the conclusion that their influence simply tapped into a mind which was receptive to such lessons. Persistence in laying the blame for my behaviour on them merely allowed me to escape from my responsibilities to me.

Was my behaviour and attitude inherited? I understand that a large body of psychological opinion supports that general position. For myself I think such opinions are "a crock." The important factor is that the decisions to steal were made by me, and I enjoyed the action. I had to live with the consequences. Blaming my behaviour on my parents (real or foster) was a way to escape responsibility. No point in trying to deal with the problem when the cause of it is beyond reach.

One thing is clear to me. I have a basic leaning towards theft. Stealing was pleasurable. It seems as if I always had that propensity, and, while I'm now in my 70s, I still notice the opportunities. Of course, so do others. There are handbags left unattended in shopping carts, cars with the keys in the ignition, cars with the windows down and items of value on the seats. What's the difference? Others ignore the chance. I consciously refuse the temptation. Like the alcoholic who admits his addiction and refuses to take that first drink, so I make the admission and likewise refuse the temptation.

I met dozens of convicts who "were not at fault." They kept coming back because they wanted to and because they were unable to accept the fact that they were the cause of their own difficulties. Ignoring the consequences is, according to some faulty proverb, supposed to indicate bravery. When the criminal intellect is involved, it merely reflects stupidity. Herein lies the answer to Warden Meighan's question, although I do not believe that he, or any other functionary in the penitentiary system in the 1940s, understood this.

There were no psychologists or psychiatrists in the B.C. Penitentiary in the 1940s. The prison system was not then being run by social scientists, but by security-conscious people. Any alteration in behaviour had to be self-generated. In many, probably the majority, there was no motive for, or interest in, self-analysis. I maintain the same is true today, notwithstanding the army of social scientists who are seemingly working on the subject.

Many of the convicts were going to do life a few years at time. A case in point: Tony C. who was in his mid to late twenties in 1943. He was doing seven years. Before that he had done five years; before that three; before that two.

I, too, could do life a few years at a time. I, too, could come back again. I could easily arrange to meet up with fellow convicts after our release and take part in spinning the wheel once more. Misery does love companionship. Criminals are basically miserable people, and can both give and find comfort by association with those who are also miserable.

The questions with which I wrestled were: Was I clever enough to commit further crimes and not get caught? Did I want to do life a bit at a time? The answer to both: No.

I had to, and more importantly wanted to, take a different course. During those some nineteen months I spent in the B.C. Pen. I had a lot of time to myself—time to think and accept that no one had caused me as much trouble and misery as I had and that no one in the future was likely to. I never stole again.

23

A LITTLE BIT OF TRUST

As a convict's time for release gets closer, officials extend a bit of trust. In the B.C. Penitentiary this was accomplished by transferring the convict to one of the gangs outside the walls.

Sometime in the fall of 1944 I was sent to an outside gang. Alex Y. and I were assigned to a carpenter-guard. Under the carpenter's instruction we built additional chicken coops. I learned how to measure and cut rafters properly, how to shingle a roof. On the sly I learned how to suck raw eggs. Being forbidden made it that much more attractive.

The next move was to the wharf gang. The wharf gang functioned alongside the Fraser River and some railway tracks. One of the convicts went out into the river with a boat and towed back logs which were adrift. The logs were pulled up onto the land and sawn into four foot lengths. These were split into sections some four to six inches thick and stacked in piles, firewood for the prison's hot-water heating system.

The wharf gang's location was ideal for smuggling contraband into the prison. Released convicts would return at night and hide the items in the wood piles, wrapped in parcels about two feet long and four inches thick.

The smuggled goods usually consisted of chewing gum, chocolate bars, and cigarettes. Sometimes there was whisky, sometimes heroin. We might find out later what the items were.

The wharf gang would be tipped off about the timing and would load the parcels along with the stacked wood onto trucks. The convicts in the boiler house removed the parcels and gradually got them distributed to the expectant inside gang.

On one particular rainy day we were loading the stacked wood onto a truck, but the guard on duty (I recall his name being Scraggs) stood close by instead of walking around as he usually did. The loading procedure was to have two convicts, one on each side of the stacked wood, pick up a split piece by its ends and swing it up onto the deck of the truck where two other convicts re-stacked it.

We were getting closer to the parcels. If the guard didn't move we were in trouble. I kept my hand around the end of the split piece we were then throwing up onto the truck and let my hand get smashed between the wood and the deck of the truck. That stopped the operation. The guard took me over to the first-aid kit and bandaged my hand. Another convict took over my part and the parcels got onto the truck. I went along with the truck to the hospital section of the penitentiary and got further treatment. It wasn't a serious injury, just some lacerations. If I hadn't done that, someone else would have done something to attract the guard's attention.

The tools we used were kept in a large shed alongside the work area, retrieved in the morning and locked away at night.

One day we had to move a large, box-shaped container from one part of this shed to another. Putting a couple of rollers under the container would make the task easier.

Scraggs, using a small piece of wood for a fulcrum, inserted a pry-bar under the bottom of the container so it could be levered up enough to put one of the rollers in place. It didn't go as planned; the pry-bar slipped off the fulcrum and pinned his hand to the cement floor. He was immobilized and we were free—in theory.

We could have casually walked away along the railway tracks and disappeared. That was the first automatic thought. Get out of here. I rejected the idea almost as soon as it popped into my head. Others must have done the same. We were all short-timers; just a few weeks or months to go. No one said a word about it; each individual must have concluded that it would be stupid to escape. Instead of running we helped Scraggs get free from his pinned-down position.

Scraggs should have had us convicts do the job. He was a guard. He was supposed to guard us and keep us from escaping. It was a dumb move on his part and if his superiors had found out what had happened he would have been fired. We kept it to ourselves. If it had become known that we turned him in, we would no doubt have suffered. We were not only in a different class from guards; we were in the lowest class.

24

ELATED BY REJECTION

I was wearing my new suit, my new shoes, my new shirt, my new socks. I was carrying my old duffel bag which contained what few clothes I had upon entering the B.C. Pen. I had $10.00 in my pocket, the minimum amount payable to a released convict (prison pay was 5 cents a day out of which tobacco was bought—a weekly net income of 8 cents). I had a bus ticket to Vancouver. I also had my Canadian Army call-up notice which was handed to me on the way out. It was springtime, 1945.

First stop: the B.C. Electric tram station at Carroll and Hastings Streets. I changed into my own clothes, and put my duffle bag into a locker.

Second stop: a pawn shop where I sold my prison-suit for $5.00. The proprietor, recognizing what I was offering, said "Looks like a jail-made suit." No comment.

Third stop: The Roman Catholic Church on Richards Street. Prison gossip was that the Church was good for a dollar or two. Had I been to confession lately? "Well, no Father, I've had nothing to confess for some time; not much chance for sin out there." Had I received communion lately? "No, Father, not for some time." "Come to Mass this Sunday." "Yes, Father, and thank you." Add $2.00 to my bankroll.

Fourth stop: The John Howard Society on Pender Street. No handout, but advice about a place to bed down while looking for work. I felt confident that the Army would not want me.

Fifth stop: the Army barracks at Little Mountain. Other convicts had told me different strategies they used to stay out of the Army. Alex Y., a heroin addict, told Army officials that he used dope and couldn't wait to get into the medical corps. He was rejected. Maurice G. said he looked forward to getting a gun in his hand; having the legitimate right to shoot people was a godsend. He was rejected; he might shoot the wrong people.

Convict-level information said the guy to deal with was the psychiatrist. Convince him you are not what the Army wants and the Army won't take you. The war in Europe was almost over and the Army was not that desperate.

The receptionist wore the chevrons of a sergeant. I sat at the side of her desk while she looked over my Army call.

"Why are you so late in getting here?" The implication was that I was a draft dodger.

"I just got out of the penitentiary this morning."

"Oh."

Throughout the whole interview I challenged her by staring her in the eyes, trying to appear like a hard-line crook.

First came some vital statistic questions, the answers dutifully entered on the form in front of her.

Then, it was nationality, citizenship, or something similar.

"Canadian."

She told me she couldn't enter Canadian because it was not an accepted nationality or citizenship at the time.

"What is the nationality or citizenship of your parents?"

"I don't know."

"Your name sounds English, so I'll put that down."

"I'm not English; I'm a Canadian and I don't want English put on my record."

The Sergeant said, "Well, we'll enter 'unknown'."

Being in the Army would be an extension of prison time. I wouldn't need to concern myself about meals; they would be provided. A place to sleep: provided. Clothes: provided. Freedom: restricted. Obedience: demanded and enforced. Release: some unknown time in the future, if the war didn't kill me.

The Army would have been a suffocating blanket. To prove myself to me and my commitment to do it right I had to be put to the test as quickly as possible. Army life could easily dilute my resolve and probably would. The simple passage of time in a protective environment would seduce me. Like the raging hangover of the boozer who promises "never again" I might develop the same kind of forgetfulness and rationalization.

The Army's psychiatrist (the last stop prior to handing out the uniforms) repeated, almost word for word, the first question by the Sergeant. The answer was the same. Then there were other questions. What did you do to get sent to jail? Why did you do it? What did you think about in jail? Then came the important question: do you think you would like being in the Army?

My answer, somewhat rehearsed, but truly reflecting my feelings, was that I had just spent nineteen months with rigid discipline being imposed every day. I had had as much discipline as I could stand. Being taken into the Army would impose more and I didn't think I could handle it.

I was rejected, and elated. The reality is that I didn't con the psychiatrist; neither did Alex Y. or Maurice G., even though they gloated that they did. I think the truth was that the Army didn't want people who had a criminal record.

I could have "gone home to mother." I could have obtained money from her and Dad to get back to Kimberley. I could probably have got a job with the C.M.&S. That would have been the easy route, one I didn't want to take. I felt I had to return to the scene of the crime, but not to find the culprit; I knew who that was. I had to find that other person within me and do it on my terms.

During the next few months I went to places which I had robbed. Standing outside them I talked to myself, saying things like, "I stole from this store, but I don't do that any longer." Melodramatic? Probably, but I was the only one in the audience; the only one listening; the only one to influence. I had to drive the past into oblivion; bring closure to it and start off afresh.

The Canadian Army wasn't the only army in existence. From the Little Mountain barracks I went to the Salvation Army.

25

IN STOCKINGED FEET

The Sally Ann took me in. The officer at the hostel didn't ask questions about confession, communion, church attendance or religious beliefs. He simply told me that I could live there for a short time until I had established myself with a job and had enough money to live somewhere else. The Sally Ann offered a helping hand, not a hand out.

The Sally Ann did not, as did the Roman Catholic priest, suggest that I attend church services; a refreshing distinction. I had gone to the Protestant Church services in the penitentiary, but that was a social outing. Church attendance got convicts out of their cells for an hour or so. It allowed convicts to arrange meetings with others, to exchange gossip, contraband goods, or written notes (kites). The services and the singing meant nothing to most of the attenders. It was a weekly break from the monotony and a relative break from discipline.

I bought a cheap alarm clock. I bought a second-hand pair of work boots. I got a day-time job sorting scrap metal at Atlas Metals on Hastings Street. I got an afternoon-shift job at the Wallace shipyard on False Creek. I walked to the Atlas Metals yard every week-day morning, left at 2:00 in the afternoon to walk to the shipyard. I walked back to the hostel after midnight. No sense wasting money on street cars. I needed every penny I could salt away.

The second-hand work boots blistered my feet, so the walking between jobs was done in my stocking feet. One of the good parts about working at Atlas Metals was that I could get paid every day. In a few days I bought a better-fitting pair of boots.

Through Alf's wife I discovered that the woman I spent my first intimate encounter with was living in Vancouver. Following some nineteen months in an all-male environment I eagerly went to visit her. She was as pleased to see me as I was to see her but nothing permanent developed.

For the following few years I was simply exercising my freedom to go where I wanted to go, do what I wanted to do, and make damned sure that I did nothing which might remotely lead me back to prison. I had no vision about my future, no grand plan.

But one thing was clear. Whatever I attempted, I had to give it my full attention and work like hell to make a success of it. After the orphanage and the foster homes and prison, I had the bare minimum of self-confidence and self-respect.

I worked, made money, and spent it. I worked as an iron moulder in three different foundries. Using a photography-shop portfolio as a sample, I tried selling family portraits door-to-door. That wasn't successful. I dug holes for in-ground oil tanks, mowed lawns, sanded chairs in a furniture factory, filled sacks with coal, worked as a part-time bartender, fixed clutches and installed brake linings in an automobile repair shop.

My mind was clear about one thing: don't apply for a job by saying that you can't do it. Whatever it was, I could do it. I hired on as a nipper (a miner's helper) at Granby Consolidated's mine at Copper Mountain, a few miles south of Princeton in B.C.

I got ready to go underground by watching what others did in the dry (the room where we changed into work clothes). We went straight down in a cage (an elevator) to what was the 5th level—about 1,200 feet below the surface. Upon leaving the cage, I motioned Ole Ardell, the miner I was to work with, to one side and told him that I had never worked underground in my life.

He said he was glad I told him, for he would have discovered that in about 30 seconds. He told me what to do, what different lengths of steel (drills) were for, why there was a relationship between the size of the bits (heads) and the length of the steels, how to set up the drilling machine he used, how to put fuses and dynamite together. He made me into a hard-rock miner. Within three months I had my blasting papers.

There's a lot of water in an underground mine. It is used to cool the drilling bits and keep down the dust. In some instances it drains away along the tunnels (drifts) and out of the mine. In some mines it is pumped back up to the surface.

Because of the wetness it was difficult to keep cigarettes burning, so a lot of miners chewed tobacco or used a moist and ground up form of tobacco called "snoose" which they shoved into the side of the mouth between the cheek and the teeth. Chewing tobacco came in the shape of a bar called a "plug." A plug of tobacco had to be kept moist.

There were portable toilets, but they were usually some distance away. Those working underground usually urinated into the running water at the side of a drift.

In one location there were three sets of miners and nippers working close to one another. We would eat together sitting on empty, wooden dynamite boxes. One of the nippers, a young kid about my age, for a lark more than anything, was always bumming a chew of tobacco from one of the miners.

One day this miner said that his plug of tobacco was getting dry. He walked over to the side of the drift and pissed on it. Shaking the excess moisture off the plug he offered it to the young kid. That ended it.

I went to work in the coastal logging industry in B.C. I got a job setting chokers—a strong-back, weak-mind job. Certain loggers (fallers) sawed through the trunks of trees which then fell to the ground. The fallen trees had their branches removed and were sawn (bucked) into varying lengths.

Setting chokers involved forcing my way through this jungle of logs, rocks, and brush while pulling a length of steel cable (the choker) behind me. One end of this choker was then wrapped around a log and locked into place somewhat similar to the way in which a belt buckle locks one's pants into place.

The other end of the choker was fitted or hooked onto a cable which was attached to a machine that pulled the log out of the jungle to a central place, a "landing."

Certain types of women's necklaces are called chokers; setting chokers was also called setting beads.

This particular choker-setting job was at a small logging operation (a gyppo) in which a tractor (a cat) was used to haul the logs out of the bush and to a landing. It was called a "cat show." The tractor operator was called a "cat skinner." From him I learned how to operate a "cat." The next logging job I got was as a cat skinner.

Another type of logging operation was referred to as a "high-lead show." A high-lead show used a machine called a "yarder" which had huge cylindrical devices (drums) upon which cables were wound, just as sewing thread is wound onto a spool. The yarder was secured to the ground, a stationary machine.

The cables from the yarder were fed though huge pulleys (blocks) at the top of a tree (a spar tree) and out to the area where the trees had been felled and bucked. The operator of this yarder was called a yarding engineer or a "donkey puncher."

Cats would sometimes have a set of drums fitted onto their backs turning them into yarders—in loggers' parlance, double-drums. One day I was given the job of moving one of these double-drums to a new site dragging all the cables with me. At the new site I became the donkey puncher.

The logging industry had been organized for many years by the International Woodworkers of America (IWA). I joined Local 1-71 while working for a gyppo on South Pender Island.

26

THE SCHEMER

In 1948 there were twelve local unions of the IWA in British Columbia, all encompassed in what was called District One.

In the fall of 1948 I went to work at Camp A in the Englewood Logging Division of Canadian Forest Products at the northern end of Vancouver Island. My local was 1-71, generally referred to as the Loggers' Local. Each logging camp was called a sub-local.

The Loggers' Local covered the mainland coastal area of B.C. northward from Point Atkinson to the Alaska border, the smaller islands between Vancouver Island and the mainland, the northern end of Vancouver Island, and the Queen Charlotte Islands.

This huge territory made it impractical for the Loggers' Local to have monthly meetings. It did, however, have an annual meeting in the winter and a semi-annual meeting in the summer, both held in Vancouver.

In October of 1948 District One met in Vancouver and made a decision which nearly destroyed the IWA in B.C. For a few years preceding 1948 there had been conflict between the District and the International Office of the Union, as well as a conflict within the District.

This International Office-District conflict was part of the postwar campaign against communism. Many unions had militant officers and many of these were accused, rightly or wrongly, of being Communists. The International Officers of the IWA were of the opinion that District One and most of the IWA locals in B.C. had officers who were either Communists or sympathizers. There were also accusations of financial irregularities.

The October, 1948 meeting of District One decided, by a vote of 74 to 12, to break away from the IWA and replace it with another union, The Woodworkers Industrial Union of Canada (WIUC). Only one local opposed this action, 1-357 whose jurisdiction was in and around New Westminster.

I arrived at Camp A in the week following the District's decision to disaffiliate. There was confusion in the Camp about the move: it was a shocker. No warning. Like a swift kick in the ass with a steel-toed boot.

Following an arrangement which had been worked out over the years, negotiations for a collective agreement between the IWA and the forest industry were not conducted separately for each logging camp or sawmill. The entire coastal forest industry negotiated through an organization called Forest Industrial Relations (FIR). The IWA locals on the coast negotiated under the umbrella of District One. The resulting collective agreement was called a Master Agreement.

Just prior to the October Council meeting the IWA and FIR had reached an accord for a new Master Agreement which contained a wage increase, but was silent about board and lodging charges for those who had to live in camp bunkhouses.

There was not only confusion in Camp A, and other logging camps, about the status of the IWA; there was anger over this new Master Agreement. With no protection relating to board and lodging charges, they went from $2.00 to $2.50 a day immediately after the Master Agreement came into effect. That move took back about half of the wage increase.

All Camp A's sub-local officers resigned, some because of the confusion, some to support the WIUC.

In the early days union organizers were denied access to logging camps. They had to sneak into camps after dark, had to sleep out in the bush and eat whatever food loggers smuggled out to them. Companies didn't want any union interfering with what they considered their God-given right to treat workers any damned way they pleased.

If a logger was caught bringing food out for an organizer he would immediately be fired. If any logger became known as an active IWA member he would be unable to get work in the camps. The one major hiring agency in Vancouver for loggers was called Black's. The word was that Black's would simply blackball loggers who were known as active IWA members.

A number of these old-time loggers were in Camp A when I got there. They faced a personal and internal conflict. Should they follow the people whom they knew as solid trade unionists and in whom they had faith, or should they stick with the IWA? There was a strong emotional drag each way.

The First-Aid Attendant at Camp A was Harry Beamer. Two other loggers and I would, after supper, play cards with him in the First-Aid shack. Beamer was IWA. One of the card players was WIUC, the other non-committal. I was a confused IWA member. By agreement the union fight didn't enter the card-games.

From the age of twelve when I was shunted off to the Children's Aid Society I lived in houses and institutions which to me were only buildings and could never be classified as home. Setting out on my own, I lived in a simple house-keeping room with a hot plate. That was essentially my home.

My room in Camp A's bunkhouse was my home and I wanted it to be particularly mine. To dress it up a bit I bought some lacy curtains and hung them over the standard roller blind supplied by the logging company. I put a discarded Union Steamship bedside carpet on the floor.

Was I ridiculed? No. In fact I got comments from a few other loggers that the curtains and carpet gave the place a nice touch.

I'd wanted to learn how to type and came to camp with a second-hand typewriter and a touch-type instruction book. Beamer came to talk with me one night and, maybe because of the typewriter, suggested I become the IWA sub-local secretary. He reasoned that the IWA was the official union, the one certified under law as the bargaining agent. It was the union which camp management, both by law and the Master Agreement, had to recognize. Any grievances in camp could only be processed and dealt with by the IWA. The WIUC had no status.

So, I became sub-local secretary simply because Beamer kept pushing me in that direction. He got the new address of the Loggers' Local and I struck up a correspondence. I wasn't elected; I just got vacuumed into the vacancy. Beamer wasn't tagged Beamer-the-schemer for nothing. I enjoyed learning to type and enjoyed writing. I subsequently learned that my typed letters to IWA offices in Vancouver left a good impression with officers of both the Local and District One.

27

RESPONSIBILITY

About 20 members attended the Annual Meeting of the Loggers' Local in the winter of 1948-49. Because of my correspondence from Camp A I was asked to run for one of the positions on the Local's Executive Board as one of three trustees. I was of two minds. I wanted to accept because I saw that being on the Executive would open other opportunities within the union movement. It offered a chance to move ahead, to become more than a transient wage earner. On the other hand I had been out of prison for only three years and felt vulnerable.

Attraction was stronger than doubt. In any event, what did I have to lose? I accepted the nomination and was elected by ballot in all the camps. Trustees examine the financial records of the Local and report to the Annual Meeting. I knew next to nothing about financial records or bookkeeping but there were three of us and maybe I could learn.

In the summer of 1949 I was hired as an organizer and assigned to the Loggers' Local. Being a greenhorn I was chaperoned for a short time by another organizer. The first logging camp we went to was the O'Brien Logging Company's Camp C near Powell River. My chaperone, Fred Fieber, called the meeting to order and immediately, without warning, introduced me and said that I would speak. What an embarrassment. I hummed and hawed and stumbled through what I remember as being an incomprehensible explanation of the law governing collective bargaining. In a few moments I came to a dead stop. I didn't complain to Fieber. That would have been whining. But I was more fully prepared when we got to the next camp.

Over the winter of 1949 I met a young woman, Edith Horvath, and we were attracted to each other from the start. She and her three sisters had come to B.C. from Saskatchewan during the Second World War to work in defence industries; two of them lived in New Westminster. She had a quiet, soft-spoken voice and I thought at first that she was shy. I was wrong. She laughed easily and enjoyed both hearing a joke and telling one. We got along well together.

While working at Camp A we corresponded. The letters were not romantic and gave no hint of our being anything more than casual friends. Whenever I came to town we saw each other but I had no thought that our involvement would be more than it was at that moment. She was just my friend. If she had hopes for something more she didn't express them to me.

Edith was very close to her sisters and a lot of our time together was spent visiting with them. One sister was a good friend of the manager of the Best Hotel in New Westminster. We would often drop into the Best for a few glasses of beer or see a movie once in a while.

We slowly became more than friends and moved into something deeper. A mutual acquaintance, Les Farkes, told us he was going to get married. That prompted Edith and me to discuss our own relationship. Was marriage what we both wanted?

At the Annual Meeting of the Loggers' Local in the winter of 1949-50, the attendance was better than the year before because we prompted loggers with the message: "It's your union, show up and make it function the way you want it to."

The Annual Meeting nominated me as President. Like the nomination for Trustee in the preceding year, I went through the same agonizing self-debate regarding this nomination and came to the same conclusion. I wanted to be President.

I was the only nominee and a virtual shoo-in during the subsequent balloting among the logging camps. I became the President of the Loggers' Local, a local which at one time had some 5,000 members. In the spring of 1950 the membership was in the 400 to 500 range. Most loggers held back until the dust settled.

Another, and more important, event took place during the winter of 1949. Edith and I were married in December at a double wedding ceremony along with Les Farkes and his bride Elsie. I took it as a given that a man and a woman who spent a lot of time together were expected to get married; that was the culture of the day. Edith felt the same way.

I was twenty-four years old and didn't have the faintest idea of what love was or what it meant. Living together as an unmarried couple was taboo, something we never talked about or contemplated.

Our son, Robert, was born in August of 1950. I wanted to be present in the delivery room, to hold Edith's hand and comfort her however I could; if nothing else, at least vicariously experience the miracle of childbirth, of our child. Our family doctor and the hospital disagreed. I was forbidden to be there.

A few hours after his birth I was able to hold our baby son in my arms. Sure, he was reddened and wrinkled but more than that he was beautiful. He helped me to feel beautiful, too. I cried then with happiness and joy and even now the resurrected memory and the writing about it brings tears.

As President of the Local I had to be away from home a lot, which placed a strain on our marriage from the beginning. Most of 1949 and 1950 was spent travelling to logging camps and working to rebuild the IWA to the position and stature it had prior to the 1948 disaffiliation move. It was mostly a steady and regular slogging and a gradual improvement in membership. The Local's office was at Carrall and Hastings Streets. Hiring agencies which were used by logging companies to recruit workers were also in this area as were hotels in which many loggers lived during the winter closure of camps. Our winter activities mostly dealt with Unemployment Insurance and Workers' Compensation problems faced by loggers. I was also home for these few months.

28

CHALLENGES, CHANGES, AND CHOICE

The IWA, prior to 1948, used a 40-foot cabin cruiser named the Loggers' Navy to service logging camps which were not accessible by road. The Loggers' Navy was kept by the WIUC but, as a result of court action, they had to return it to the IWA because it was IWA property. For a short period the IWA chartered a fishing boat, the Lady Alice, to service the camps. The IWA also hired people to operate these boats; Phil Cootes for the Lady Alice, and Oswald (Ozzie) Mattila for the Loggers' Navy.

Part of my time as an organizer was spent on the Lady Alice and the Loggers' Navy. The Lady Alice was 38 feet long and not designed for comfort. Fortunately it was only in use for a short time. When the Court returned the Loggers' Navy to the IWA Phil Cootes travelled to Vancouver to skipper it back to Alert Bay. In the meantime I was visiting the logging camps at the northern end of Vancouver Island.

On the scheduled meeting day it was cold, rainy, and as miserable as the west coast can get. By late afternoon I figured that the Loggers' Navy wasn't going to show up because of stormy weather in the Gulf of Georgia so opted for a hotel room. There was none to be had. There were beds for rent at the rear of Alert Bay's only laundry so, with sodden shoes and drenched clothes, I sloshed my way there. No luck. It was filled too. Where next? I trudged to the police station, identified myself and my plight and asked for advice. The constable on duty was friendly and helpful. He told me I could sleep the night in one of their cells. Thinking the situation somewhat ironic I asked, "You'll leave the cell door unlocked, of course?" "Sure," he replied. "You're not being charged with vagrancy." Then: "You're lucky this isn't a Saturday night. If it was we would be filled up, too."

The Loggers' Navy had been built in a shipyard at Squirrel Cove specifically for the Loggers' Local. It was a forty foot cabin cruiser with a sleeping and cooking area in the after part. She cruised at about eight knots an hour.

Because of the bunks along each side, the hull had the curvature of something like half an orange. A twenty-mile an hour wind from the southeast in the Gulf of Georgia would produce waves about three to three and half feet high which would be enough to cause the Navy to roll from side to side, making travel nearly impossible.

A number of bodies of water along the coast of B.C. are "bottlenecked." Because of the rise and fall of tides huge volumes of water are forced through narrow passages creating something akin to rapids in a river.

Skookumchuck Narrows is such a "bottleneck." It connects Sechelt Inlet and Jervis Inlet. At each change of the tide up to 200 billion gallons of water surge through the narrows in a roaring torrent of whirlpools, cascades, and eddies. Even a modest three-foot tide will result in this deluge reaching 15 knots an hour.

The time to travel through the narrows is when the tide has reached the level at which it starts to reverse its movement, often called "slack tide" or "slack water." Ozzie and I, using a federal government booklet setting out the precise times when the tide would be slack, had gone through the narrows a number of times at "slack water."

On one unforgettable trip into Sechelt Inlet we discovered that the tide book was incorrect, off by a couple of hours. Ozzie was at the wheel. We moved into the narrows on an incoming tide and the rushing of the water clearly showed that something was wrong.

The boat couldn't be turned around. We were stuck and forced to "go with the flow." Ozzie steered to the outer edge of the whirlpool whose centre was three or four feet below the boiling, frothing, white-capped level of the water. Ozzie had the engine at full-throttle. Even at that the whirlpool heeled the boat over and sucked us towards its centre. It was touch and go whether we would get through safely. We did but were both white from fear. It could have so easily gone the other way.

We immediately notified the Local's office so it could contact the people who published the tide book. The Local was told that a bulletin correcting the mistake had been issued. We probably should have contacted the government officials before sailing to see if any up-to-date information existed. We certainly did from then on. Nothing like the threat of death to smarten you up.

The time I spent on the Loggers' Navy was fascinating. It wasn't just the spectacular scenery of B.C. coastal waters. It was a learning experience, a quasi-apprenticeship. Thanks to Phil Cootes and Ozzie Mattila I learned how to read charts, calculate travelling time, set a compass course and steer by it, "read" the lights displayed by other boats; how to do virtually everything needed to navigate in inland waters.

The Loggers' Navy was a welcome visitor to logging camps. The more isolated the camp, the more we were welcomed. We brought news about the union's activities and a form of entertainment.

Most logging camps didn't offer much in the way of amusement. It was work, eat, play poker, read, and shoot the breeze. From the National Film Board we borrowed a movie projector and films about safe logging practices. Nearly everyone in camp, management included, turned out to see the movies.

In Jervis Inlet there was a logging camp at Britain River. We pulled into it one weekend and almost the first person I saw had been in the B.C. Pen. He was assigned to the machine shop a short time prior to my being moved to an outside gang.

"Hey," he said, "I think I know you from New Westminster."

"Well," I replied, "I worked there for a while, but I don't remember you."

"I'm sure of it. You worked in a machine shop. You ran a milling machine."

"I worked in an automotive repair shop there, Walker and Sons. I rebuilt clutches and installed brake linings, but I don't know anything about a milling machine. Where did you work?" I asked, hoping to get the discussion away from what I did. But, he wouldn't budge. He knew me and was persistent about it. I was just as persistent. It broke off with his saying that he was pretty sure he knew me.

I got my first lesson in being discrete about union funds while on a visit to the Morgan Logging Company's camp on the Queen Charlotte Islands. Many old-time loggers would pay their union dues in cash, sometimes for months in advance. I'd give them a receipt and then write a cheque on my bank account, payable to the Local, to cover the receipts issued.

Logging camps usually had a "poker shack." I enjoyed playing poker and one evening sat in on the game at Morgan's. The following day I was in the cookhouse talking with the staff. Out of my sight were a couple of camp-level employees. I heard one of them say, "That goddamned union guy was playing poker last night with our union dues."

I went around the corner and told them of my cheque-writing procedure. No apology was offered but I think they accepted the explanation. That was the last time I sat in on a poker game in a logging camp.

Being a union organizer required innovation. During this period I had taken a correspondence course in photography from the New York Institute of Photography. I bought a second-hand, old-time 4" by 5" press camera. The only time you see them now is in ancient black and white Hollywood films with flash bulbs about the size of lemons.

There was a small logging operation northward from Squamish

with the only transportation to it being the Pacific Great Eastern Railway (now the B.C. Railway). Like a flash from that old press camera I got a brain wave about organizing the camp.

I got off the train carrying my press camera and went to the office of the logging company. I told them I was writing an article for MacLeans about logging in the area and asked permission to take some photographs and talk with some of the loggers as well. Because there would be no train until the next day, I asked if I could stay overnight in their bunkhouse.

I was apprehensive about being discovered as an IWA organizer and being run off the property, but if that had happened I'd figured out what to do: sleep alongside the railway tracks and sneak back into camp the next morning just as the loggers were getting up. I was sure that my organizing task would be made easier by telling the loggers that the company had ordered me off the property.

I waited until after supper before talking with the loggers. My first questions related to logging practices, then moved into the area of unionism by asking about the IWA. Some of the loggers responded by saying that they were IWA members but that the camp wasn't organized. That was all I needed. Nearly all of the loggers signed up with the IWA that night and we subsequently got certified by the Labour Relations Board. I did submit an article and pictures to MacLeans, but the editors there weren't able to see the merits of the story.

We got a letter from a logger (Bill Michaels) in Stewart asking us to come and organize the operation. He told us that the company was antagonistic to unions. He told us where he lived in town and suggested we be cautious. The only access to Stewart was by plane or boat (Union Steamships). I took Union Steamships to Stewart, getting in on a Saturday evening.

I located Bill Michaels' house, but he had gone into the hills goat hunting and wouldn't be back until Sunday night.

Stewart was a sparsely-populated old mining community north of Prince Rupert and at the head of the Portland Canal. It is close to the

B.C.-Alaska border with the town of Heider, Alaska being only a mile or so away. The mines had closed down some years before, turning Stewart in a semi-ghost town. Like many small communities it was gossipy and a stranger in town would become the new subject to be talked about.

The Letizia was a small hotel owned by John Meneghello and was named after his wife. There was a small lunch counter on the main street. I went there on the Sunday for a snack and some coffee. I sat at the counter close to another person. The usual "Good-morning" pleasantries were exchanged.

Even though he knew the answer, he asked, "You new in town?"

"Yeh, I came in on the steamer last night. I'm staying at the Letizia."

"That's a nice, quiet place, the Letizia. Uh, are you in the mining game?"

"No," I replied, "I'm just visiting, just looking around."

"Mining was what Stewart was all about a few years ago, but not any more. Right now the main thing going on here is logging. You in the logging business, or something like that?"

"Oh, no," I said, "I'm just visiting; you know, kind of like a holiday."

By Sunday afternoon I was either an undercover policeman or a Canada Custom's or United State's agent investigating possible cross-border smuggling.

We got the loggers organized and certified. The logging company was Western Wood Products Ltd. and was a United States based company, with the management being U.S. citizens. The local people were generally favourable to unions for, during the hey-days of mining, the International Union of Mine, Mill and Smelter Workers was an integral part of Stewart's society.

In 1954/55 a pulp mill was in the construction stage at Hinton, Alberta. Mike Sekora, another IWA organizer, and I were assigned to Hinton to organize the loggers into the IWA. These loggers were reported to be working for contractors and not for the company which would own and operate the pulp mill.

Access to the logging camps was restricted. One night Mike and I walked about a mile through the bush and forest land to get to one of these camps. In the bunkhouse we were able to start getting the loggers to join the IWA.

The bunkhouses were what we called "ram pastures." Maybe fifteen to twenty beds in a row with a stove in the middle. Mike and I were at one end when a man burst in, shouting, "Get out of here, you guys! You're not wanted!" We didn't move.

Then he and Mike got into a shouting match about us being foreigners—not Albertans—and Mike, lying in his teeth, roared back with: "What the hell are you talking about? I was born in this goddamn province."

While this was going on I said, "Any of you guys want to talk about the IWA, let's go down to the other end." Quite a few came with me.

The man who had roared into the bunkhouse couldn't be in two places at once. He stormed out screaming, "I'll call the police and they'll get you out."

The building of the pulp mill drew hundreds of people, giving it a boom-town complexion. Mike and I shared a two-bed room in what was then the lone hotel in Hinton. The hotel was always full, always crowded. There was no night manager and it was common to find people sleeping on the floor of what passed for a lobby. Two R.C.M.P. constables lived in the hotel. Mike and I got to know them casually.

In the morning following our trek into the logging camp we went into the cafe for breakfast. It was crowded so we couldn't immediately get seats. We stood behind the two mounties who were sitting with their backs to us. I said good morning to them and then, "I hear you got a call to go out to one of the camps last night."

They both spoke almost simultaneously. One said, "What do you mean?" The other, "We got more important things to do."

Before dealing with the Alberta Labour Relations Board we had to make sure who was the employer. We got hold of one of the contracts between the pulp-mill company and the contractors. It showed that the contractor wasn't the employer.

My knowledge of photography was helpful. Using a slow-speed, fine-grain film I was able to photograph each page, blocking out the name of the contractor who loaned us the contract. The resulting photographs were used to show the Labour Relations Board that the employer was the company having the pulp mill built, and that the contractors were simply logging-camp superintendents. The Board agreed with us.

In the mid-1940s a Royal Commission inquiry into forestry in B.C. concluded that our forests were in need of a management plan.

The response of the government was the establishment of Forest Management Licences, under which forest-harvesting rights on huge tracts of forest land would be made available to companies engaged in logging and log-processing activities. In return for getting access to non-competitive timber, companies were to engage in reforestation programs to ensure there would be trees in the future.

The first Forest Management Licence was given to The Columbia Cellulose Company which received access to some 750,000 acres of forest land in the north-western part of the province. It built a pulp mill in Prince Rupert to process the timber logged off these lands.

The major part of its logging activity was in the Terrace area. The International office speculated that coastal, high-lead logging operations would be permitted in the area; a departure from past practices.

I went to Terrace in the spring of 1951 to assess the situation, get a feel of the area, and determine what might be needed for our organizational campaign.

I returned in the fall and successfully organized Columbia Cellulose's loggers into the IWA.

By this time our membership had increased to the point where we could hire more organizers and assign them to specific areas. I decided to locate in and work out of Terrace to service the north coast and the Queen Charlotte Islands.

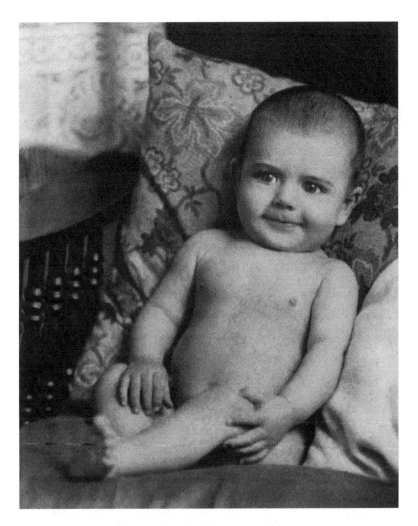

Anticipating life at six months.

Aboard the ocean liner MONTCALM en route to England.
circa 1930

In my Boy Scouts' uniform with Mrs. Woodd in Kimberley. House decorated in honour of British Royalty.
circa 1937

Y-5565

Mug shot upon entering the B.C. Penitentiary, September 9, 1943, at the age of eighteen.

Working at a lathe in the automotive repair shop of Walker and Sons, New Westminster, B.C. circa 1947

As M.L.A. for Skeena (1953-1956) climbing stairs in the Legislative Buildings at Victoria, B.C.
circa 1954

CCF M.L.A.s
1953 to 1956

Back row, left to right:

Frank Howard (Skeena), Anthony "Tony" Gargrave (Mackenzie), Frank Calder (Atlin), John Squire (Alberni), McRae "Rae" Eddie (New Westminster), Vincent "Bill" Segur (Revelstoke), Rupert Haggen (Grand Forks-Greenwood).

Front row, left to right:

Arthur Turner (Vancouver East), Arnold Webster (Vancouver East), E.E. "Ernie" Winch (Burnaby), William "Bill" Moore (Comox), Leo Nimsick (Cranbrook), Randolph "Ran" Harding (Kaslow-Slocan), Robert "Bob" Strachan (Cowichan-Newcastle).

Robert about three or four years old with his mother, Edith.

A fifty-five pound ling cod I caught at Klemtu, B.C. while campaigning during the 1958 federal election.

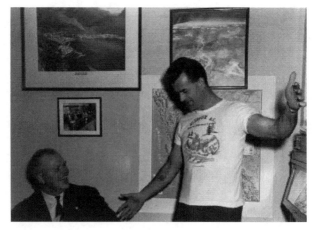

Showing Murdo Martin, M.P. for Timmins, the size of salmon in B.C.'s Kispiox River.
circa 1961

Robert Clifton, Treasurer (?) of The Native Brotherhood of B.C.,
giving me gifts to commemorate my receiving the Indian name
Weget.
Vancouver, B.C, circa 1960s

Danny Sailor, famed for participating in loggers'-sports days, hands
me a set of bells for use during sports day in Terrace, B.C. The
contest was to see which logger could climb the tree the fastest, ring
the bells, and get back to the ground. I climbed the 90-foot spar
tree and hung the bells at the top.
circa 1960s

Northern Sentinel

VOLUME XXVI NO. 19   Kitimat, B.C.   Thursday, May 10, 1979   PRICE 20 CENTS

RURAL VOTE COUNTS

Howard Wins Skeena

Gleeful upon again becoming M.L.A. for Skeena on May 10, 1979.

Family joyfully celebrating Christmas in Terrace, B.C.
Left to right: Frank, son Robert, step-daughter Danielle, step-son Anthony, Julienne. 1984.

Joane Elizabeth Humphrey (J.J. McColl) and I were married on June 22, 2002 at Hornby Island, B.C.

29

THIRTEEN—A LUCKY NUMBER

Politics in B.C. has often been classified as nutty. Political parties have found it expedient from time to time to camouflage themselves, to put on different coats or dresses, to rouge themselves up like street walkers. Weird things have taken place here, no doubt about it.

My first vote was cast at the 1949 provincial election. At the time I didn't know what had taken place following the 1941 provincial election but found out later that two arch and historic enemies (Conservatives and Liberals) decided, in the vernacular of the times, to "shack up."

They set up housekeeping in Victoria as the Coalition Government, but maintained separate domiciles in the constituencies. There were no in-laws and each considered the other a sort of twin-bed, temporary companion. The knot they tied was a slipknot.

In 1952 these collusive Coalitionists split up. The separation was messy; instead of holding each other by the hand they held their hands around each others throat. No wonder the general public thought that politics in B.C. was dominated by "crazies."

Terrace was in the Provincial Constituency of Skeena, its politics dominated by the Liberals. George Home, Secretary of the B.C. Federation of Labour, suggested I run as a CCF candidate in Skeena at that 1952 election. Sounded good to me, but I didn't live there. I lived in New Westminster with my wife Edith and our young son Robert. If I was to be a candidate, I thought that moving to Terrace was politically necessary. Edith was reluctant. It would have been a dramatic change for her, a form of isolation. She was close to her sisters and felt at home in New Westminster. In Terrace I would be away from home more often and she would be alone in a strange town with our two-year old. Edith was not an outgoing person and would have found it difficult to make new friends. I was disappointed, but we didn't move.

Harold Winch was Provincial Leader of the CCF. I met with him at his home in Vancouver to talk with him about being a candidate and to tell him of my criminal record. There was no would-you-like-a-cup-of-coffee stuff. It was business. Harold was dark-haired and intense. His eyes seemed to penetrate, rather than just see. He was a powerful public speaker with a strong voice. He suffered from an involuntary tenseness of his vocal chords which gave his voice an occasional hesitancy, something that gave added impact to his public presence.

Winch's advice was straightforward: if the matter was raised, admit to it. Don't lie. Don't equivocate. Put it down as teen-age stupidity. It will probably get you defeated, but that's the price you'll pay. He told me the CCF didn't have any organization in Skeena and there was no hint of anyone there wanting to be the CCF candidate.

The two major union federations in North America in 1952 were the Congress of Industrial Organizations (CIO) and the American Federation of Labour (AFofL). The B.C. Federation of Labour was part of the CIO, and had hired Tom MacKenzie as an organizer to attempt to organize construction workers who were then being employed to build a power plant at Kemano to generate electricity for the Aluminum Company of Canada (Alcan).

MacKenzie worked out of Terrace, but it was a hopeless job for him. The AFofL construction unions and Morrison-Knudson (the company building the Kemano project) signed a collective agreement with all hiring done through those unions.

One of Morrison-Knudson's first tasks was to clear away the forest. This involved loggers who were IWA members but who were forced to join an AFofL union. We tagged this as an invasion of our jurisdiction and the only way to correct it was to try to get into Kemano and organize them.

Morrison-Knudson, though, was running the show. It could decide whom to let into Kemano and it didn't want any union jurisdictional squabble on its hands. The effect was that I couldn't simply pack a bag and get onto the site.

Fortune came my way in the form of a government inspector I knew who, by law, could get to Kemano. I ran into him one day in Terrace. He had chartered an aircraft to get to Kemano and conspiratorially agreed to take me along. He also agreed to make his visit coincide with the arrival of a Union Steamships passenger/freight boat.

As soon as the plane had tied up to the floats at Kemano I melted into the crowd of workers getting off the boat. A bus took us along the ten-mile valley road to Camp 5, the main construction camp.

Camp 5 was filled with workers getting off shift and those getting off the bus. I put my suitcase against a building where I could keep it in sight and, to be as inconspicuous as possible, got into the line-up for mail. Milling around with the crowd I found a bunkhouse being used for storage.

That night I slept in my clothes on a bed spring. Because I didn't have an identification badge I wasn't able to get any food. No supper that night; no breakfast in the morning.

About noon I walked towards the sawmill, hoping to be able to talk with the sawmill workers during the noon break.

Someone from a nearby office saw me and came out to enquire who I was and what I was doing there. I told him I was an IWA organizer and wanted to talk with the sawmill workers.

He simply said, "Come with me."

We went into the office building where he had me sit down across from him and his desk.

Without any preliminary he told me, "This afternoon there will be an airplane going to Vancouver and one going to Prince Rupert. Which one do you want to take?"

From Prince Rupert I went back to Terrace and the expected provincial election.

MacKenzie was a great help during the election campaign. He had been a candidate at an earlier election and had that experience to draw upon. I was the novice with a limited formal education. At one meeting I contended that the Coalition Government had misled people. I knew the word, but had never heard it spoken. My "misled" came out "myzuld." MacKenzie tactfully pointed out my mistake but thereafter privately called me "the myzler."

Our first task was to contact those who were CCFers. That was the easy part. Following the 1949 election the CCF in Skeena virtually disappeared. The CCF's provincial office in Vancouver could only provide the names of six people. Of these six, one had died and another had moved to Campbell River. MacKenzie's advice was to make personal contact with each person.

The first need was to discover if any of the four in Skeena was interested in the nomination; the second to ask each person for the names of others who were CCF'ers. Every lead was followed up and at each negative response about candidacy I said that I was interested. We didn't have a formal nominating convention, just meetings in Terrace and Smithers at which my candidacy was approved. By this time we had signed up about 50 CCF members.

It was a fools-rush-in venture. I was an outsider, a parachute drop. E.T. Kenney, the incumbent M.L.A., was a local celebrity and job-creating hero. As Minister of Lands and Forests he brought Columbia Cellulose to Terrace, and Alcan to Kitimat to build an aluminum smelter. At the breakup of the Coalition he also was made Minister in charge of highways and crowed about getting a substantial increase in the highway-building budget for Skeena.

Another negative aspect was the IWA. Feeling aggressive after winning out over the WIUC, the IWA declared war on the coastal forest industry by establishing a "No contract-no work" policy for the 1952 negotiations. That meant the IWA would go on strike if no new collective agreement was reached by June 15th.

Election day was June 12th and I was playing both roles in this "good-guy (candidate), bad-guy (IWA)" routine. One day I would be urging loggers and sawmill workers in Terrace to prepare for the possibility of a strike on June 15th. Another day would see me wearing "my other coat" and arguing that the CCF was the only Party responsible enough to bring common sense back to government.

Terrace was located on the western side of Skeena; Smithers, about 140 miles away, at the eastern side. The pre-strike preparations were concentrated in Terrace. In addition to "changing coats" I did a lot of travelling and had a minimum amount of sleep.

I had one pair of decent trousers, a sports jacket, and one dress shirt (white). I kept the trousers reasonably well pressed by using a portable steam iron. I washed the nylon shirt and hung it up to dry every night. By the end of the campaign it had a yellowish tinge.

All of my travelling and living expenses of the campaign were modest. Tom MacKenzie had a car which we used from time to time, but I also did a lot of hitch-hiking. Many CCF members offered me beds, meals, and rides to the next community.

Between Hazelton and New Hazelton is the community called Two Mile. MacKenzie and I were given the name of a CCFer there who would no doubt help during the campaign. We got to Two Mile and called on this supporter. We had no place to bed down so asked him if he could put us up for the night. He was somewhat hesitant, but did say there was a room above an unused barn which had been rented to a mining engineer who was absent for a few days.

Our host told us he was too busy to take part in the campaign and couldn't afford to make a financial contribution. We later learned that he was not a CCFer, but was the main organizer in Two Mile for the Social Credit Party.

There were a number of Native villages in the Hazelton area. There were no Aboriginal people in Kimberley and I was taught nothing about them in school. Hollywood, with its flair for turning fiction into fact, had given me and millions of others a false impression about Indigenous people.

My education about the history, culture, and life of Natives began in 1952. They were given the right to vote in provincial elections in 1949. Frank Scott, a long-time north coast resident, convinced the CCF that Frank Calder, a Nisga'a, should be the CCF candidate in Atlin. He ran and was elected. Atlin had within it four Nisga'a villages along the Nass River.

In 1952 Calder travelled with me to a few of the villages in Skeena and gave me sound advice relating to Native people.

A common—not derogatory—reference was that there was such a thing as "Indian time." Things get accomplished without reference to the clock. Calder told me not to look at my watch when visiting in homes or at meetings.

My first encounter with "Indian time" was at Kitwangak. I had made arrangements to hold a public meeting at 7:00 P.M. in the community hall, and had posted notices about it. I made sure I got there early. I sat on the steps of the hall and waited. 7:00 o'clock came and went, as did 7:30.

About 7:45 (I had cautiously glanced at my watch) a man came to the hall, opened it, went in, and came out with a trombone. He strode around the village calling people to the meeting by playing the trombone.

We got going about 9:00 P.M. and wound up about 2:00 A.M. Some people asked questions; some made speeches in English; some made speeches partly in English and partly in what they referred to as "my own language." Everyone was polite and courteous. This meeting was one of many I attended. They would last until everyone who wanted to speak had the opportunity to do so, following which a general understanding would determine that the meeting should come to an end.

Highway 16 was on the opposite side of the Skeena River from

Kitwangak and travel from one side to the other was by way of a reaction ferry. This was a ferry which had a platform for cars and people built athwart-ships of two pontoon-like floats. The floats faced in the direction of the river's flow and the ferry kept from sweeping downstream by being attached to pulleys and a cable stretched across the river.

Using another set of cables and pulleys, the ferry operator would move the floats at an angle to the flow of the river and the ferry would react to the current and move across.

At 2:00 A.M. the ferry at Kitwangak was not operating. I slept in the railway-station waiting room. There was no point in looking at my watch; there were no lights in the station and it was pitch black outside. "Indian time" was a revelation.

I did a lot of door-knocking in Native villages. Hagwilget is a reserve close to the confluence of the Bulkley River with the Skeena River. It was there I met Donald Grey, an elderly gentleman, and visited with him in the kitchen of his house.

He was chopping up some darkly-coloured substance on a block of wood. I asked him what it was. "It's seaweed," he said, "and it's all I got to eat. I don't have enough money to buy much grub."

I went away feeling so sad and so sorry for him. I was tempted to give him a few dollars, but it was an election campaign and I couldn't gamble with the possibility of being charged with bribing a person to vote.

Much later I learned that seaweed is part of the regular diet of Natives along the coast and is considered a bit of a delicacy for people who live inland.

I got to know Donald Grey and visited him often. One time I reminded him of that moment in his kitchen when he was chopping up what is called "Thlu-usk" in the Tsimshian language. He laughed and said he was only having a bit of fun with me. As a token of our friendship he gave me an old stone adze which was used to cut wood before the Europeans came and introduced iron.

As far as the election was concerned all I had going for me was my own enthusiasm and public dissatisfaction with the antics of the Coalition.

The Coalition Government, expecting its own demise, brought into law a system of voting which got its first use in 1952. This system, dubbed a single transferable vote, allowed each voter to mark the ballot in preferential order, using numerals. The voter would give his first choice candidate number "1", his second choice number "2", and so on.

On election night, all first choices would be counted. If no one received a majority the candidate with the lowest number of first choices would be eliminated and the second choices on those ballots added to the totals of the remaining candidates. This procedure would continue until someone obtained the required majority.

Our election campaign was humble. Money was scarce, expenses were minimal. As I recall, our campaign costs were about $250.00. There was no television and no local radio. We ran a few small ads in the two local newspapers. We had a couple of leaflets printed. They were distributed to homes by volunteers. I did a lot of door-to-door canvassing.

The highlight of the campaign was a visit by our Provincial Leader, Harold Winch. He spoke at public meetings in Smithers, Hazelton, and Terrace.

I enjoyed the campaign. It was fun. Each day was a new adventure. Each day I met new people. One quip relating to politics is that it is better to be thought a fool than to open your mouth and prove it. I knew very little about Skeena so I listened more than I spoke. I had no illusions about winning the election and kept telling our supporters that it was a tough fight. It was.

Kenney was re-elected with 58.6% of the vote. I got 41.4%. 19 Social Credit M.L.A.s were elected. The CCF got 18; the Liberals 6; the Conservatives 4, and 1 Labour. W.A.C. Bennett became leader of the Social Credit Party and, with the support of the 6 Liberals and 4

Conservatives, became Premier.

On June 12th I failed to get elected as M.L.A., but on June 15th the IWA didn't fail to call a strike which lasted for about six weeks. It could have got me jailed.

We were picketing a sawmill in Terrace. The owner was furious so he got a judge to issue a Court Order ordering us to stop. If the injunction was disobeyed I'd have to go to court to show why I shouldn't be sent to jail for contempt.

Our lawyer said to ignore the injunction because it didn't have some specific information attached. So we ignored it. After the strike was over I had to appear in a Vancouver Court. Our lawyer's argument was accepted and I was exonerated. I wasn't afraid of a jail sentence, but was damned pleased to get off.

It was pressure-cooker time for me and the tension took its toll. I developed a duodenal ulcer. Our family doctor laid it out for me. No cigarettes, no alcohol, no fried foods, no coarse foods such as corn, no this or that for a whole year. He must have guessed that all his advice wasn't sinking in because he then told me that if I didn't follow this regime he would have me on the operating table and cut out part of my stomach.

"It doesn't matter to me," he said. "That's what I do. It isn't my stomach, it's yours. If you want me to take part of it out, I'll be glad to accommodate you."

Smart move on his part. It struck home. So I followed his diet for the year, followed his advice about dealing with tension, cured the ulcer and haven't had a recurrence.

Alcan's power-house construction at Kemano was in full swing in 1952, with some 5,000 workers on the job. There had been no concerted effort to register voters so the 1952 voters' list for Kemano contained a paltry 194 names. Only 47 of them voted.

Because of the existence of a minority government we expected another election soon. Having got a taste of it I wanted to run again. One of the problems was that my wife and I, and our 2 year old son, still lived in New Westminster.

I rented a post-office box in Terrace to give me a local address and spread the word through our IWA membership that I was moving to Terrace as soon as possible.

The follow-up election was called for June 9, 1953, again using the single transferable ballot. I spent the first part of the campaign in Kemano registering voters and passing out campaign cards which would easily fit into a wallet.

Two suitcases came with me to Kemano. One was for my clothes, the other was filled with voter registration cards.

Using a card table, I "set up shop" outside the recreation hall. My hand-lettered sign saying "Want to vote in the provincial election? Register here!" was taped onto the wall. I gave everyone who registered one of my campaign cards which told them they were registered in Skeena and could vote for me anywhere in the province on election day. The card also said "For two weeks annual vacation with pay vote CCF."

One worker tore up my campaign card, threw it on the floor and vehemently told me he wouldn't vote for the "f... CCF." "Well," I thought, "I can play that game, too. I'll just rip your bloody registration card to shreds." After I had cooled down I decided I was wrong. If I had destroyed his card I would be stealing his right to vote. No difference between that kind of theft and stealing anything else. So I played it straight.

Work at Kemano went on twenty-four hours a day at a number of different work sites. The graveyard shift (midnight to 8:00 A.M.) had lunch at 4:00 o'clock in the morning. On at least a half dozen occasions I eagerly got out of bed at 3:00 to meet with and register these voters during their lunch break. For the afternoon shift (4:00 P.M. to midnight) I was "on the job" at 8:00 o'clock.

The construction company provided motion pictures. Before the movie started I would get on the stage and announce that I'd be at the back of the hall with registration cards.

One area (called Wachwas) was set aside for families who lived in trailers. It was door-to-door there.

I stayed in Kemano for about two weeks and left with 1,132 registration cards. These I delivered to the Registrar of Voters in Smithers and got the officials to establish 6 polling divisions at Kemano. Many of those whom I registered left Kemano before election day and the number of votes cast was 440. Some of those whom I registered would have voted in other parts of B.C. using the absentee system of voting. The number of absentee votes cast was 582, up considerably over 1952.

It was a close race. The Liberals asked for and got a recount before a judge. Every ballot was recounted. I became the first CCF-M.L.A. for Skeena with a margin of thirteen votes.

30

LEARN BY DOING

I wasn't attracted to the CCF because of any theories it held regarding sociopolitical matters. I joined because I was a trade unionist; because corporations had the ear of government and workers did not.

I was attracted to the trade union movement because its philosophy was to work together for the common good. Dad was working class. While he was not an active trade unionist he brought this work-together philosophy with him from England. It rubbed off on me.

Naturally I was elated at being elected to what is often referred to as the highest court in the province. I also considered that being an M.L.A. was the logical extension of trade union activity. The process of becoming the bargaining agent for a group of workers and of negotiating with an employer was, and still is, controlled by a law which suits the convenience of corporations. Being an M.L.A. would at least give me the chance to tell the Legislature about the concerns and hopes of workers.

Edith accompanied me to the opening of the Legislature following that 1953 election. I think she was more excited than I. My lasting memory of that day was to see the late Jack Webster (then a reporter for the *Vancouver Sun*) rushing along one of the corridors in the Parliament Buildings. In his haste he slipped on the smooth and shiny floor and tumbled into a heap of embarrassment.

Facilities for M.L.A.s were primitive. We had elected fourteen Members. The office for all of us was one large table in one room. Around this table each Member had a space about three-feet wide. It was there that we did all our paper work, all our reading. Off a corridor there were two small cubicles with a telephone in each. These cubicles were also used when dictating letters. That was another problem. We had the services of only one stenographer.

Much of my correspondence was either hand-written or personally typed. One bit of advice I followed was to scour the local newspapers for references to births and marriages and then write congratulatory letters.

I received one reply, from a family in Smithers telling me how poor they were and asking me to lend them a hundred dollars. Another letter I wrote, to a young mother regarding the birth of a child, was received by the seventy-five year old grandmother. I soon stopped writing that type of letter.

Living accommodation was temporary. During that first session of Parliament I rented a house-keeping room. Afterwards four of us shared a two-bedroom suite in a downtown apartment hotel. We drew straws for the bedrooms. I ended up sleeping on one of the cots in the living room.

Arnold Webster was Provincial Leader of the CCF at the 1953 election. He replaced Harold Winch who had retired from the provincial scene to run as a federal candidate. First off I told Arnold about my criminal record. His reply was: "I'm glad you told me. I would have been disappointed if you hadn't."

M.L.A.s are not referred to by their given or family names in the Legislature; the title is Honourable Member. Arnold Webster was more than an Honourable Member; he was an honourable person. A former High-School principle he was tough-minded, yet gentle and dignified. He was respected by everyone who had any contact with him.

The raucous and sometimes abusive debating techniques employed by people like Premier Bennett and Flying Phil Gaglardi distressed him. His view was that such tactics tended to blacken and deny the importance and value of a law-making body. He told caucus he felt terribly uncomfortable in the Legislature. To me he was like a time-traveller from the past, from an era when dignity and integrity were honoured. Webster got elected too late in his life and felt the need to retire from politics too soon. Had he stayed he might have been able to bring a larger degree of civility to the Legislature.

Winch was never able to get over the fact that he was not chosen to form the government in 1952. He had been the CCF's Provincial Leader for many years and had an uphill fight at every election.

He felt cheated by the Liberals in 1952 who told Lieutenant-Governor Wallace they would support Bennett to form a government. Winch couldn't understand why the Liberals would endorse the person who had done so much to destroy the Coalition and, consequently, the Liberals.

What Winch seemed to have missed is the fact that then, as now, pro-capitalistic political parties will always cuddle when it suits their purpose.

Government is involved with civic matters, with law; capitalism's involvement is with a process. Where conflict arises between civic matters and process it has to be government which is the arbiter for it has the wider responsibility. Political parties with pro-capitalistic biases contend that capitalism, through its pursuit of profit, will provide benefits to society. Capitalism may provide goods and some services, but government intervention has produced the societal benefits.

A great deal of laissez-faire political chatter today employs words such as freedom and liberty. Freedom for whom? Liberty for what? We must keep in mind that capitalism wants freedom from government intervention; human beings want freedom from exploitation. The greater the amount of freedom from government intervention, the greater the potential for corporate exploitation.

During sessions of the Legislature I retained the position of President of the Loggers' Local but took myself off the payroll. During the time that I was both M.L.A. and President none of the meetings of the union ever tried to give me instructions or exert any pressure about my conduct as an M.L.A. The position was respected by the local. I was a representative of all people in Skeena and needed the freedom to make decisions on their behalf as I saw fit.

Such respect was not observed by two corporate representatives in Skeena. Their position was clear: Don't challenge their corporate interests.

Fred Adames, Personnel Manager of The Columbia Cellulose Company's logging division in Terrace, approached me one day to talk about labour-management relations. He raised the subject of strikes, saying, and I recall his words clearly: "It's your duty as M.L.A. to put down strikes. They are not in the public interest."

I told him that was nonsense and that a strike, or threat of one, was the only lever working people had if they were not satisfied with wages, hours, or working conditions. He backed off a bit and rephrased his words to the effect that I should not encourage strikes.

Being an M.L.A. was full-time work. Financially, though, it was a part-time job. The practice was to have one session of the Legislature lasting about six or seven weeks in the spring of each year. In the early 1950s a Member was not paid an annual salary, only an indemnity for the loss of income from any other job while attending sessions.

This sessional indemnity was also to cover living expenses in Victoria and any other costs an M.L.A. would incur while servicing his or her constituency. Some M.L.A.s, myself included, had to have another source of income.

At one point I thought it would be in the best interests of my family and myself if I resigned from the IWA and found some other job so I'd be able to spend more time at home. I applied for a job at Alcan's smelter in Kitimat. I was interviewed by the Personnel Manager, R.S.S. Wilson. Because of his initials the work force tagged him as RSsquared.

RSsquared's approach was clear and simple. He told me it would be embarrassing if I made some unkind comments about Alcan in the Legislature and then came back to work for them after the Legislature adjourned. If I wanted to work for Alcan I would have to resign as M.L.A. That ended the interview.

Political parties which declare they support the capitalist system, by that declaration, invite corporations to link up with those parties. They have a common goal: government is there to serve the interests of corporations. What Adames and RSsquared said merely reflected the general corporate opinion and demand about the purpose of government.

Bennett was a supporter of the concept that government can best serve the interests of society by aligning itself with the corporate sector. He was clever. He was able to get votes from the average citizen and money from corporations by giving the impression that he would protect each from the other.

There was no doubt as to who ran the show. It was Bennett who was both Premier and Minister of Finance. He controlled his government and the Social Credit caucus.

What shocked me during my first session of the Legislature were the procedural rules of the place (The Standing Orders). When my union met, it was those in attendance who made decisions; any Member could move a motion to instruct the officers to do whatever it was the Member wanted. If the majority voted for the motion, the officers were obligated to carry out the instruction. I was used to that; it was my sense of democracy.

In the Legislature it was upside down. The rules prohibited the moving of any motion to instruct the government to do anything. Any motion seeking to send a message to the government had to be preceded with a twisted and coiled preamble such as: "This House is of the opinion that the government should consider the advisability of..."

I was also shocked to discover that it was out of order for a Private Member to move any motion or introduce any Bill which would entail the expenditure of public funds. Those rights were reserved only for

Cabinet Ministers. Neither could a Private Member introduce a Bill to amend the Constitution.

Premier Bennett looked upon the Legislature as more of an inconvenience than as an integral part of our political democracy. He had scant interest in lengthy debates and lengthy sessions. The first session of the Legislature following the 1953 election lasted just four weeks.

Speaking in the Legislature was vastly different from speaking to a group of loggers. This was a new and daunting arena for me. Seasoned and loquacious warriors were ready to pounce on and verbally demolish anyone in an opposing political Party. Usually it was only the first speech of a newly elected Member that was listened to without interruption.

One maxim of political life is to speak in parliament as soon as you can. Jump in with both feet and take the consequences. My first opportunity was during the Throne Speech debate of that first session. Nothing of consequence, just another maiden speech about roads.

The major constituency problem in Skeena was the condition of the roads and this became my primary concern. The main road (Highway 16) was simply two lanes of rocks, dust, potholes, and washboard. As winter frost melted in the spring, roads became cratered with mud holes and were virtually impassable.

Travelling salesmen might drive westward from Prince George along Highway 16, but wouldn't make the return trip. They'd ship their cars back to Vancouver by boat from Prince Rupert.

Local residents installed sheets of steel beneath the engines of their cars to prevent having the crankcase punctured. Two spare tires were a necessity.

It wasn't all work and no play, though. During this 24th Parliament (1953 to 1956) Lieutenant-Governor Wallace (the L.G.) hosted a state dinner for those of us who were the back-benchers, officially Private Members. It was a multi-course, sumptuous affair like something I'd only seen in movies.

There were three or four different wine glasses at each setting. Sit-

ting across from me were two Social Credit M.L.A.s. Both were teeto-
tallers. They turned their glasses upside down, smugly indicating they
didn't want wine. I wasn't familiar with the etiquette at such dinners,
but common sense told me that this was something of an insult to the
host. It seemed to me they need only have said "No, thank you" to the
server.

Near the conclusion of the dinner we were offered bowls of brandied dates and figs. It was a help-yourself serving. The two Socreds
who had turned down their glasses couldn't get enough of these treats.
Rae Eddie, M.L.A. for New Westminster, leaned across the table and,
with a glint in his eye, asked them if they knew that the sweets were
brandied. Looks of consternation. No more dates or figs; no glasses to
turn upside down.

I sat next to John Squire, M.L.A. for Alberni. We had chatted
throughout the dinner, marvelling at each course, and asking each other
what this was and what that was. The last offering was a bowl of clear
liquid with a flower floating on top. It was placed beside each guest. I
asked Squire what it was. He didn't know either. He dipped a spoon
into it, took a taste, and said that it tasted like lemon. We then noticed
what other more sophisticated guests were doing. It was a finger bowl.

On another occasion the L.G. hosted a reception for all M.L.A.s.
Afterwards five or six of us decided to go out for some Chinese food.
Included in the group were two Liberals, Art Laing, Leader of the Lib-
eral Party, and Bruce Brown from Prince Rupert.

At the restaurant Laing excused himself and, upon his return, told
us that he had phoned the L.G. and that he was going to join us.
When he and his aide-de-camp arrived the owner of the restaurant
advised everyone that he was going to close the doors, but that cus-
tomers could stay to finish their meals. Whisky was on the house, served
from tea-pots.

We were there for quite a while, the L.G. dancing with women
who belonged to some bowling club and who had remained when the
place closed. I have this mental picture of the L.G., with his coat on a

chair, dancing in his shirt sleeves with someone in baggy slacks and a sweat shirt emblazoned on the back with something like "Joe's Bowling League."

Arnold Webster and I were two newcomers to the CCF caucus. The other Members had at least one session's experience. Because Webster was Leader of the Opposition, he got—quite rightly—advice and guidance about functioning in the Legislature. I was on my own and had to grope through the rules of the House as best I could, getting bits and pieces of information from other Members of caucus.

It was a learning process. The first bit of advice came from Bob Strachan, M.L.A. for Cowichan-Newcastle. "Don't be disappointed if proposals you advance are not accepted by government. The government does not want to appear to give anyone in Opposition credit for anything, no matter how valid that anything might be."

He told me that the acceptance of the CCF by the general public would be advanced by media coverage and the information we could provide for our constituents when reporting back to them at public meetings after a session had concluded.

Even media coverage is chancy. To support that he cited an experience of Arthur Turner, long-time M.L.A. for Vancouver East. It was really a story which Turner himself told. "I had prepared my maiden speech," so said Turner, "over the course of a number of days, and had silently rehearsed it. I gave the speech on a Friday. The next day I looked through the newspapers to see how it had been covered, and all I could find was one small line about the Legislature which said Friday was a dull day."

Did I accomplish anything during my stint as M.L.A.? I can recall but one item. My interest in photography had led to selling photographs and photo-stories to different publications. I subscribed to the magazine *Arizona Highways* in an attempt to learn composition from its superb photographs of that State.

One day I crossed over to the government side of the House and sat next to Ralph Chetwynd, Minister of Railways and Minister of

Trade and Industry. I gave Chetwynd a number of copies of *Arizona Highways* and suggested a similar publication relating to the scenic wonders of B.C. should be undertaken. Thus was born *Beautiful British Columbia*.

Did I contribute anything? Yes, but it took years for it to come to fruition. In April of 1954 I moved a motion which asked government to consider setting up a Women's Bureau in the Department of Labour. Labour Minister Lyle Wicks replied that he wasn't interested in even considering the idea because there were many individuals and groups to speak on behalf of women.

Lydia Arsens, a Socred and the only woman M.L.A. at the time, objected to my motion as well, saying that she couldn't believe an employer would allow conditions to exist which would be detrimental to either men or women. She also said that if women were in jobs that were injurious to them, it was their own fault.

Did I learn anything? To a politician publicity is more important than substance; favourable, more important than bad; bad, in small doses, more important than none. The vital ingredients of news items had to be your name and your political party.

31

SURRENDER

This Chapter is more declaratory than autobiographical. I think it's a necessary prelude to information and events set out in subsequent chapters.

Motion pictures told me about human beings who were called Indians. The plots were always the same. The Indians were the bad guys; they always lost. The U.S. Cavalry and the cowboys were the good guys; they always won.

Many people living along the coast of British Columbia who had been designated by the so-called white man as Indians objected to being so identified. Their position was logical and understandable: Columbus didn't know where he landed in 1492. They preferred to be called Natives.

It's now considered politically correct to use the phrase First Nation. To be truly correct and respectful we should refer to specific nations of people using their proprietary names (e.g. Nisga'a, Tsimpshian). In a broad, generic sense it's appropriate to use First Nation or Aboriginal.

Becoming an M.L.A. in 1953 gave me the opportunity to learn about and appreciate the history and culture of Indigenous people. More than that it put me in the unique position to understand the reasons for their frustration and anger.

In the beginning I sensed an aloofness on their part and a reluc-
tance to talk with me. I wasn't surprised. After all, I was just another
white man. All I could do was hope that their unwillingness to reveal
would ease off.

While the full chance to learn came about at the 1952 provincial
election, I'd been given an earlier glimpse of what it meant to be an
Aboriginal. When I was IWA secretary at Camp A one of the loggers
came to my bunkhouse one evening to join up.

After he had signed the necessary form he said, "You don't remember me, do you?" I had to tell him, "No, I don't."

He lowered his voice to a conspiratorial level and said, "I was with
the Dome Gang in the B.C. Pen when you were there."

"Yeh, now I remember. You were the guy that Blackie used to call
a 'bow and arrow'." Blackie was another convict.

We then got into a lengthy discussion about our lives. He told me
he wasn't going back, either. Once was more than enough.

We talked about Natives. He said to me that most kids were told
at home to hate the white man because of the way Natives were treated
by the government appointed Indian Agents.

He related that his grandmother called Reserves nothing more than
concentration camps.

That conversation could not have taken place if we had not had
the common experience of jail. In one sense we were "brothers" and
spoke a common language. We understood, accepted, and because of
our commitment to go straight, respected each other on a level beyond
the ordinary relationship of one human to another.

That Camp A discussion gave me a feeling of sensitivity about the
life and conditions of Aboriginal people that was helpful when I became M.L.A.

Voting in a provincial election for an M.L.A. was a "new" adventure for Native people. They couldn't vote in federal elections and had
very few, if any, earlier direct experiences with government. What relationship did exist was channelled through the narrow conduit pipe of

the Federal Government's Indian Affairs Branch.

I seriously wanted to help change the lot and life of Aboriginal people. I wanted them to look upon me as a friend and supporter. No bones about it, I also wanted them to vote for me in future elections.

I did a number of things which I hoped would establish a sense of trust. I found out that people who were not First Nations simply entered a Reserve as if it were a public park. I decided I wouldn't visit a Reserve unless I asked the Chief Councillor for permission. Such a request may have surprised a Chief, but it was never refused.

In visiting Native villages I got the sense that two of them were more friendly than others. I asked each Band Council in those two (Kispiox and Kitwancool) if it would appoint one person through whom I could communicate. At Kispiox it was Stephen Morrison and at Kitwancool it was Robert Good. This system was gradually expanded to other villages.

In each village there are family and tribal groups which sometimes are at odds with one another. I didn't want to get into any of those squabbles so working with the elected Band Council was the safest and best way.

Gradually I got invited to meetings, feasts, and potlatches. I attended a gathering one evening at Kitsegeucla. Afterwards about a half dozen older men stayed. We sat around a wood-burning stove until well past midnight and I listened while they talked and told stories. In addition to some of their history I learned a few words of the Git'ksan language.

Much later I attended a feast at Kitsegeucla. Many of the speakers used the Git'ksan language. When I spoke I told the assembly about the earlier late-night meeting and that I had learned some of their language. I said I was surprised that no one who spoke at the feast had used any of the words I had learned. That got a big laugh.

At the formation of the Dominion of Canada our Fathers of Confederation placed Indigenous people and reserve lands exclusively at the mercy of the federal government. Section 91 (24) of the British

North America (BNA) Act (Canada's Constitution) says: "... the exclusive Legislative Authority of the Parliament of Canada extends to... Indians and Lands reserved for the Indians." By exercising this constitutional authority the Parliament of Canada passed a law called the Indian Act. It controlled all rights and liberties of Aboriginal people. Matters such as education, health care, property rights, marriages, civil rights, burials were governed by the feds; for the rest of us it was a matter of provincial jurisdiction.

The Indian Act also set out who could be classified as an "Indian." Being an "Indian" was not a matter of inheritance or birthright, it was a matter of a legal definition. A ludicrous example of this relates to marriage. If an Aboriginal man married a white woman she, under the Indian Act, became an "Indian" and would lose her right to have access to alcohol. On the other hand if an Aboriginal woman married a white man she lost her legal status as an "Indian" and would gain the right to have alcohol.

Booze was employed as a bribe to get First Nations people to give up their status. The Indian Act made it illegal for them to possess alcohol. It was also illegal for anyone to supply it to a Native.

If Natives gave up this Indian-Act status they could have access to alcoholic beverages. The federal government issued a card to prove they could buy it. There was no law called The White Act, but the idiomatic expression of Natives who succumbed to the bribe was: "I'm under the White Act."

An opinion existed for many years that the physiology of Aboriginals was inferior to that of others, and, as a result, they couldn't handle alcohol. I've drunk with Native people many times and found their reaction to booze no different from anyone else. The argument that they are unable to handle the stuff was absolute government bullshit.

Those who developed the law about prohibiting Natives from having access to liquor, because they felt they couldn't handle it, were hypocrites. On the one hand they said they wanted to protect Natives because they had such a frail and sensitive biological make up. On the other hand they said that such people didn't need protecting once an application was made to give up their Indian-Act status.

Calder used to give this denigrating opinion about the effect of alcohol on First Nations people. He said, "A drunken Native would stagger about and fall down; would use abusive language; would want to argue and fight; would get sick and vomit. He was almost as bad as a drunken white man."

The Indian Act was drafted and brought into law by a bunch of politicians and bureaucrats who felt they were the pre-eminent group and that Native people were somehow less than human. That attitude was, and still is, offensive and self-serving. It is often recited by those who are so insecure personally that they have to put someone else down to feel good about themselves.

Prior to British Columbia entering Confederation in 1871 there were negotiations regarding the number of M.P.s and Senators for the province. This number was related to the population. One of the contentions put forward by the federal authorities was that Aboriginals should not be counted as part of the population; they were just like "the deer in the forest."

The Indian Act set up a mechanism for Natives to elect a group to manage affairs on a reserve. This law simply denied the inherited cultural processes of choosing Chiefs, and substituted for it a procedure used for choosing municipal governments. The Indian Act referred to these elected people as a Band Council. Another imposition by officialdom in Ottawa to eliminate a cultural identity and inheritance.

Many years ago public servants who administered the Indian Act in local areas were called Indian Agents. The connotation was that this person was an agent for Natives and acted on their behalf. Then a change took place. The Indian Agent got a new title: The Superintendent of Indian Affairs. This smacked of more authority.

If a Band Council decided that a part of its reserve land should be sold and thus removed from reserve status, the Indian Act process for so doing was called a surrender. That word surrender sums up succinctly the attitude of government towards those who were here when the Europeans came.

Restrictions about land, booze, marriage, Band Councils, voting, and much more all gave the same message: abandon your possessions, your inherited individuality, your culture. Give in to a foreign power.

Here we are, more than 135 years after Confederation, and only at the starting point of trying to repair the damage done by successive governments and the Fathers of Confederation, one of whom, William Henry Steeves, may have been an ancestor of mine.

Like it or not; governments continued to tell generations of Natives that they were dumb and couldn't make a go of it on their own. They were told that they had to be isolated and that government would care for them; clothe them, feed them, build houses for them. First Nations people were inculcated—educated is too polite a word for what happened—with the idea that they were incompetent.

The result of generations of "benevolence" by governments is a group inferiority complex. This, of course, has rubbed off onto individuals. I've sat up with many Natives well into the small hours of the morning, drinking wine, all of us revealing ourselves, our fears, and our frustrations.

For more than a century Aboriginal people were put down. The total effect of this cultural and individual destruction can be summed up in six words. The saddest admission I ever heard from some of my Aboriginal friends, and I heard it many times, was: "Let's get drunk and be somebody."

Some First Nations people think that the best strategy is to strike back, to set up road blocks, and make inflammatory statements about how much is owed to them. That route is the easiest one. It takes no courage to wear a mask.

Those who take the easy way hurt themselves. Every time they occupy some government offices, put up a road block, wave a rifle, or wear masks and old army uniforms they injure the larger cause of getting redress for past indignities. They may be looked upon as heroes by some of their compatriots, but even their most staunch supporters feel enraged at times.

There are many Native communities where common sense and dignity prevail, but these either get no attention from the media or, if they do, the attention is usually a one-time reference. The media is more interested in social warfare than in success stories.

I personally hope that more individual First Nations people will develop the guts to stop whining about the past and provide within their own communities the type of leadership which is statesmanlike. It takes more courage to be a statesman than it does to be a belligerent and wave a rifle.

32

A DOUBLE STANDARD FOR BOOZE

One subject uppermost in the minds of Natives during the 1952 provincial election was that of alcohol. As a candidate in that election I
gained a limited and brief introduction to the question of booze. When
I became the M.L.A. I made it my business to learn all I could about
the history of Natives and alcohol.

Following the 1949 provincial election the Coalition Government
decided to give Aboriginals limited access to alcohol, a decision which
caused people more grief than did prohibition.

The election of Frank Calder as M.L.A. in 1949 was a factor in
this move. The Lieutenant-Governor of B.C. hosted a social evening
for those elected at the 1949 election, an evening at which alcohol
would be served. Harold Winch asked B.C.'s Attorney-General, Gordon
Wismer, if the police were going to arrest Calder for violating the Indian Act and arrest the L.G. for supplying the booze.

But Wismer and the government ignored the violation. It would
have been embarrassing to do otherwise. Still, it got the government's
attention.

The Canadian Government (Liberal) undertook to revise the Indian Act in 1951. The Liberals typically endorsed both sides of the
question of alcohol availability under the Indian Act. The changes to
the Act said: No and Maybe. A cruel change.

Those 1951 amendments still denied complete access to alcohol, but offered a limited exemption if a province requested it. The offensive wrinkle was that such an exemption would only apply if alcohol was bought and drunk in a public place licensed by a province to sell alcohol. In B.C. the only licensed public places were "beer parlours." The only alcohol they could sell was beer. This is where Natives went.

The main beneficiaries were beer parlour owners and breweries. The provincial Minister of Finance at the time, Herbert Anscomb, was a Director of Coast Breweries Limited.

In 1951 it was obvious to those on the inside of B.C.'s Coalition Government that it was going to self-destruct. The Liberals dominated the Coalition and knew that an election was imminent. The general public and the media also believed this.

The 1951 Indian Act amendments were promulgated on September 4, 1951. On October 26th the government of B.C. requested an exemption which was granted on December 15. When it suits their purpose, governments can move quickly.

There was a beer parlour in New Hazelton. At closing time it was common for the R.C.M.P. bun wagon to be parked at the door. Any Aboriginal person who came out of the beer parlour and who looked intoxicated would be hustled into the bun wagon and carted off to jail to face a fine of not less than $10.00 and not more than $50.00 or to a three-month jail sentence or to both.

One evening I got back to the New Hazelton Hotel at closing time and witnessed the R.C.M.P. herding people into the bun wagon. One of the constables spoke with a Native woman and, in some infantile attempt to determine intoxication, said to her, "Come here; let me smell your breath." Her reply was an uncomplicated challenge to the stupidity of the question and of the law, "How'd you like to smell my asshole?"

I laughed and, in the presence of the constable, said to her, "Good for you." The constable turned away, got into the bun wagon with his partner, and drove off.

I went to the R.C.M.P. offices and spoke with the person in charge of the detachment about the practice of waiting outside a beer parlour. He said they were only enforcing the law.

The result of that visit, though, was that the R.C.M.P. in the Hazelton area became more respectful. They didn't simply wait for people to walk out of a beer parlour and be taken to jail. They dealt with the problem only if a nuisance or a fight arose. The R.C.M.P. in other areas became more tolerant also.

Regardless, this two-faced standard of one law for Natives and another for everyone else remained in place for years.

33

RIGHT PLACE AT THE RIGHT TIME

Because I had undertaken to serve the north-coast area of the Loggers' Local, I was able to maintain a regular and steady presence in Terrace even though I didn't reside there.

Edith, Robert, and I finally moved to Terrace in 1955 and had to live in an auto court; not the most prestigious accommodation for an M.L.A. and family, but it was all that was available.

I had married too soon. I wasn't ready for marriage; wasn't able to give marriage a chance; wasn't able to devote the time necessary to help make a family develop into a cohesive unit.

Edith was a good person, a good mother, and Robert was fortunate to have such care and devotion. But Edith and I quarrelled a lot about my work. I was intent on pursuing a career in the trade-union movement or in politics. Edith would have been content, as Robert told me years later, if I had worked at an hourly-paid job which kept me at home.

Still, in Terrace I was home more often than when we lived in New Westminster. All the Local's administrative work was handled by Fred Fieber, our Secretary-Treasurer. The office of President became more and more titular, which was fine with me, but I still had the northern part of our Local to attend to as well as going to Vancouver from time to time.

Edith often suggested that I quit as President and find some other job in Terrace. The application to work for Alcan was killed by RSsquared's demand. I didn't want to go back to the logging industry. Politics had become a benign infection; my interest in it increased.

When I'd gone to work for Canadian Forest Products at Englewood in 1948 I was in the right place at the right time. The attempted sundering of the IWA and formation of the WIUC created confusion and a vacuum. If it had not been for that abortive move I would have had virtually no chance to become an officer of the IWA. I would have likely continued on drudging at whatever work presented itself. Instead, I got scooped up along with a number of other woodworkers and flowed along with the crowd.

When I went to the Terrace area to organize the loggers working for Columbia Cellulose Company I was once again in the right place at the right time. Getting the IWA organized in an area that historically had lower wages and more onerous working conditions than existed on the coast was beneficial to the workers in the area, to the image of the IWA, and to me as the IWA representative who was on the scene. Fortuitously I was there for the 1952 and 1953 provincial elections.

Bennett, having received the benefit of his baby (the single transferable vote), arranged to have the Legislature repeal it during his second term as Premier. The provincial election in 1956 used the traditional system of marking one's ballot with an X. Social Credit knocked me out of the race by 63 votes. Although I didn't realize it then this defeat as M.L.A. once again put me in the right place at the right time.

34

A LUCKY SO AND SO

One of Duke Ellington's lesser-known compositions is "I'm Just A Lucky So And So." In 1956 and 1957 I was a lucky so and so. Being defeated at the 1956 provincial election was a tragedy which later became a blessing.

1956 was a year of turmoil on the federal political scene. Prime Minister Louis St. Laurent's Liberal Government had made a deal to promote and help finance the construction of a natural gas pipe-line from Alberta to eastern Canada, built by a company called Trans-Canada Pipe Lines. Trans-Canada was controlled in the United States and had experienced difficulty getting the project financed by Canadian institutions. The Liberals came to its rescue by proposing to advance up to 90% of the cost of building the Alberta to Winnipeg section. A Bill to accomplish this was introduced into the House of Commons on May 8, 1956 with a deadline of June 6th for its passage. Both the Conservatives and the CCF vigorously opposed the Bill because Canada would be putting up taxpayers' money to finance an American project.

To get the Bill through the House by the deadline the government cut off the debate on six of the seven clauses, allowing only the Minister in charge of the Bill (C.D. Howe) to speak. This contemptuous attitude towards Parliament and the Liberal Party's sneering criticism of any objections provoked extensive media coverage and an enraged public response.

I read Hansard voraciously in an attempt to get a handle on the pipe-line issue. I gave up after awhile. There were pages upon pages of points of order and irrelevant speeches, a labyrinth of words, the purpose being to get as much anti-Liberal media attention as possible.

The federal constituency in the north-west part of B.C. was also named Skeena. We called it Federal Skeena. Federal Skeena was a large area; about 125,000 square miles, easily twice the combined areas of Nova Scotia, New Brunswick and Prince Edward Island. Even the British Isles and Ireland would fit into it. Within its boundaries were three provincial constituencies and parts of two others.

Economically it embraced both hard-rock and open-pit mining, ranching, logging, saw-milling, aluminum smelting, pulp mills, dairy farming, and salt-water fisheries. Many of the communities were miles apart.

Federal Skeena, from cattle ranches in the eastern area to rugged and soaring mountains in the west, is staggeringly beautiful.

The climate is as variable as the terrain. Winter temperatures range from around 0°C. on the coast to -40°C. in the interior. When the warm, moisture-laden air from the Pacific strikes the mountains tons of snow fall on them. At the mining camp of Granduc Mines (a copper mine near the Alaska border) the snowfall one winter was close to ninety feet.

Historically Federal Skeena had elected Liberals. The Conservatives won the riding in the mid-1920s, and then for one short term. The CCF won the riding in 1945, also a one-term shot. The Liberal M.P. elected in 1949 and 1953 was E.T. (Ted) Applewhaite from Prince Rupert.

Ted was a fine, well-regarded person. He was gentle, respectful, and considerate. In a two-way fight he won Skeena in 1949 with 58.2% of the vote, defeating the CCF M.P. One reason for the huge Liberal vote was the fact that the Conservatives didn't run. The Liberals and the Conservatives, cosily together at the provincial level, decided to play the same game in Federal Skeena to ensure that the CCF was defeated.

Applewhaite's status in Federal Skeena was injured by two major factors. One was the furore over the federal government's support of, and involvement in, the gas pipe-line. That involvement was mercilessly exploited by the Conservatives, with the debate raging on for weeks.

The other difficulty for Applewhaite related to the sale, by the federal government, of a shipyard in Prince Rupert. This shipyard had been fully used during the Second World War. People in Prince Rupert had a strong emotional attachment to it.

Applewhaite lost ground by trying to explain and justify the sale. Had he taken the opposite position, his stature wouldn't have become so tarnished.

I, being that lucky so and so and in the right place at the right time, ran as the CCF candidate in Federal Skeena in the 1957 federal election. My taste of politics at the provincial level stoked the embers of my ego. My inner voice said to me that this is what I wanted. I was attracted by the prestige of public office. I also wanted to be able to help people in their struggles with the eastern dominated Federal Government. I had a few things going for me.

As President of the Loggers' Local I was well known on the Queen Charlotte Islands, especially among loggers. In the fall of 1956 I moonlighted by becoming a salesman for an industrial supply company, Paragon Supplies of Vancouver. This enabled me to travel to the parts of Federal Skeena east of Smithers selling for Paragon and selling myself as the federal CCF candidate for the expected 1957 federal election.

The eastern part of Federal Skeena was strongly Social Credit. In that area a number of lakes had been dammed up to reverse the flow of water and channel it westward to supply Alcan's power-generating facility at Kemano. A number of communities and much land was flooded.

E. T. Kenney was the government minister responsible for the deal with Alcan to flood the area. People were incensed at the flooding, and at Kenney and the Liberal Party. They elected a local man, Cyril Shelford, as the Social Credit M.L.A. in the 1952, 1953, and 1956 provincial elections.

The Social Credit Party picked Arthur Murray, a Prince Rupert resident, to be its candidate in Federal Skeena in the 1957 election. Nomination Day was May 13. Murray refused to file his nomination papers so Social Credit had no candidate. He didn't publicly explain his refusal.

It was privately known, though, that Premier Bennett didn't think Social Credit had a chance in Federal Skeena and had refused to approve any financial assistance to Murray. Social Creditors were made to look like fools.

I took full advantage of the situation by telling Social Credit supporters that the Conservatives, not having been able to elect anyone for the past 30 years, had no chance. The choice was between me and the Liberals. Because of the flooding in the eastern part of the riding, this tactic went over well.

On June 10, 1957 I won Federal Skeena with a modest 39% of the vote. The Conservatives, led by John Diefenbaker, formed a minority government with 113 M.P.s to the Liberals' 103. There was no doubt in my mind that a follow-up election would take place, a repeat of the events which occurred in B.C. in 1952 and 1953.

Because Federal Skeena was such a large area containing many small communities, it had not been possible to visit all of them during the 1957 campaign. Shortly after the election I visited these communities, a kind of post-election campaign. I held public meetings and explained who I was and what I would try to do. There was surprise everywhere. Whoever heard of a politician coming to town after an election?

I went to Native villages and told them I would try to get the residents the right to vote in federal elections.

In 1952 I had learned that Aboriginal people living on a Reserve could not vote in federal elections. To me it was an insulting travesty that they should be denied the right to vote by the very people who had the constitutional authority over them.

Edith, Robert, and I drove to Ottawa making it a holiday on the way. We spent the first day there looking for a place to live, finally settling on an apartment-type hotel. My next move was to call on M.J. Coldwell, the CCF's National Leader, affectionately called M.J. Our caucus consisted of 25 M.P.s; many were long-time Members. I told M.J. about my criminal record which was still an important concern of mine. I don't recall exactly what he said except that he thanked me for telling him.

I called on Howard Conquergood, "Conkie", educational director for the Canadian Labour Congress (CLC). I met Conkie at educational seminars when I was with the IWA, and simply wanted to renew acquaintances. Conkie urged me to set up a special mailing list for those in my riding who dealt with the public, people like taxi drivers, hairdressers, barbers, bartenders.

I used the M.P.'s free-mail system to tell those on my mailing list what was happening in Ottawa and what I was doing.

At our first caucus meeting M.J. proposed that we not move any want-of-confidence motions and not support any moved by anyone else. He stated that we needed to give the Conservatives a chance to show what they could do.

I, for one, raised objections to M.J.'s proposal. I told how Bennett had manoeuvred to get an early election in 1953 which gave him a majority government, and that the Conservatives would similarly manipulate to their advantage.

I also argued that the CCF membership expected us to be aggressive and to fight in the House of Commons for what we believed in. If we didn't put up a fight we would enter the expected follow-up election as weaklings.

Caucus decided to move a want-of-confidence motion at the first opportunity; M.J. was forced to comply. After the meeting Alistair

Stewart, M.P. for Winnipeg North, told me he approved of my position. He said M.J., an M.P. for 22 years, had become soft over those years and tended to compromise more.

Those of us who were new M.P.s met with Stanley Knowles, M.P. for Winnipeg-North Centre, one evening to get advice, information, and guidance. Knowles was a long-time M.P., an institution in his own right, honoured and respected by all. He was the CCF's procedural expert in the House of Commons. At that meeting with Knowles I can only recall two matters. He went to great lengths to tell us about his filing system. He also told us in detail about the M.P.'s pension plan. I wasn't interested in the pension plan. I was interested in what could be done to increase my chances of re-election. Doug Fisher, also a new M.P., said, "Stanley already qualifies for the pension. Well, I want to qualify also but I have to get elected a few times first. My vision is for my future but Stanley appears mired in the past."

Knowles's life was the House of Commons. He lived and breathed it. Tommy Douglas, in later years and with affection, said that Knowles was so enamoured of the House that he stayed after adjournment to pick up scattered pieces of paper.

Prime Minister Diefenbaker had appointed George Hees as the Minister of Transport. Before the House of Commons was called into session, Hees came to Prince Rupert for some ceremony relating to his portfolio. I spoke with him for a few minutes and congratulated him on being chosen at the Transport Minister.

He told me that the House of Commons was really a rather gentlemanly place. I remember him saying, "Sure, the debates can get raucous and accusatory, but when it's all over M.P.s can be friendly over coffee or something like that."

Having had the experience with W.A.C. Bennett's methods of debate in B.C.'s Legislature prompted me to take Hees's words with the proverbial grain of salt. But, his comment did have some truth to it as far as Coldwell and Knowles were concerned. Maybe their years in the House had mellowed them to the point where friendship with M.P.s from other parties was more important than pursuing CCF policies with vigor. Maybe their personalities were such that gentlemanly behaviour was second nature. Whatever the reason I found both of them to have had a mind set about newly elected M.P.s. I felt we were expected to stay in the background, to defer to long-time Members, to postpone any desire to carve out a personal niche. In other words—we were to be seen and not heard from too often.

In 1957 facilities for back-bench M.P.s were better than what I'd experienced as an M.L.A.—but not by much. We shared office space and secretarial assistance; two M.P.s to an office. One secretary was shared with an M.P. who was in a different office. Secretaries were located somewhere on the ground floor. It was a hassle to make phone calls, to dictate letters, to do any reading and studying of issues. I typed most of my own letters and used the facilities of the CCF's National Office to mimeograph reports to my specialized mailing list. Doug Fisher, with whom I shared the office, did most of his work in a secluded corner of the Parliamentary Library.

Conkie also advised me to make as many friends as I could with members of the Press Gallery on Parliament Hill. "It isn't that you will get special treatment from them," he said. "It will serve to keep you up-to-date on what is happening and what is likely to be newsworthy."

I made a few friends in the press gallery, some from B.C., which made it a bit easier. Tom Gould, Charles King, Ken Kelly, and Norman DePoe come to mind. But I found the Press Gallery to be a gossip centre with reporters almost interviewing one another. Conkie was correct about not getting special treatment. If an item was newsworthy, it would get written up and submitted. If it wasn't, the reporters I knew wouldn't waste their time on it.

The 103 Liberal M.P.s were leaderless following the 1957 election, former Prime Minister St. Laurent having announced his retirement. In January of 1958 they elected Lester B. (Mike) Pearson. It always amazed me how Pearson was able privately to admire and kowtow to the power elite and publicly exhibit an aloofness from it. He seemed to say that it's there and I respect it, but I don't want it for myself. Perhaps that is what Mrs. Pearson was saying with her famous comment: "Behind every successful man there stands an amazed woman."

The Liberals had not moved any want-of-confidence motions in the House and had voted against those moved by both the CCF and Social Credit parties. Pearson's election as Liberal leader required him to show his mettle. He had to move a want-of-confidence motion against the Conservative Government.

John W. (Jack) Pickersgill, Liberal M.P. for the Newfoundland Constituency of Bonavista-Twillingate, was figuratively a consecrated and venerable member of Ottawa's Liberal Party elite.

Pickersgill had spent a great deal of his adult life in the back rooms of power. In 1946 he was an executive assistant to Prime Minister King. Newfoundland entered Confederation in 1949, its first Premier being Joseph (Joey) Smallwood. Smallwood credits Pickersgill with being mainly responsible for persuading the Canadian Government to accept Newfoundland as a province.

Pickersgill was chosen by Premier Smallwood as the Liberal candidate for Bonavista-Twillingate at the 1953 federal election and was elected its M.P. He was re-elected in 1957 and was a major influence among Liberal M.P.s.

The Liberal Party historically has taken both sides of thorny issues. It seems the philosophy behind Mackenzie King's war-time comment that it was "Conscription if necessary, but not necessarily conscription" was Picksergill's unamendable policy.

On January 20th, Pearson made his first speech in the House as Leader of the Opposition. He concluded it by moving a motion, written by Pickersgill, which called upon the Conservatives to resign and allow the Liberals to be sworn in as government without an election. That sort of arrogance did Pearson and the Liberals a lot of damage. Even though Pearson was able to become Prime Minister in later years that January 20th motion denied him a majority of M.P.s.

This Liberal arrogance gave Prime Minister Diefenbaker all he needed to convince the Governor-General to dissolve Parliament and proceed to an election which was held on March 31, 1957.

The most catchy Conservative slogan in that campaign was "Follow John." Voters followed John in droves giving the Conservatives 208 seats and reducing the Liberals to 48. The CCF also got slaughtered. I was one of the eight CCF M.P.s elected.

35

A ONE-MAN BAND

On November 5, 1957 I introduced into the House of Commons Bills which sought to give Aboriginal people the right to vote in federal elections. As far as I know I was the first M.P. to take such action. The Bills were not debated.

I had the services of "half a secretary." I was the other half, spending hours and hours doing secretarial work. The National Office of the CCF had a mimeograph machine and an addressograph machine. The addressograph was a clunking and clattering device which stamped letters onto metal plates and was activated by a typewriter keyboard. These plates were then used to address envelopes.

I spent much of my spare time and many weekends punching out these metal plates, addressing envelopes, and mimeographing my form letters to Native people. I was virtually a one-man band.

I had the names and addresses of all elected Chief Councillors in Federal Skeena. From the Indian Affairs Branch of the Department of Citizenship and Immigration I obtained the names of many other Chief Councillors and First Nations leaders in Canada. To all of them I mailed copies of the two Bills along with a covering letter which asked people to express their support for the two Bills both to the M.P. from their area and to the Minister of Citizenship and Immigration, the Honourable Ellen Fairclough.

In the first session of the new Parliament following the 1958 election I again introduced the same two Bills and did a repeat of the mailing. These Bills also were not debated.

In the second session of that Parliament, 1959, I again introduced the Bills and again mailed copies of them to First Nations people. In this session the Bills came up for debate.

These two Bills were identified as Public Bills in the hands of a Private Member. Such Bills were available for debate only for limited periods of time, something like one hour per week.

At the end of the hour, if the debate continued to that time, the Bills went to the bottom of the list and were unlikely to be debated again that session. In Parliamentary lingo, they were "talked out."

My two Bills were "talked out", but I was able to send my speech on them to those on my mailing list.

I explained that the right to vote would attract candidates and political parties to make contact with this new group of voters. One beneficial result would be a greater understanding of the needs, rights, and desires of Aboriginal people.

Not all Indigenous people supported my move to give them the vote. The Grand Confederacy of the Iroquois Nation told me that they were a Nation long before Canada came into existence and they had no desire to vote for what, to them, was a foreign power.

At a convenient moment I crossed over to the government side of the House and sat beside Prime Minister Diefenbaker. I asked him what the intentions of government were with regard to giving Natives the right to vote. He looked at me with his piercing eyes and said, "This is strictly private, but we are looking at it." I took his words to mean that the government was going to move.

The Speech from the Throne opening the 3rd session of Parliament on January 14, 1960 contained this sentence: "Legislation will be introduced to give Indians the franchise in federal elections."

The Honourable Ellen Fairclough introduced the two necessary Bills on January 18th. The debate commenced on March 9th and they were given third and final reading on March 10th. After three years of effort my campaign had paid off. I was elated.

Would the Conservative government have introduced the Bills to give Natives the right to vote if it not been prodded to do so? I don't know. I feel confident that I had a large part of winning that right for them.

When I got back home I went to see Federal Skeena's Returning Officer, Alex Bill. I urged him to appoint residents of the Reserve as Deputy Returning Officers and Poll Clerks to run the election machinery in the Native communities which would be added as a result of their obtaining the right to vote.

The experience at the provincial level was that Natives were often by-passed and others appointed to run the provincial election machinery. Discrimination was involved. Provincial authorities considered Aboriginal people to be incompetent.

Alex Bill was completely in support of appointing Native people, and he did so.

I gave him the names of each Chief Councillor for each Reserve. Alex Bill was a very competent Returning Officer and would no doubt have obtained these names in the ordinary course of his duties.

My purpose was twofold. Get whatever credit I could and, with my eye on a future election, have Natives fully involved in the detailed operation of a federal election at the community level. I had enough experience to know that they were just as able as anyone else to run an election.

I once attended a Nisga'a Tribal Council meeting at Greenville on the Nass River at which a secret ballot had to be conducted. The procedure the Nisga'a followed was first to choose a balloting committee of two people. These two, the equivalent of a Deputy Returning Officer and a Poll Clerk, sat at a table. Each voter, out of earshot of the other voters, whispered to the balloting committee his or her vote. The committee marked the vote in the appropriate column on a sheet of paper which was then covered so the next voter would not be able to see how anyone voted.

A similar procedure exists at a federal election. If a voter is unable to mark the ballot, because of poor eyesight for example, he or she can get the Deputy Returning Officer to mark the ballot as instructed. The Deputy Returning Officer and others at the table take an oath that the vote of any voter will not be revealed to anyone else. The Nisga'a omitted the oath part. They didn't need it. Trust was the key element. It worked wonderfully.

36

A VERY SERIOUS PROBLEM

The BNA Act gave the subject of divorce to the Parliament of Canada, but no Canada-wide divorce law existed in 1957. With the exception of Nova Scotia, Newfoundland, and Quebec all provinces were governed by the divorce law of England as it was in the 1800's. Adultery was the only reason for divorce except in Nova Scotia where cruelty was added.

Those in Quebec and Newfoundland who wanted a divorce had to go to Ottawa and get Parliament to pass a Private Bill (Divorce Bill) granting the divorce. A Private Bill results in a law applicable only to those who are specifically identified in it. Prior to 1930 this same bizarre procedure applied to Ontario.

Divorce Bills commenced in Canada's Senate because the Senate charged a lower fee for the Bills than the House of Commons did, a deliberate move, making it appear as if the Senate had some purpose. Following passage by the Senate these Bills were forwarded to the House of Commons.

Over the years, thousands of Divorce Bills were passed by Parliament. In both the Senate and the House they had to be given first, second, and third readings, plus committee stage. The Senate established a committee to hear the evidence in each individual case. Witnesses were sworn and could be cross examined. Exhibits such as clothing could be presented.

The House Rules provided that each Bill be dealt with separately. But M.P.s couldn't be bothered with that procedure. Standard practice was to lump a number of Divorce Bills together and pass them with one motion. For example, on November 22, 1957, 64 Bills were passed en bloc.

J.S. Woodsworth, an M.P. who later became the founding National Leader of the CCF, in the late 1920s began asking questions in the House about individual Divorce Bills; questions about children, financial support, and other familial matters. Government responded by having Parliament pass a law giving Ontario the divorce law of England as it was on July 15, 1870. Because of political power wielded by the Catholic Church it was too dangerous to apply the same law to the Province of Quebec.

CCF M.P.s, following upon Woodsworth's efforts, once in a while would question certain Divorce Bills, but such forays were fleeting shots and didn't result in any change to the system.

Harold Winch was elected M.P. in 1953. At a CCF picnic he related the circumstances about one Divorce Bill. In sworn testimony before the Senate's Divorce Committee a private investigator, looking for proof of adultery, said he placed a ladder against the wall of a two-storey house, climbed the ladder, looked in the bedroom window and saw the participants in the bed.

Winch said, "The investigator must have had X-ray vision. He could see through walls." It was subsequently shown that the bedroom was on the opposite side of the house to where the ladder was placed. The divorce was granted anyway.

One of the 8 CCFers re-elected in 1958 was Arnold Peters from the Northern Ontario riding of Timiskaming. He and I had a lot in common. We both had been in the IWA; we had worked in hard-rock mines; we had been active trade unionists.

In the first session following the 1958 election Peters and other CCF M.P.s, myself included, did what CCF M.P.s had done in the past. We debated some of the Divorce Bills.

Robert McCleave, Conservative M.P. from Halifax, was Chairman of the House Committee on Miscellaneous Private Bills which dealt with Divorce Bills. McCleave told the House that about 30% of them were of the "hotel and motel" type. McCleave didn't say it was illegal to arrange for adultery to be discovered, but it was common knowledge that hotel and motel rooms were rented for this purpose. Later I learned that one hotel even designated a room which was dubbed "the discovery room."

Howard Green, Minister of Public Works, told the House that having to deal with divorce cases was "… a very serious problem…" but he made no suggestion about any corrective action. At the 1960 session Peters started raising questions about individual Divorce Bills. He asked me if I would give him a hand with them. "What's your objective?" I asked. Peters' response was, "If we continue to raise questions and debate these Bills, the Conservatives might do the same as the government did in Woodsworth's days."

We talked about it for some time and both felt that the newly elected Conservatives, under John Diefenbaker, would be amenable to the idea. Governments which replace old, hide-bound ones that have been in power for decades are usually more open to change. It was worth a try so I agreed to join Peters.

But, we did have a concern. The subject of people from Newfoundland and Quebec seeking divorce was not something which affected either of our constituencies. We had no idea how this would go over back home. It wasn't a matter of any personal concern either.

However, we agreed that M.P.s should not be divorce-court judges. It was demeaning. It also injected party politics into what should have been a purely legal question. Senators and M.P.s had no business deciding how married people should handle their private and personal affairs.

At the time we had no idea what we were getting into, what the future might bring. It was a short-term venture and we thought that common sense would prevail.

We also thought it would be fun to find any inconsistencies in the evidence accepted by the Senate Divorce Committee. That would bolster our argument that government take action to extract Parliament from its divorce factory role.

Peters and I then started "talking out" each Divorce Bill that came up for debate. As I recall it, one or two entire days during the session were set aside for Private Bills plus the hour from 5:00 P.M. to 6:00 P.M. twice a week. There was a time limit on speeches (40 minutes). It meant that Peters and I had to be in the House each assigned day at the appointed time. When one's 40 minutes were up, the other took over. During the entire Private Bill days we simply alternated all day long. Attendance in the House reached new lows when we got into the Divorce-Bill hour. I recall a quorum as being ten Members and often that was the number who were there.

Our tactic meant that we were blocking all Divorce Bills. We had doubts but believed it might create an influential political force. If hundreds of divorces were "talked out", we reasoned that enough political pressure would compel the government to take action.

During the course of talking out these Bills we lurched from asking a few questions about each case to reading hours of testimony taken by the Senate's Divorce Committee. Government ignored us completely. We concluded it wasn't going to make any move to deal with the situation. There were hilarious and sometimes ludicrous moments during these hours. Teen aged young people were employed as attendants (pages) in the House of Commons. They brought glasses of water and messages to Members.

At the commencement of each Divorce Bill debate they were excluded from the House. Someone figured that titillating or even salacious matters might be discussed and that it would be improper for young ears to "tune in." That someone, though, missed an important point, namely that the pages could read everything in Hansard the next day.

I felt sure that the pages knew all about this stuff anyway. I raised that very matter one evening, but the pages were removed anyway.

We discovered that exhibits could be filed with the Senate Divorce Committee. These exhibits were kept in brown envelopes and were available to us. We got some of them so we could use whatever the contents were to add to our arsenal.

On one occasion I held up a lacy, black girdle. My contention was that M.P.s had better things to do than examine someone's underwear. The Hansard reporter didn't hear Peters' quip, "Well, not in public anyway."

Peters and I, with our trade-union background, knew we had a tough fight ahead of us. We knew that we had to "hang in there" and show no weakness or doubt.

We refused to discuss our blockade with the CCF caucus. We thought it would endanger our objective if six other people became officially involved. If caucus authorized our campaign, it could easily de-authorize it. Two caucus Members, Hazen Argue and Bert Herridge, told us they disagreed with what we were doing. Winch worried about potential damage to the CCF.

We made a confidential overture to the government House Leader, Gordon Churchill, and suggested that if there were a Royal Commission into the subject we would discontinue the blockade. We never knew if he passed this on to Prime Minister Diefenbaker because Churchill didn't report back.

On April 18, 1962 Peters asked Prime Minister Diefenbaker if the government "… has given any consideration to the establishment of a royal commission to undertake a study of parliamentary procedure with respect to divorce." Diefenbaker's reply was: "… that is a matter… for parliament to decide." It was his evasive way of saying "No."

On January 30, 1963 I asked the Prime Minister "… what progress had been made towards finding a solution to the subject matter of divorce." Diefenbaker's reply was: "… the subject matter of divorce is in the same position as it has always been."

Diefenbaker's attitude was easy to understand. He was Dief the Chief; he wasn't going to let a couple of CCF upstarts force him to move.

Churchill's attitude towards us was also easy to grasp. He was a colonel during the Second World War and carried his authority into public life, treating Peters and me like AWOL privates who had been arrested.

Peters and I created a lot of enemies, not all of whom were expecting to obtain a divorce. Other M.P.s were furious; some implied that we were a couple of thugs denying people their legitimate rights. We both felt that we didn't come to Parliament to be loved, or even to be liked.

We were threatened; one petitioner promised to shoot us. That unnerved us but the threat had been made verbally with the petitioner identifying himself. We couldn't treat it seriously and told him that the threat and his identity would be forwarded to the R.C.M.P.

We were offered $5,000 to let one particular, but unidentified, Divorce Bill pass. The offer was made through a third party, an M.P. from Quebec, and passed on to us by Murdo Martin, the CCF M.P. from Timmins. We refused the offer.

Edith, Robert, and I were living in a rented apartment in Ottawa. We would get phone calls at home from people who, because of our blockade, couldn't get a divorce. All this did was shatter our home life. Finally I had enough when, at 3:00 o'clock one morning, I got a call from a woman screaming curses at me. That was it. I had my phone disconnected and a different number assigned to Edith's maiden name.

Michelle Chartrand was the provincial leader of the CCF in Quebec. He told us he was approached on a number of occasions by petitioners, and lawyers representing petitioners, asking what could be done to get particular Bills passed. The gist was: You know these guys. What do they want? What can we offer? Chartrand said he told each of them that he knew us, knew what our objective was, and that it would be a waste of time for him or anyone else to approach us.

Week after week, for some three years we "talked out" the Divorce Bills. Nicholas (Nick) Mandziuk, Conservative M.P. from the Manitoba riding of Marquette, was Chairman of the Miscellaneous Private Bills Committee in December of 1961. He told the House that 901 Divorce Bills were then blockaded and waiting.

A number of times Peters and I discussed the possibility of painting ourselves into the proverbial corner and having to continue the blockade into an election. We decided we had no choice. If we backed off, we lost everything. We would lose the campaign to get divorces out of the House but, more than that, we would lose our self respect and the respect of everyone else, even those who were viciously opposed to what we had done. There was no doubt, no equivocation, no backing off.

On April 19, 1962 an election was called for June 18th. Peters and I were now faced with a very serious problem.

37

THE NEW PARTY

David Lewis was "Mr. CCF" for many years. He was virtually an institution, primarily responsible for keeping the administrative section of the Party alive. The thrashing the CCF took at the 1958 election had prompted Lewis to take steps to have it replaced by "a new, broadly-based political movement."

One of the first moves was maneuvering Stanley Knowles into the position of being a vice-president of the CLC. His function was to entice various labour unions to take part in the development of this "new party."

The eight of us who were M.P.s were considered by the CCF hierarchy to be an unessential element, if not an outright impediment to its development.

The only one of the eight who might have been considered part of the CCF's "old guard" was Winch. But he, though former Leader of the CCF in B.C., was never a part of the Toronto-based faction which controlled the CCF at the national level.

Erhart Regier and Bert Herridge from B.C. and Hazen Argue from Saskatchewan were also outsiders. The remaining four CCFers—Doug Fisher, Murdo Martin, and Arnold Peters from Ontario, and I from B.C.—were brand new and strangers to the CCF executive.

The opinions of caucus regarding the development of the "new party" were neither sought nor even wanted. We were considered too intellectually incompetent to be drawn into the ongoing plans.

There was a two-level gap: youth and lack of experience. The four of us who were newly elected were thought to be too young to grasp the fundamental philosophy of the CCF and were simply apprentices to the art of politics. We weren't even a factor.

We elected Argue as our House Leader. He was ambitious, energetic, and brimming with ideas. He contended that the Liberals, in search of a replacement for the retiring Louis St. Laurent, would be concerned more with internal Party squabbles than with trying to be an effective Opposition. We felt we could fill that vacancy.

With only eight of us it was easy to have consultations about House tactics and responses to government legislation. Argue would often stride into our offices asking, "How can we make this a CCF day? What can we do to get some publicity?"

We worked hard; we had to debate every issue which came before the House; we had to have at least a faint understanding of the subjects. We had to be aggressive.

I made speeches during that period on subjects which I knew practically nothing about. We had no research team and no speech writers. I read past issues of Hansard and plagiarized what others had said. I didn't know spring wheat from Cream of Wheat, but spoke about it anyway.

Our efforts to be the "real" opposition prompted the government to consider us a nuisance; the hierarchy of the CCF felt the same. We were anathema to the legacy of Woodsworth and Coldwell. They were respected gentlemen; we were rude intruders.

Someone in the Liberal Party (Prime Minister St. Laurent I believe) said that CCFers were only Liberals in a hurry. That salvo stuck and influenced many to think that way. I believe Coldwell and Knowles were flattered by it. They looked upon themselves as liberals, seventeenth and eighteenth century ones who lived within the framework of liberalism as it developed and existed in those times.

A number of ideas which CCFers championed and which they fought for in election campaigns were adopted and put into effect by Liberal governments. How easy, in that context, for CCFers to accept that they were Liberals in a hurry.

The gulf between the CCF party and the caucus arose and grew wider because of a mutual lack of trust in that period between 1958 and 1962. In 1960 a by-election took place in Peterbourough. Even though this "new party" had not been formed, Walter Pitman, a New Party candidate, was elected. His campaign was managed by CCFers.

When Pitman came to Ottawa he told us he had been advised by the CCF's top brass not to sit with the CCF caucus, but sit as a New Party M.P. He refused and sat with us. His revelation proved to us that the caucus, in the eyes of the CCF's hierarchy, was not only irrelevant, but disposable.

Were we angered at being by-passed? Yes. But we were committed to keeping the CCF alive at the parliamentary level and internalized our frustrations. The last thing we wanted was to have the media gleefully salivating over any rift.

Even though we were kept in the dark about much of what was developing we did have an intense interest in who might be the leader of this "new party", for we were all likely to seek re-election under that new banner and the new leader.

Tommy Douglas, then Premier of Saskatchewan, was often touted as the best leadership candidate. Caucus authorized Harold Winch to talk with Douglas. Winch reported that Douglas said no.

I was in Saskatchewan on a speaking tour and on my own called on Douglas and asked him about his leadership intentions, if any. He confirmed Winch's report: he had too much important work in Saskatchewan and his desire to implement Medicare in that province was the priority.

When Coldwell announced his intention to retire as National Leader the caucus decided it couldn't operate in a vacuum. Argue had been an effective House Leader and was ambitious. He was more a follower than a leader, but he was all we had.

Argue agreed that he would seek the National Leadership of the CCF and be a leadership candidate at the founding convention of this new party. He committed himself to announcing these intentions at a meeting of the CCF's National Council.

We later discovered that the Party was appalled at Argue's move and at the decision of caucus to support him. At the National Council meeting a committee was set up to draft a policy on leadership matters and Argue became a member of that committee. The committee's report was unanimous. It recommended that the coming CCF National Convention not elect a National Leader but elect someone as a Parliamentary Leader, a fancy name for House Leader. Argue, by not standing up to the power brokers and by going along with the committee's report, had double-crossed caucus.

Fisher, Peters, and I were furious at Argue's betrayal and told him that if he came back to Ottawa without retracting his support for the Parliamentary Leader idea he would be dumped as House Leader. Argue did retract and thereby also double-crossed the National Council. It was later that Douglas declared he'd run for the leadership.

Did Douglas decide to seek the leadership of this "new party" early in the game and keep that information from Harold Winch and me? Did the move by Argue to be a leadership candidate so frighten the Party's brass that they intensified their pressure on Douglas to make the move? These were serious questions to us. I believe Douglas decided early in the game but kept caucus in the dark. After all, caucus was not considered an essential element in the broad scheme of things.

Because I'd supported Argue at the leadership Convention, lots of lifetime friends said, "What are you doing? Tommy's the guy!" I told them that we'd tried earlier to find out from Douglas if he'd be running and when he said "No" I'd made the commitment to Argue. I told them that once having done that I couldn't back down.

At its founding convention the "new party" got a name: The New Democratic Party. It also got a leader: T. C. (Tommy) Douglas. Argue, making the traditional loser's declaration that the vote be unanimous, said, "I will never let you down." That went over well. He was a good and honourable fellow.

But shortly after Douglas was elected Argue did let us down; more than that, he let himself down. He defected to the Liberals. I was not only angry at him, I was angry at myself. He had made a fool of me. Make a fool of me once; there is no second opportunity.

A few days after Argue sold out I was in the Centre Block of the Parliament Buildings waiting for an elevator. The elevator arrived. The doors opened. There were two passengers, Hazen and Jean Argue. Argue wouldn't meet my gaze. I used a ten-letter word to tell him what I thought of him. To the elevator operator I said, "I'll wait for the next trip."

What were the dynamics which led Argue to join the Liberals? Jack Pickersgill, in his memoirs, *Seeing Canada Whole*, tells us that from 1958 to 1962 it was Liberal strategy to avoid friction with the CCF. He says that Pearson asked him to maintain a liaison with Argue, which he did. Pickersgill tells us that he had come to know Argue well, and that their personal relations had remained friendly.

Argue never reported to caucus that he had been approached by Pickersgill to establish a liaison with the Liberals and that he had agreed. No one else was approached by Pickersgill. The reason Argue was singled out involves one Ross Thatcher.

Thatcher was elected in 1945 as a CCF M.P., but quit the party in 1955 to sit in the House as an independent, then as a Liberal. Argue and he became close friends and kept up that friendship even after Thatcher moved to the Liberals.

Thatcher knew Argue's weaknesses probably more than anyone and would clearly see the advantage of informing Pearson and the Liberals that Argue was easily seduceable.

38

A LUCKY SO AND SO, PART 2

The scene is Third Avenue in Prince Rupert. The date is May 21, 1962. The time is 1:45 P.M. The participants are prominent people, all Big Liberals. They are walking up and down a small portion of Third Avenue smiling and waving to pedestrians and shop keepers.

At about 1:55 P.M. they enter a building and proceed to the office of Alex Bill, Returning Officer for Federal Skeena. They present the nomination papers for John Watt who is to be the Liberal Party's candidate in the June 18th election.

Alex Bill examines the papers and tells them they are not in order because certain signatures are not witnessed.

Panic ensues because the deadline for the acceptance of nomination papers is 2:00 P.M.—just moments away.

A telephone call to Canada's Chief Electoral Officer in Ottawa confirms that Alex Bill's interpretation and decision is correct.

I heard of this blunder while in Telkwa, a community in the eastern part of Federal Skeena. I immediately sent a telegram to John Watt expressing my personal regrets, and, of course, released the telegram to the media.

Winch, when I ran as a provincial candidate in 1952, told me not to let anyone else handle the nomination papers. In his sometimes near-staccato style of speaking he said, "Do it yourself. You get the signatures of those who are going to nominate you. You check to make sure they are on the voters' list. You take the nomination papers to the Returning Officer. And file them early. Don't wait until the last minute."

This mistake by the Liberals was a blessing. It allowed me and our campaign team to commiserate with known Liberals and tell them they could vote Conservative and perhaps help John Diefenbaker to be returned as Prime Minister. Alternately, they could vote for me and thus ensure that Federal Skeena didn't go Conservative. We had no hesitation in telling them something they already knew: we were not going to form a government.

Conservatives tried their damndest to make our divorce blockade an issue. Howard Green came to Skeena and scathingly condemned me. All that did was give me the opportunity to toss back at him his words that divorce being in Parliament was "a very serious matter." It also let me tell the voters that if they wanted an M.P. to go to Ottawa in order to divorce people from Quebec, they should vote Conservative.

The Conservative campaign backfired. A.D. (Bill) Vance was their candidate in both 1958 and 1962. In 1958 the Conservatives got 30% of the vote; in 1962 they got 23%. By contrast my vote went from 39% in 1958 to 59% in 1962.

Our appeal to those who otherwise would have voted Liberal had paid off. It also meant that I had nowhere to go but down.

Peters was also re-elected in Timiskaming. Our divorce blockade had passed the crucial test of an election. We were vindicated; our strategy and objective were approved by voters.

In 1961 the CCF was transformed into the New Democratic Party (NDP). The election of 1962 produced an increase for the Liberals (from 48 to 100) and for the NDP (from 8 to 19), and a decline for the Conservatives (from 208 to 116). For Tommy Douglas this was his first election campaign as National Leader. It wasn't good. He failed to get elected. Erhart Regier, from Burnaby, B.C., voluntarily resigned his seat; Douglas ran in the by-election and got into the House of

Commons that way.

With the Conservatives holding on to government in a minority position it was obvious that another election would take place within a few months. Peters and I continued our divorce blockade, but the political parties in the House paid more attention to manoeuvring for the expected election than to dealing with divorces from Quebec.

After running unsuccessfully for Parliament a number of times, David Lewis was elected in 1962 for the Toronto riding of York South. He was articulate, multi-lingual, and intelligent. But his ability to anticipate events two or three steps into the future left many of those whom he persuaded unsure what it was he had in mind, what his objectives were.

My first personal experience with Lewis was during the Parliament elected in 1962. He came into my office one day and said he would like to talk with Arnold and me. He told me he'd spoken with Peters and we could meet in Peters's office.

Lewis started by saying he wanted to talk about the divorce blockade. He applauded us. "You have done a masterful job of bringing divorce reform to the attention of the general public and of forcing the Liberals and Conservatives to consider changing the law." He said that we were heroes.

I was honestly flattered by his comments and I think Peters was, too. Peters and I had been considered by many people in the upper echelons of the CCF as irresponsible upstarts who were injuring the Party's image of nobility and respectful behaviour developed over the years by Woodsworth and Coldwell. To be told by the great David Lewis that we were heroes was heady stuff.

Lewis then astounded us by suggesting that we would be even greater heroes if we agreed to discontinue the blockade. If we agreed, he said that he would then go to both Prime Minister Diefenbaker and Opposition Leader Pearson and urge them to make a public statement that they would deal with the matter of divorce. He said that he knew them both well enough to feel confident that they'd agree.

We told Lewis that Diefenbaker had at least three years to make a move, but had refused. We told him that Jack Pickersgill had tried by a procedural device to destroy the blockade, but had failed. We told Lewis that we had just gone through an election during which the divorce blockade was an issue, and had both been re-elected. We told him we didn't see any point in giving up now that we had basically won the fight. Because of the minority government situation we were obviously going into another election fairly soon and whoever formed the government was going to have to find a solution. If we gave up, there would be no incentive for the government to do anything.

He asked us to think about his proposition and let him know what we decided. Peters knew Lewis better than I and told me that Lewis would come out as the hero-type "honest broker" for getting the two major parties to make some statement about dealing with the divorce blockade. He said that this was the way that Lewis operated. We decided to let Lewis's proposition fade away, to say nothing to him. Lewis didn't follow up the matter and in the succeeding election of 1963 was defeated.

During a strike in northern Ontario Peters and others had been charged with assault. Lewis was the lawyer retained by the union to defend those so charged, but Peters was the only person who had to go to trial. He was found not guilty because he wasn't involved in the event which led to the charges. Peters told me Lewis tried to lever him to drop the divorce blockade by using the you-owe-me-one type of pry.

Many in the CCF were critical of Lewis; they considered him always to be less than completely open with his suggestions and objectives. I had no personal knowledge of his alleged dealings and manipulations, only the general rumour and gossip, which I had taken with the proverbial pinch of salt.

However, Lewis's suggestion that we abandon the divorce blockade and the subsequent conversation with Peters left me with the feeling that Lewis was too cunning and crafty for me. Being buttered up as a prelude to asking for a favour, one which would benefit him, resulted in my never trusting him.

Maybe Lewis's exceptional intellect led him to believe that others weren't as smart as he and needed to be cajoled into doing things. That smacked to me of arrogance and over the years of my association with him I saw more and more of it. I'm reminded of the question Oscar Levant put to his friend George Gershwin, "Tell me, George, if you had to do it all over would you fall in love with yourself again?"

At the 1963 election the Liberals ran a candidate in Skeena, John Magor from Prince Rupert. The Liberals got 24% of the popular vote, the lowest in many years. Magor contributed to his disappointing tally by telling Aboriginal people that they were stupid to vote for the NDP. The message received was that Magor called them stupid. They responded with a bit of delightful and quiet retaliation.

When Magor visited the community then known as Kitamaat word passed quickly that he was in town and knocking on doors. At one home he was invited in. The residents said they had some things to do in the kitchen and asked him to sit and wait in the living room.

He sat; he waited. No one came back into the living room. He must have assumed that the residents were too busy to talk with him; he left and went to the next house. He was invited into this house as well and asked by the lady of the house to wait a few moments because her husband was busy. She went into another room. He waited, but no husband or anyone else came to talk with him. He finally got the message and left Kitamaat.

39

SUCCESS

During Diefenbaker's term Doug Morton, the Conservative M.P. from Davenport in Ontario, had introduced a Private Members's Bill giving the Senate the exclusive authority to grant divorces. That Bill received all-party support and went through all stages in one day. It was what Peters and I had set out to accomplish. However, the Senate still had to pass the Bill.

The Chairman of the Senate Divorce Committee was Arthur Roebuck, a Liberal senator since 1945 and former Attorney-General of Ontario. The Divorce Committee was his raison d'etre. The Senate refused to pass the Morton bill. Roebuck said that such a move would leave the impression that divorcing people was the only function of the Senate. My reaction was, "How true."

The 1963 election gave the Liberals a minority government. Prime Minister Pearson appointed Jack Pickersgill as Government House Leader. The House Leader does the drudge work, arranges the business of the House, sets the agenda, calls bills for debate; he is the "work horse."

Pearson gave Pickersgill a short and clear instruction about our divorce blockade: fix it.

Pickersgill, nicknamed "Pick" or "Jumping Jack", was a shrewd and cautious manipulator with no shortage of imagination. He wanted the blockade out of the way and did not want the Liberals tainted by its resumption; divorce was still a touchy subject in Quebec.

His executive assistant, Alistair Fraser, represented him in the negotiations with Peters and me regarding the blockade. Fraser did an excellent job. He was careful, considerate, and a gentleman at all times; indispensable in those discussions. I regret he was not given credit in Pickersgill's memoirs for the part he played.

Pick's proposal was that we make the first move by letting the backed-up divorce bills pass. He contended that this would prove to the government, the media, and the public that we were serious about finding a solution. Sounded like David Lewis. The blockade was our only lever. We rejected his proposal.

Consequently he promised that he would keep the hundreds of blockaded divorce bills from being called for debate while we discussed a plan to settle the matter. We had many meetings. We didn't fully trust Pick. He probably didn't trust us either, but a plan did evolve.

Our original goal had been to get Divorce Bills out of the House of Commons, but as Peters and I examined each divorce case in detail our objective changed to the broader question of divorce reform.

Except in Nova Scotia, the sole grounds for divorce was adultery. Brutality, desertion, alcoholism, drug addiction, child abuse could exist, but those situations were not accepted as legal reasons to dissolve a marriage. The marriage may have broken down, but the law said it was still intact.

It was common knowledge that collusion was used to show that adultery had taken place. One private investigator's evidence before the Senate Divorce Committee in 1961 was that he and his partner went to the third floor of a particular apartment building to find evidence of adultery. He said, "I tried the door knob and the door was not locked so we walked in and there was a light on. There were beer bottles around and there they were in bed together. They paid no attention to us."

Finally these two people noticed the private investigators and gave them the required identifying information. When asked how long the investigators stayed in the apartment, one of them said: "Oh, just a few minutes, didn't stay too long because he was a little hostile."

Peters and I found this farce played again and again in numbers of divorce cases: the door was unlocked or open; the names of the people obtained; the man turned a little hostile and the investigators left the premises. It was as if a blank form existed with spaces for names, addresses, and dates.

We mailed letters to co-respondents who had not appeared before the Senate Divorce Committee, telling them that they had been so named and asking if they had any comments about the case. One person replied that he was a co-respondent in more than one case and wanted to know which we were writing about.

Of 242 letters to co-respondents, 114 were returned with notations such as, "no such street number", "not listed in directory and not at that address", "moved", "no forwarding address", "does not work here."

Our position regarding the substantive changes needed for a nation-wide divorce-reform bill was an impediment to our negotiations with Pickersgill. He wanted no part of divorce reform. Reluctantly we had to abandon the idea.

Phase one of the plan which emerged was to have Mandziuk introduce a Bill patterned after the Morton Bill of 1960 and pass it with either limited or no debate. Pick assured Peters and me that the Senate would pass the bill because the Liberals had the majority in the Senate.

Phase two involved passing all the backed up divorce bills.

Phase three was that the Speaker of the Senate would appoint an officer of the Senate, a Commissioner, to consider divorce petitions, hear evidence, and recommend for Senate approval those cases in which adultery was proved. This procedure would separate the role of the Senate as a law-making body from that of a quasi-judicial body.

Senator Roebuck, in 1963, was 85 years old. Pick didn't want to force Roebuck out of his role as Divorce Committee Chairman, but would make every effort to have him voluntarily relinquish his activity in divorce cases. The implementation of phase four, which was the appointment of an additional judge to the Exchequer Court of Canada to replace the Commissioner, would be postponed to a more appropriate time.

Peters and I still believed that too much of this phased-in plan depended upon other players and a future time. In a rare show of unanimity all phases of it were put into effect. Peters and I were finally vindicated. Our goal of getting divorces out of the House of Commons was reached. Success was our reward.

Bob McCleave, Conservative M.P. from Halifax, was Chairman of the House Committee which dealt with Divorce Bills when Peters and I started our filibuster. Obligated to see that those Bills got through the House, he did his best, but Peters and I stood in his way. Our blockade made his parliamentary life miserable. We respected him for his tenacity and regretted he was no longer an M.P. when a solution was finally reached.

When Pierre Trudeau became Minister of Justice in 1967 one of the bills he introduced dealt with divorce reform to give Canada its first nation-wide divorce law. Trudeau, in his memoirs, says that proposed legislation relating to divorce had been gathering dust in departmental files for six years (since 1961). The divorce blockade which Peters and I had mounted clearly prompted the Conservatives to draft divorce-reform legislation. They didn't have the guts to bring it to the House.

Trudeau's revelation showed that Peters and I accomplished more for divorce reform than all the other concerned Parliamentarians put together.

Canada's parliamentary system has spawned an awesomely powerful structure, one not too far removed from a dictatorship. At elections we vote only for someone to represent our area in the House of Commons. We do not, and cannot, elect someone to be Prime Minister. The person who is leader of the political party which has more M.P.s elected than any other party becomes Prime Minister.

The Prime Minister is all powerful. He alone decides who will be Cabinet Ministers. He can fire any of them at will. Jean Chretien. Louis St. Laurent, John Diefenbaker, Lester Pearson, Pierre Trudeau, Brian Mulroney—all wielded the same power. I'm not being analytical about this; merely setting out the facts.

Activity in the House of Commons is governed by rules. These rules have been developed over the years to limit the power of the House of Commons and vest it in the hands of the Prime Minister's hand-picked Cabinet Ministers. For example, no one but a Cabinet Minister can introduce a Bill which involves the expenditure of public funds.

That sort of restriction applies to government back benchers (Private Members) as well as to Members of any other party. The total effect is that Private Members have no power to do anything specific. In theory government is responsible to the House of Commons. In reality it is just the opposite. The Prime Minister and his Cabinet have the control and the House is servile.

Having to function in that atmosphere makes the success which Peters and I had regarding divorce matters all the more amazing. What we did was discover a loophole in the House rules and exploit it to the full. That made our victory all the more rewarding.

40

BULLSHIT

In 1962 Diefenbaker and the Conservatives had been trounced at the polls, but Diefenbaker still had enough seats to form a minority government. Another election in 1963 resulted in the Liberals forming a minority government. During the campaign there had been concern among voters that we might elect another minority government and more instability. Douglas, our National Leader, said publicly that if there was another minority government it should be kept in office for at least two years to work on the problems facing Canada. I picked up on Douglas's statement and made it a personal pledge in Skeena.

It turned out that Douglas's words were an erasable campaign promise. In 1964 the NDP moved a want-of-confidence motion relating to Medicare. I took the position that I was bound by what Douglas had said and told caucus that I would not vote for the want-of-confidence motion. I didn't. I could have taken the easy way out and been absent from the House when the vote took place. I didn't do that either. I voted along with the Liberals against my caucus's motion.

Following the vote Paul Martin, Sr. said to me, "That took a lot of guts."

Douglas strode into my office the next day and upbraided me for voting against Medicare, charging me with hypocrisy. I replied, "If you want to see a hypocrite look in the mirror." I adored Tommy and as soon as I said it I was sorry, but I didn't apologize. It was something I should not have blurted out, but I was totally pissed off by his comments.

Douglas was not one to hold a grudge; he was too much of a gentleman to do that. Afterwards he never mentioned my outburst or his displeasure with my vote.

That vote resulted in a number of NDP M.L.A.s in B.C. worried that I was going to "cross the floor" and sit with the Liberals.

Robert Strachan was provincial leader of the B.C. NDP at the time. He happened to be in Ottawa shortly after that vote and said to me, "There are rumours that you're going to join the Liberals." "Bob", I answered, "that is simply not going to happen. I consider the Liberal Party to be the most deceitful and dishonest Party in existence. They have no philosophy except to embrace any proposal which will help get them elected. You can tell anyone that this rumour is strictly bullshit."

41

VINCENT DE PAUL

Vincent De Paul, born in 1581, was ordained as a priest at the age of 20. Captured by Turkish pirates and sold at an early age into slavery he reportedly converted one of his owners to Christianity and was released. He spent his life helping the poor, the abandoned, and the enslaved. In 1737, seventy-seven years after his death, he was canonized.

One of Saint Vincent de Paul's prayers was: "We should strive to keep our hearts open to the sufferings and wretchedness of other people, and pray continually that God may grant us that spirit of compassion which is truly the spirit of God."

Many charities, societies, and institutions have been formed to extend homage to his memory. One such institution was Saint Vincent de Paul Penitentiary on the outskirts of the City of Montreal, Quebec. Construction started in 1873. It was the first post-confederation penitentiary built in Canada.

In 1962, 89 years after it was built, the prison was struck with a devastating riot. One convict was killed and a couple of dozen others wounded. Quelling the riot took five hours of intense military-style action involving the prison guards, Canadian army, and local police. Five of the buildings were severely damaged by fire. Cost? An estimated $2,500,000.

Shortly after becoming an M.P. I started visiting penitentiaries.

My interest was prison reform. Sometime in 1962 Harold Winch, knowing this and of my criminal record, suggested that we check out the post-riot situation at Saint Vincent de Paul. The Commissioner of Penitentiaries, Alan McLeod, was our tour guide. Of course, we saw what the prison officials wanted us to see. Much of the charred and blackened remains of the buildings had been removed. It was just an old, grey, dirty-looking maximum security prison with about a thousand cells and the same number of convicts.

Both Harold and I knew that communication with any of the convicts would be strained and unproductive. Not only were we strangers, we were being chaperoned by the very people who had fired weapons at some of them during the riot.

What I remember most about that visit were the "bucket cells" in the old part of the prison—with no flush toilets, just a bucket for overnight use. In the morning the cells would be opened. Convicts would carry these buckets to a central, human-waste disposal facility and dump the contents into it. They would then proceed to pick up their breakfast and, with the tray in one hand and the bucket in the other, parade back to their cells.

When I was in the B.C. Pen I heard many stories about convicts being severely punished following prison riots. Some of the stories involved guard brutality. So, after the 1963 election I returned to Saint Vincent de Paul alone (Winch wasn't interested) and was guided around by one of the guards. I spoke with many convicts. I didn't ask questions. I told each one who I was and that I wanted to find out everything I could about the riot and living conditions then and now. I said that I wanted the information so I could press for immediate changes in the prison and get it demolished as quickly as possible. Some of the convicts told me about living conditions, about rats, cockroaches, and bedbugs being rampant throughout. Some gave me their views about the riot and the prison's administration. At least one convict trusted me.

Upon his release he came to Ottawa to meet with me. Like many ex-cons he probably would not like to be identified so I'll simply refer to him as Yves. I offered to let him live with me in my apartment until he could get settled. Before returning to Toronto he stayed with me for about a week. From him I learned which areas of the prison to visit, what questions to ask, which convicts to interview. He told me that he and others had been clubbed and kicked by guards to the point of near death. After the riot he was charged with destroying government property. At his trial an Anglican priest and a doctor testified that he had been beaten. The judge gave him one day to be served on top of his original sentence.

His was a gruesome story with huge ramifications—too many, I thought, for one person to handle. So I drew Arnold Peters into the scene. He and I had worked well together and I was tuned in to his abilities as he was to mine.

Peters and I went to Saint Vincent de Paul with Yves requesting that he be our guide. Warden LeCorre refused to let him in. In retrospect it was a dumb thing for us to suggest. If he had been allowed entrance it would have been a hero-worship sport wherever we went. His presence could have provoked another riot.

Our main purpose was to interview convicts, but Peters wanted to see the inside of the prison so he would better visualize what might be described to us. After that tour we told the prison officials that we wanted to talk in private with specific convicts. We met with each one separately in a conference room.

The first guy we spoke with wanted to know if the room was bugged. We couldn't assure him that it wasn't, but pointed out that it was the room set aside for lawyer-client meetings.

We told each inmate that we wanted all the information we could get about the riot and prison conditions and that anything he told us would be confidential unless he gave us authorization to use his name. When some began talking they wouldn't shut up. After all, this was a break from the usual routine and a special event for those who had been in segregation (locked up for 23 1/2 hours every day and allowed out only to walk in a courtyard for the remaining half hour).

Each story was a horror story. These guys claimed that they had been beaten by guards, that there were "goon squads" comprising other convicts, that certain inmates enjoyed special favours, that the administration of the prison made deals to accommodate homosexuals, that the use of informers had been set up by the administration, etc.

We had taken a couple of packages of cigarettes to give to anyone who wanted to smoke. Soon the packages were empty. I went to the door, knocked on it to get the attention of the guard outside, and asked him if I could bum a cigarette or two. Eventually we used up his supply. The inmates probably got a great charge out of smoking a guard's cigarettes. The next day we returned the borrowed smokes and gave him a couple of extra packs.

Since the riot one of the guys (I'll call him Louis) had been in segregation for over 2 years. He, too, had been charged with destroying government property and was found guilty. The judge nailed an additional fourteen years onto his original sentence. He poured out his tale with such vividness that he became almost incoherent. We had to ask him a couple of times to slow down. He curled up on the floor to dramatize his claim of having been beaten and kicked by sadistic guards.

Louis wanted his story to be told and gave us authorization to use his name. I've chosen not to repeat it here because he is now, and has been for many years, well established in society. We arranged to visit him in the segregation unit and obtain his written declaration. Peters and I followed the plan we'd worked out with him. I talked with the guard to keep his attention off Peters. When Peters, outside the cell, felt it was O.K. he reached in and pocketed the written statement. Louis had kept it in the sole of his shoe while waiting for us. I then excused myself and went along to the cell.

According to Louis, we got there at the right moment. A few days later, he said, and there might have been bloodshed. Each convict on the segregation tier had been allowed to keep a meal-time spoon in his cell. Louis told us that some of them, himself included, had been sur-

reptitiously sharpening the spoons by rubbing them on the concrete.
Convicts were released from their cells one at a time for the half-hour
daily exercise and once a week for a shower and a shave. The washing
facilities were at the end of the tier. The plan was for one of the convicts to grab the tier guard as a hostage and then try to negotiate with
prison officials for better treatment. Desperate people will do desperate things to rectify an intolerable situation. Louis said that he faced
doing the rest of his time in segregation. He had nothing to lose.

Peters read the statement in the House of Commons on November 27, 1964. Members of all parties sat in stunned silence as the rev-
elations of cruelty and horror were revealed. Peters and I had read the
letter together before deciding how to deal with it. In our opinion the
extra fourteen years Louis got was such a raw deal that we decided to
go to bat for him. It was at that point that I'd revealed to Arnold my
own criminal record. I suggested that he read the letter in the House of
Commons because I felt that if I read it, and if it became known that I
had a record, the cry might go up that is was a ex-con championing the
cause of criminals. If that happened I feared it would injure our efforts
to see that justice was done for the guy.

The riot took place on June 17th, 1962. On June 21st the Commissioner of Penitentiaries appointed a Board of Inquiry to look into what
was officially called a disturbance. Its Chairman was J.C.A. LaFerriere,
Director of the Penitentiary Service's Inmate Training Division. As far
as I know its report, dated December 6, 1962 and labeled **CONFI-
DENTIAL**, has never been made public.

A few quotations from it are necessary. Its summary says:

"1. The riot could have been quelled at the beginning if custodial officers on duty had taken proper
action.

2. The staff of the institution were not trained nor
instructed on how to deal with emergencies. They were
uncertain, hesitant or reluctant to use firearms or other
means at their disposition to quell this disturbance.

They had no riot or emergency plan to follow.

3.   Some officers have acted in a commendable manner while some others have failed to do their duty.

4.   The causes of the riot and the extent to which it developed can be attributed to the maladministration of the institution.

5.   The recommendations of the Board of Inquiry can be summarized as follows:

a) That appropriate action be taken in the cases of officers mentioned in para. 3 above;

b) That a separate inquiry be conducted in the administration of the institution prior to June 17, 1962."

It is not my intention to dwell on the detailed causes of the riot, but I think it necessary to enter a brief quotation from the section of the Board of Inquiry's report headed **MALADMINISTRATION**. Under paragraph 121 the following appears:

"121. The impression arising from the inquiry is that nothing worked within the Penitentiary. The administrative structure was defective at all levels…"

With respect to the recommendation for a separate inquiry in the administration of the prison I emphasize that Warden LeCorre became the warden on June 1st, less than three weeks before the riot. Prior to that time Mr. Gregoire (Butch) Surprenant was warden. I have been unable to discover if such an inquiry took place.

Because Louis had so openly declared that he had been beaten by prison guards Peters and I felt he would be in continual danger if he remained in Saint Vincent de Paul. We made a number of representations to the Minister of Justice and to the Commissioner of Penitentiaries to have Louis moved out of Saint Vincent de Paul to another prison. They responded favourably and he was transferred to Kingston Penitentiary and put in the general prison population. While there he had four reconstructive surgeries to repair the damage to his face from the beatings

Louis's story, and the follow-up by Peters and me, created a lot of pressure, mostly from the media, for government to deal with the situation at Saint Vincent de Paul. Government decided to open the prison to the media. Commissioner McLeod and Public Works Minister, Jean-Paul Deschatelets, led a contingent of 50 to 60 news-gathering people through the penitentiary. I went along. McLeod told me that his predecessor would roll over in this grave if he knew of the media tour.

I saw one of the convicts whom Peters and I had interviewed and went over to speak with him. He said that the day before had been a busy one for the prison population. "They (meaning the guards) had us cleaning everything. We were even picking up stray pieces of paper and goddamned fallen leaves from the yard."

At the end of the tour Deschatelets spoke to a press conference and declared that Saint Vincent de Paul would be replaced in two years. Good news that would not have been possible without the courage and determination of Yves and Louis, and the companion action of Peters and me. It took more than two years, but the prison was closed.

Peters and I made representations to have the government issue a pardon to Louis or extend to him the Royal Prerogative of mercy by releasing him from prison immediately. We felt he had received enough punishment. On June 17, 1968, six years precisely from the date of the riot, he was released. He says he was given no explanation about the release. I can only guess that government opted for the Royal Prerogative route and passed the appropriate Order-in-Council.

Where was the spirit of Saint Vincent de Paul when it was so badly needed? Obviously not at the Saint Vincent de Paul Penitentiary.

42

WEGET

From 1962 to 1968 Canada had four general elections and two B.C. provincial general elections—an average of one every 13 or 14 months. I was a successful candidate in each of the federal elections and saw our vote in Skeena remain above 50% each time.

I also worked assiduously for our provincial candidates. It was almost perpetual motion and, for the Party, perpetual debt.

In the House of Commons our caucus had changes of personnel at each federal election. Some were elected only once, making it difficult, and in some instances impossible, to develop any firm relationship. It was like trying to make friends in an elevator.

In addition to Arnold Peters and Bill Knight there were three other M.P.s with whom I felt a companionship. Tom Barnett from Comox-Alberni, John Skoberg from Moose Jaw, and Les Benjamin from Regina-Lake Centre had work-experience backgrounds similar to mine. We spoke the same language.

Each change resulted in a re-alignment of responsibilities of individual caucus members. I was able to concentrate on the Indian Affairs Branch, fisheries, and prisons. I became less involved in caucus matters and more involved in constituency work.

In a city, especially in a high-rise apartment, a person hardly knows his or her next-door neighbour and is largely wary of them. This was not the case in Federal Skeena.

I enjoyed visiting the many small communities in the riding. Everyone knew everyone else. There was an intimacy and friendliness which was, and probably still is, foreign to an urban or city constituency. Over the years I visited every community; some had only a handful of residents. It was not uncommon to drive more than 100 miles to get from one to the other.

Personal appearances in small communities helped my continued success at election times. Even those who disagreed with my political philosophy admitted, sometimes grudgingly, that I was doing a good job by keeping in touch.

Pleasant Camp is the name of the Canada Custom's border-crossing into the northern reaches of Alaska's panhandle. The custom's officers and their families were astonished when I showed up there one day. "My God", said one officer, "I've never seen an M.P.!"

Sometimes I stayed for two or three days in smaller communities such as Telegraph Creek and Kitkatla sleeping in the homes of Party supporters. During these visits I talked with everyone about whatever it was they wanted to talk about. If religion was raised, I refused to discuss it. I said it was a highly personal matter and should not be mixed with politics. Given my views about the subject I would probably have lost votes.

The racial discrimination which denied Natives full access to alcohol was finally eliminated. Credit for it goes to the then Mayor of Prince Rupert, Pete Lester, and a Prince Rupert lawyer, Jim Harvey. Harvey's reading of the Indian Act was that Aboriginal people could decide whether or not alcohol could be allowed on their Reserve.

Harvey had drafted a resolution for the consideration of any Band Council. This resolution asked the Indian Affairs Branch to conduct a referendum, the question being something like: "Are you in favour of allowing alcohol on this reserve?"

The Indian Act was confusing and stupid regarding alcohol. If a referendum passed it would mean that Natives could have alcohol on the reserve and, because of the 1951 changes, in a facility licensed to serve liquor. The stupid part was that they couldn't buy alcohol in a liquor store and take it home.

It was Harvey's opinion that the passage of a resolution by any Band would put the Provincial Government on the hook. The province could object to, or accept, the decision made by referendum. If it accepted the decision, then any adult band member of any reserve which passed a referendum could buy alcohol and take it home.

What about a reserve which voted "dry?" Harvey believed that the province and the federal government would have to allow any adult Aboriginal to buy alcohol and have it in his possession anywhere in the province. He just couldn't take it to his home reserve.

My role was to send this proposed resolution to Band Councils with a letter of explanation. Some reserves voted "wet" and some voted "dry." The effect was exactly as Harvey assessed it would be. Harold Sinclair from Kitwangak was a Vice-President of the Native Brotherhood of B.C. in 1950. In that year he petitioned the B.C. Provincial Government asking that his people be given the same rights to alcohol as existed "… for our white brothers…" The government ignored the request and continued to allow discrimination to prevail. Thanks to Jim Harvey that discrimination was finally wiped out.

The Native Brotherhood of B.C. is an organization of First Nations people along the coast of the province. Formed in 1931, it's the longest-lasting Aboriginal organization in Canada.

As the M.P. for Skeena I was guest speaker at an annual meeting of the Native Brotherhood in Vancouver in the early 1960s. I can't pinpoint the date, but Robert Clifton from Hartley Bay was an officer (Treasurer, I believe) of the Brotherhood at the time.

At the end of my speech Guy Williams, the Native Brotherhood's President, and Robert Clifton overwhelmed me by bestowing upon me the name Weget, an esteemed, honoured, and powerful name. Translated into English it means a big or powerful person. Then, amidst great hilarity, they presented me with a sweater, a pair of mitts, and a hat all knitted by a woman from the Cowichan Band on Vancouver Island.

Robert Clifton told the assembly that Weget was a name belonging to Gitga'ata. It is also a name belonging to, and used by, other Nations. Properly the name is only on loan to me; it will revert to its tribal owners at my death. Out of respect for the Gitga'ata and their culture I can only hope that I have done nothing to bring dishonour to the name. I have always been proud to have the use of it.

Robert Clifton was President of the Native Brotherhood in 1954. I'll always remember his visit to the Legislature and the gaff of Labour Minister Lyle Wicks. Wicks rose in the Legislature and welcomed Robert Clifton. However, by a slip of the tongue, he referred to him as Clifton Webb, a Hollywood actor. Thereafter, when friends of Robert would meet him, they would often ask: "How's Clifton Webb today?"

The Git'ksan of the upper Skeena River have four matrilineal groups of extended families often referred to as "tribes", one of which is Gis-Gaas. At an outdoor ceremony in the summer of 1967 the reigning Chief (in the Git'ksan language Simauget) of the Gis-Gaas at Kitwangak adopted me before a number of witnesses as a member of Gis-Gaas.

Carvings or paintings of animals or plants (called crests) are used to identify "tribes." As an adopted member of Gis-Gas, the Killer Whale became my crest. It's carved into a ring and a bracelet, each of which is part of my being.

After years of working on behalf of Native people it was an emotional moment to be adopted and thus feel a special relationship with sisters and brothers of the same clan, not only amongst Git'ksan, but amongst all other Aboriginal Nations.

43

A CLOUD WITH A SILVER LINING

Prior to the 1962 general election Edith, miserable living in Ottawa, decided to return to New Westminster. Our son, Robert, went with her. We saw very little of each other following her move. Our marriage, strained and difficult at most times, finally disintegrated. I voluntarily provided the grounds for our divorce.

The atmosphere and demands of political activity are hostile towards a marriage or even a casual relationship. One leads the life of a wanderer, often away from home for days, even weeks at a time. In the 1960s Parliament Hill was a small village of at least a thousand people, about one-quarter of whom were M.P.s, many living in Ottawa without their spouses. Sexual temptations exist within such a milieu and can easily create marital tensions.

Whether or not liaisons develop, spouses tend to lead separate lives, to move away from each other both sexually and intellectually. They often became strangers who inadvertently tug at the marriage, isolating children from one, if not both, parents. Edith's moving back to New Westminster isolated Robert from me.

He was sixteen when he returned to Ottawa to live with me. If he was anything like me at that age, at least he'd thought about sex. One day I told him that I would like to discuss sexual matters with him. I grasped his look and response as being disdainful.

"If you want to," he said.

"Yeh, I do. I just want to make sure you understand about men and women, uh, how they get along, uh, how they make love, uh, have sex together and what to look out for."

His response shook me up. "I think it's dirty."

After a few seconds I asked, "What do you mean?"

"I just think it's a dirty thing to do." He got up from his chair and ran up the stairs to his bedroom. I didn't follow him. I didn't want to intrude, but I also didn't know what to say.

Sex can be a delicate subject at the best of times for a parent to discuss with his or her children. For me, it was more difficult; Robert and I had been away from each other for 4 years. Sure, we talked on the phone and I saw him whenever I could, but that hadn't been enough.

His reply told me that something wasn't quite right. My first thought was that Edith, because of the tensions between us, had knocked the idea of male-female relationships.

The next indication of something out of the ordinary took place when I walked past him as he was talking on the telephone. Into the phone he said, "Put in some words."

Clearly he didn't want me to hear what he was saying. So I did a sneaky thing.

I had his mail forwarded to my office so I could read one or two of his letters. I wasn't proud of this, but I was concerned and needed to find out what the score was.

We talked about it in my office. I confessed to him what I had done, why I had done it, and gave him the letters.

Gently I said, "Robert I think, from the letters, that you have, uh, homosexual tendencies."

He angrily replied, "So what? It's my business."

"Yes, Robert, it's your business, but I am concerned that you might not know about the dangerous part and I'd like to talk with you about it."

"All you'll want to do is make me change."

"No, I will not try to change you. I don't understand homosexuality, that's true. I'm not attracted to it, but I'm not opposed to it either. I've read of instances when homosexuals…"

"Dad, the word is gay, not homosexual."

"Yes," I said, "I've read that too, but maybe I'm too old-fashioned to use that expression. What I was saying was that homo…, er, gay people sometimes get beaten up by kids who think it's wrong. Also, there are some pretty weird people out there who are gay themselves. I don't want you to be injured, that's all."

I don't know if he trusted me at that time, but what I did and what I said broke the ice. It laid the foundation for us to talk more freely, not only about being gay, but about other things as well.

Sunday, April 2, 1967. I went to my office to check over accumulated mail, something I often did. One of the envelopes was marked "Personal and Private." I opened it. For more than twenty years I'd feared this moment. Blackmail.

"Send five thousand dollars in ten, twenty, and fifty dollar bills, not new, to… care of General Delivery, Vancouver, B.C., in a small box wrapped in brown paper. If received within twenty-one days of March 15 you will be repaid at one hundred dollars a week for one year beginning May 4. If not I will totally ruin you by distributing proof of your past to friends, relatives, political associates and appropriate authorities. Likewise, if you involve any authorities or attempt to establish my identity. If you comply you won't be bothered again and will be promptly repaid. I'm sure you realize this loan is in both our interests.

An old friend"

I'd expected such a communication for some time. I had, over the years, told a number of people about the jail term. I wasn't proud of the event, but it was necessary that people I worked with knew of it. But, the only way to keep a secret is keep it to yourself; tell others and it will become public knowledge.

E. Davie Fulton, Minister of Justice with Prime Minister

Diefenbaker, knew. Senator Guy Williams years later told me that Fulton had access to my file in the Penitentiary Service and wanted to use the information during an election campaign. Williams, and others, persuaded him not to.

Some time later I went to the Commissioner of Penitentiaries and asked to see my file. Everyone who gains access to such a file has to list their name and date of access in ink on the cover. Only one person had gained access to my file prior to my seeing it. That person's name and the date had been vigorously scrubbed out.

Knuckling under to blackmail is a losing game. Pay up once and you are stuck. I had decided a long time ago to move against any blackmail attempt quickly and firmly. Harold Winch was right on the mark in 1952 when he told me not to hide or deny.

Even so, I sat for a long time wondering if there was an alternative. I could ignore the letter; wait for the public disclosure and then confess. That would put me in a defensive position. If no public disclosure was made, I could not live, day after day, with the threat that to-morrow might be the day.

I could write a reply to the letter and tell the author to "stuff it." The result would be the same as ignoring it.

I could offer to lend the author the money, because that's what the letter said the $5,000 would be. Two problems with this option: I couldn't raise $5,000. I would have been hard pressed to raise $500. Secondly the author would not want to be identified. I took the letter to the R.C.M.P.

Some years earlier I had told Robert of my criminal record. Robert was now seventeen years of age. I told him of the blackmail attempt and let him read a copy of the letter. I told him what I planned to do. I suggested that if any media people approached him he should refuse to comment. I didn't want him drawn into any controversy either with his friends or people at his place of work.

Robert was a very lovely person and I was deeply moved by his response. He told me, simply and clearly, he would stand by me and support me and be proud to do so.

I told a number of groups in the Party: our caucus, the NDP provincial executive, and our constituency association. I told them what I planned to do and that the burden was mine alone.

While I was in Terrace the extortionist was arrested. On Sunday, April 16th I voluntarily appeared on Terrace's Television Station, CFTK-TV, and laid out the story of my childhood and the penitentiary sentence.

Following that broadcast I headed back to Ottawa and was met by media people in Vancouver and, at a change of aircraft, in Toronto. In Ottawa it was more of the same. I had to face the media and go through the gruelling spate of questions as quickly as possible; have the story examined in as much detail as the media desired and then get on with my life.

About a week after I thought the media interest was satiated I was invited to appear on the CBC's FRONT PAGE CHALLENGE. By then I'd had enough and declined the invitation. It was a punishing and exhausting couple of weeks but I felt a freedom I hadn't experienced in over twenty years. Even so, I still had to face the prospect that my political career and life was finished.

Letters and telegrams flooded in. Nearly all of them were sympathetic or congratulatory. I had not expected such a response and the flavour of it was heart-warming and made life that much easier. One of the letters was from the man who owned one of the stores which I'd robbed. He told me he was angry at being held up, but that time heals such emotions. He also congratulated me for going public and owning up to the deed.

A federal election took place on June 25, 1968. My criminal record was not mentioned. In fact, it didn't seem to be a factor. This election was characterised by the great emotional binge over Pierre Trudeau. The Liberal candidate in Skeena was the same person who'd run in 1965.

In 1965 the Liberals received 30% of the vote; in 1968 they got

32%. We got 53% in 1965 and 52% in 1968.

I'm grateful to the general public for its acceptance of the fact that a teen-age blunder can be overcome and forgiven.

But, the blunderer must continue to prove to himself, and thereby to others, that overcoming the blunder is permanent.

44

THE TEN PERCENTERS

During the Liberal minority position from 1972 until 1974 Allan MacEachen, for more than twenty years the de facto federal Liberal Leader in Nova Scotia, was President of the Privy Council and government House Leader. MacEachen was wily, shrewd, and tactically very nimble.

On June 22, 1973 MacEachen introduced Bill C-203 relating to election expenses, campaign fund contributions, and income-tax credits for such contributions.

Part of Bill C-203 authorized the government to subsidize the election expenses of candidates who received at least 20% of the popular vote.

David Lewis urged the NDP caucus to support the Bill, but seek to have the subsidy kick-in-figure reduced to 10%. A few of us, I included, opposed subsidization, but we went along with caucus's decision.

The Bill was referred to The Standing Committee on Privileges and Elections. Les Benjamin from the Saskatchewan riding of Regina-Lake Centre and I were the NDP members. At the Committee stage of a Bill it can be examined in great detail, even to deciding whether a punctuation mark should be a comma or a semi-colon.

As mentioned, only a Cabinet Minister can move, and have accepted, motions which entail the expenditure of public funds. But, to show the Party that we were trying, I moved a motion to reduce the 20% figure to 10%. It was, as expected, ruled out of order.

The Committee reported the Bill back to the House in December of 1973. Bills examined by a Standing Committee could be amended in the House, provided formal written notice was given of the amendments. Such proposed amendments were debatable.

I conceived a plan to bring that 20% figure down, but deliberately concealed it from caucus. The heavies in caucus were Lewis, Andy Brewin from Greenwood in Toronto, and Knowles. Douglas, no longer National Leader, quite properly deferred to Lewis. I didn't want to present the plan to caucus because I was afraid these guys would shoot it down. I was afraid they would be more interested in getting home for Christmas than in getting the bench-mark figure of 20% reduced. There were a few other reasons as well. I didn't want Lewis to know because I didn't trust him to keep such a matter under his hat. Brewin was brilliant, a lawyer known in legal circles as a lawyer's lawyer. He, however, was a long-time friend of Lewis and I didn't know where his loyalties might lie. Knowles, a parliamentary-procedure expert, was so much of a purist about the rules that I thought him unable to employ them for strategic purposes.

My plan was simple and needed some co-conspirators in caucus. They were Peters, Tom Barnett from Comox-Alberni in B.C, and Bill Knight from Assiniboia in Saskatchewan. At the time we were only a few days away from the Christmas recess of the House. Our gamble was that we could use this as a lever to bring our plan to success.

We conspirators drafted more than thirty amendments and gave the House notice of them. Other members of the NDP gave notice of amendments, bringing the total to forty-two. The key amendment was mine which sought to increase the 20% figure to 70%.

The Big Three of our caucus were furious, with most of the fury directed at me and Bill Knight. They thought my 70% figure was only a device to scuttle the subsidy proposal because getting 70% of the popular vote was a virtual impossibility. Lewis was incensed at me, partly because of filing all the amendments, and partly because of my telling him, some time earlier, that I didn't trust him.

These amendments were dealt with on December 18th, 19th, 20th, and 21st. December 21st was a Friday; Christmas Day the following Tuesday.

On December 18th the amendments were called for debate. I raised a point of order to the effect that the report from the Committee was out of order because the Committee had included an expenditure item which was beyond the scope of the initial recommendations of the Governor-in-Council.

The Speaker subsequently ruled in my favour, but in the meantime Allan MacEachen had obtained the necessary authority. It was presented to the Speaker on December 21st.

The purpose of all our amendments was to use them as the threat of a filibuster, information which we made sure got through to MacEachen, who was quite aware of what Peters and I had done with the divorce blockade.

Lewis appointed Brewin as "hit man." Brewin's purpose was to make sure the Bill got through the House before the expected Christmas recess, and spear me whenever possible.

During the debate on one amendment, Brewin said: "Speaking for the majority of my colleagues, if not all of them… the majority of our party will restrict their contributions to the debate… to facilitate the passage of this Bill."

Brewin, in referring specifically to an amendment of mine, also said, "I do not propose to vote for it and I suggest to other members that they should not vote for it." This prompted Joe Clark, the Conservative from Rocky Mountain in Alberta, to say: "I was very much heartened… to hear the words of… [Mr. Brewin]. We can only express the hope that those words will be matched by the actions of his party."

The Conservatives wanted the Bill to pass quickly and stated that they accepted the government's 20%.

The House recessed for lunch on December 21st between 1:00 P.M. and 2:00 P.M. During the lunch break I went to John Reid, Liberal M.P. for Kenory-Rainy River in Ontario and Parliamentary Secretary to MacEachen. I told Reid that there was room for discussion if MacEachen would agree to reduce the 20% figure. Reid got back to me and said MacEachen would accept 15%. I agreed and told him we would withdraw all of our amendments except the one raising the 20% figure to 70%. This would allow MacEachen to amend it by changing the 70% to 15%. I also told Reid that if anyone else in our caucus got wind of this deal it could blow up.

The House was scheduled to adjourn at 6:00 P.M. It took some time for all the adjustments to get into place and by the time all was in readiness it was close to 6:00. It was necessary for the House to agree to sit beyond the time of adjournment in order to complete the debate on the Bill. It did. We withdrew all our amendments but the one agreed to. MacEachen moved the 15% amendment. It passed easily.

One thing I learned from working with Lewis, Brewin, and Knowles was that they were not scrappers; they were just talkers, debaters who relied on argument to convince others. They were strong with their philosophic and ideological beliefs and held to them. But I never had any indication that they would "go the extra yard." As they say: Be cautious when dealing with your enemies, but more cautious when dealing with your friends.

When it was all over I went to Brewin, Lewis, and Knowles separately and, with a suppressed smile said, "I'm sorry we couldn't get you your 10%." None of them said a bloody word.

Within our Party's ranks the word always was that the NDP caucus had brought about the reduction. The role our small group played was never recognized by the Party or even mentioned; it would have embarrassed too many people.

45

THE T-SHIRT DIDN'T HELP

Lewis was our National Leader at the 1972 general election; we elected 31 M.P.s. The Liberals elected 109, the Conservatives 107, Social Credit 15, and Independents 2. It was a victory for Lewis, one which gave the NDP the balance-of-power. No party had a majority. Both the Liberals and the Conservatives needed the NDP's support to form a government.

At our first caucus meeting Lewis contended that minority governments were in store for the next couple of elections. It was to be the Pearson syndrome of the 1960s. Lewis recommended we write to both Trudeau and Conservative Leader Robert Stanfield setting out our "shopping list" and saying that we would defeat whichever one formed the government if that list did not find its way into legislation. Lewis knew that the Liberals were a malleable bunch who would adopt any program or policy which would get them into office, or keep them there.

What Lewis didn't reveal was that Trudeau had already approached him and that a deal had been struck. Christina McCall-Newman, in her book *Grits*, says that Trudeau had made approaches to the New Democratic Party with promises of Liberal legislation compatible with their goals in return for their agreement to maintain him in office despite the minority situation.

Constitutionally it is the Governor-General who picks the person who is to be Prime Minister. The Governor-General needs to be assured that whoever he picks has the support of a majority of M.P.s.

Trudeau, a constitutional lawyer in his own right, would want to nail down such majority support as quickly as possible so he could tell that to the Governor-General. On election night there were still some three or four seats in doubt but it was clear that there was going to be a minority government.

The NDP, with 31 seats, was the only Party which could give Trudeau his much-needed majority. Trudeau, to get that majority, would have called Lewis at the first opportunity perhaps even on election night.

Responding to our support Trudeau took a number of steps that otherwise would not have been taken: personal income taxes were indexed, a Food Prices Review Board set up; former NDP M.P., Tom Berger, was appointed to hold an inquiry into the proposed Mackenzie Valley Pipe Line.

Trudeau wanted more than just support on a case-by-case basis. He wanted a longer-term arrangement. He wanted to buy time for the Liberal Party to get its act together for another election. Of course, the NDP also needed time.

I have no doubt that Lewis and Trudeau had agreed upon a longer-term plan, but nothing of that nature was ever relayed to caucus. Lewis's style was secretive. He would have hopes and expectations about schemes in which he might be involved, but keep his thoughts to himself. That way, if the plans didn't evolve as he desired, he wouldn't be embarrassed.

With Trudeau in a minority position we in the NDP seemed always to be functioning day by day. Decisions as to how we would vote on any issue before the House were made within an election-or-no-election context. If we voted with the Conservatives against the government, an election would take place.

Caucus was not unanimous about the strategy of voting to support the Liberals. There wasn't an open fight about it, just some private grumbling. Some of us, I among them, were of the view that we were selling out and diluting future campaign platforms. Every time the Liberals adopted a part of our program we lost it; it became Liberal policy.

Early in 1974 the House of Commons was buzzing with rumours of an imminent election either by the defeat of the Liberals in the House or by Trudeau asking the Governor-General—as Pearson successfully did in 1965—for dissolution.

The public never considered the NDP would form a government and they were right. Many of us feared that people would vote for stability and give either the Liberals or the Conservatives a majority, squeezing us out of the game. The Diefenbaker sweep in 1958 had reduced us to eight seats. We were scared that it would happen again.

So a few of us devised a plan to defeat the Liberals on our terms. We felt, by doing that, we would at least be a factor in the ensuing election.

With Lewis in attendance I presented caucus with the outline of this plan. It involved moving motions at the various Standing Committees to cut back on government spending. Caucus set up a committee of three members: John Harney from Scarborough West in Ontario, Bill Knight, and I as the chair. We sent a letter to each caucus member asking for their advice on what to cut.

In conjunction with our research staff we prepared a 47-page detailed document cutting the budget of every department of government, for a total reduction of slightly more than $1.02 billion. We worked with members of caucus to make sure everyone knew what was involved and how each department would be affected.

We were interested in advancing the NDP, yes. We also wanted the cuts to be acceptable. Our proposed budget cuts did not involve programs benefiting the public. For example, we proposed reducing the budget of the Department of Regional Economic Expansion by some $112 million. This Department was used as a pork-barrel for channelling funds to favoured constituencies. The money saved by our plan could be used to reduce personal income taxes or increase Old Age Pensions.

Each department's budget was to be referred to a House of Commons Committee for examination. The first Committee to meet for the consideration of the budget would see our members move motions to cut the budget for that department.

We didn't want the Conservatives to grab this issue and take it away from us. When that first Committee met we would simultaneously give notice of our intention to move similar motions in each committee, hand-deliver the notice to the chair of each committee, and release the complete details of our plan to the media.

We were gambling that the Conservatives, who were clamouring for an election, would support our budget-cutting motions. Procedurally, when the budgets were reported back to the House, they would be reduced by whatever amounts the various committees agreed upon. If the government wanted to re-instate the budget-cuts it would have to do so by motion. If we and the Conservatives stuck to our guns the government would be defeated and the NDP could fight the election on the grounds of cutting back on government expenditures. That at least would give us a better chance than simply looking like the Liberals.

All of caucus knew what we were doing. Knight says that Lewis was in complete understanding of our intent but fearful of our methodology. Knight also says that Lewis told him that he was on Knight's side.

But when the 47-page document was presented to caucus Lewis came out against it with both guns blazing. I was taken completely by surprise and felt shattered. I remember Terry Grier, from Toronto-Lakeshore in Ontario, telling caucus that he had spent a lot of effort to become an M.P. and wasn't going to support anything which would see him face an early election. Knowles and Douglas were outraged and accused Knight of being irresponsible.

For Lewis to engage in a blistering attack upon our committee's budget-cutting plan when he was aware of it all along left me with no other conclusion than that a deal with Trudeau to keep the Liberals in office for a period of time had been agreed upon right from the beginning.

I was so furious that I quit going to caucus meetings.

Coupled with this continual difficulty, those of us from B.C. faced another problem.

On August 30, 1972 the NDP was elected as the government of B.C., with Dave Barrett as Premier. In the spring of 1973 that government introduced the Bill which would preserve agricultural land. It met with a shrill and intense attack, mostly generated by the real-estate industry. The NDP provincially was vociferously criticized for other measures. During 1973 and 1974 the eleven NDP M.P.s from B.C. not only had the discomfort of trying to sort out what Lewis might be up to, but had to face the wrath of voters over what was happening at home.

The August 30, 1972 provincial election was immediately followed by a federal election for October 30. Our workers in Federal Skeena were exhausted, as was our bank account. At my urging the NDP in Federal Skeena played a low-key role for the first half of the 1972 election campaign. Not only were we broke and worn out; we were in debt.

I felt we had a good, solid support base and didn't need to campaign very strenuously. In each of the four federal elections immediately preceding that of 1972 we had won with our percentage above 50%. The strategy worked. Our vote dropped, but we still won with 47.7% of the vote.

The 1972 strategy worked for us, yes. It also worked against us in the 1974 federal election. Too many workers said that we didn't need to conduct a vigorous campaign; we'd succeeded in 1972 and we could do it again. That wasn't the only problem.

Dave Barrett, on becoming Premier, appointed Frank Calder to the cabinet as a minister without portfolio. Calder's responsibility was to bring the federal government and Aboriginal people together with the province to commence negotiations over what was then referred to as "the land question."

Less than a year later Barrett fired Calder. Neither he nor Calder revealed the reason. I was asked by many people why Calder was fired. I didn't know. I suggested they ask Calder. In the background was the impression that this was a white man firing a Native without cause. Calder helped set the tone for this, claiming it was racist. Whatever the reason, the firing of Calder lost votes for us.

It wasn't until Barrett's autobiography was published in the mid-1990s that I learned of his side. He says that Calder and a woman had been arrested in Victoria while being drunk in a car which was parked in the middle of an intersection. When Barrett confronted Calder with this information he denied it.

Barrett says he fired Calder for lying. What I don't understand is why Barrett didn't say this at the time.

We also had the general problem of the attack, justified or not, against the provincial NDP. Too many of our supporters were unduly influenced by the broadside and either abandoned us or slacked off as workers.

The lackadaisical approach of NDP members is probably best exemplified by recounting an event in Terrace. Hartley Dent was elected the NDP M.L.A. for Skeena in 1972. I was scheduled to be in Terrace on a particular date. Ordinarily the NDP in Terrace would have arranged a public meeting or some other event to give publicity to our campaign.

It may have been that my scheduled appearance in Terrace coincided with Dent's birthday. In any event the NDP in Terrace abandoned the campaign and decided to celebrate whatever Dent was celebrating. We had no public meeting, no television program, no opportunity to enthuse our supporters, no media coverage beyond what I was able to put together in a written statement.

Half way through the 1974 federal election I came to the conclusion that we would have been better off if we'd used the issues raging at the provincial level and in effect fought a provincial campaign. By that time it was too late to change.

The Liberal candidate was from Prince Rupert, Iona Campagnolo. One of our workers, until I heard about it, wore a T-shirt during part of the campaign. This T-shirt not only detracted from our campaign; we were ridiculed because of it. The slogan on the front was: "A Woman's Place Is In the House of Commons." The slogan was "right on", but the timing was disastrous.

Our vote dropped to 30%. The Liberals won with 40% of the vote and Campagnolo became the M.P. Trudeau made her a Cabinet Minister. At the 1979 election she was defeated by the NDP's Jim Fulton. She went on to become B.C.'s Lieutenant-Governor.

We went into that 1974 election with 31 M.P.s and lost half of them. The Liberals, contrary to Lewis's opinion, got a clear majority. Lewis was defeated, a victim of his own brilliance.

Lewis was extremely articulate, a first-class orator with a manner and style which revealed his intelligence. He not only was unable to camouflage his intellect, he appeared to flaunt it.

Part of the Liberal campaign was to play up to NDP voters and make promises about such things as an easier arrangement for home ownership and equality for women. The Liberals were only capitalizing on the NDP's support for Trudeau's minority government by shoplifting segments of our policy.

The few of us in caucus who were apprehensive about keeping the Liberals in office were at fault too. We didn't push the issue; we didn't argue with the strategy. We suffered our anguish in private and, I suppose, were simply willing to go along with the majority because we couldn't change it anyway. Lewis's oratorical brilliance and influence in caucus was too strong. Maybe we were—what?—just Liberals in a hurry?

Politics is one profession where you can be fired for doing a good job. I felt I'd done that over seventeen years as Skeena's M.P. The loss devastated me. I was depressed and demoralized, but it helped just to hurry back to Ottawa and clean out my office. All my files were given to the National Archives. Almost as soon as I had got rid of all the paper I felt relieved.

Being defeated, though, was not a complete surprise. During the campaign it became increasingly evident that we were going to lose.

Even so, I was out of a job and had no contingency plans.

Sure, the turmoil and tension within caucus from 1972 to 1974 had worn me down. I had contemplated not running again, but the attraction was too strong. I loved politics.

At one time horses were used to draw fire-fighting equipment to a fire. It was said that when the fire-alarm bell sounded those horses which had been retired were just as eager as they'd always been to get back into harness.

I guess I was like one of those retired horses.

46

MORE THAN LAND WAS CUT OFF

In 1969 (we were never able to pin down a date) I met Julienne Peacock (Julie). She, like I, was divorced. She had two children, then in their teen years, Danielle and Anthony. Danielle lived with her mother in Aylmer, Quebec; Anthony with his father in Calgary, Alberta.

I met Julie through a mutual friend, Eileen Scotton who, along with her husband, Cliff, were Ottawa residents active in the CCF. They were also good friends of Julie and her husband, Don Peacock, a reporter attached to the Parliamentary Press Gallery. He and I were friendly, but I didn't meet or know anything about his family before 1969.

Eileen contacted me one day and asked if I could help a friend of hers to keep in touch with her son in Calgary by letting her use my office telephone. I said, "Sure." So Eileen introduced me to Julie.

One of the perks provided to M.P.s was the payment from the House of Commons' budget for long-distance telephone calls. I, for the first and only time, let someone else use that service. I rationalized my action by telling myself I was only helping someone in need.

Julie was dedicated to her children. She worried about Anthony being in Calgary with his father and wanted to talk with him as much as possible. Eileen's main reason for contacting me was that Julie just didn't have the money to pay for the phone calls.

Being a single parent then was a tough go, and still is. But I found out that Julie was a gutsy and determined woman, especially about her family. She had gone back to school to earn her teacher's certificate and was teaching school when we met. She also worked at a part-time job. She was going to provide her children with the best she could afford.

I didn't want my secretary to hear any of what were private conversations so the phone calls took place in the evening. I naturally remained in my office each time and, because I didn't want to hear either, busied myself with my own work.

So there we were, two divorced people, alone with each other. A casual relationship which gradually moved along towards friendship. I invited her to have dinner with me a couple of times. We told each other bits and pieces about ourselves, just enough for friends to prepare for a gentle and mutual courtship which evolved, on my part, into something more than merely an attempt to win favour.

On March 14, 1974 Julie and I were married. She was comforting and supportive about losing Skeena, which eased the trauma of my losing a job I loved.

A few months after my defeat the B.C. Provincial Government hired me as a consultant on matters relating to Aboriginal people. Norman Levi, an M.L.A. for Vancouver-Burrard, was the Minister of Human Resources who, following Calder's removal from Cabinet, was assigned Calder's former responsibilities.

There was the usual clamour about patronage. I trotted out my prideful defiance and replied that I had spent many years in the House of Commons working on behalf of Native people and knew more about the subject than almost everyone else in politics.

Shortly after the appointment I accidentally met Calder. He told me that he felt like resigning. I asked him why. All he said was: "You know why." Then he abruptly walked away.

One of my first tasks was to meet with various groups of Natives to find out how we might approach the claim that they still owned the land. There was some rivalry within the Union of B.C. Indian Chiefs as to strategy and what should be given priority.

One such rivalry related to what were called the cut-off lands. These were parcels of Reserve land which had been removed from Reserve status.

In 1912 the federal and provincial governments established a Royal Commission (The McKenna-McBride Commission) to settle certain matters relating to Aboriginal affairs. This Commission completed its work in 1916 and recommended that land be removed from certain Reserves; hence the label "cut-off lands."

Around the time that Barrett was Premier the Union of B.C. Indian Chiefs had established a cut-off-lands committee under the chairmanship of Chief Adam Eneas from Penticton. This Committee wanted priority given to its mandate.

Levi concluded that the cut-off lands question should be dealt with initially without the federal government's involvement because the cut-off lands became provincial crown lands when the reserves were reduced.

Levi held a meeting with the cut-off lands committee of the Union of B.C. Indian Chiefs and other First Nations leaders on June 24, 1975. He told the gathering he wanted to see the cut-off lands matter settled amicably and asked for suggestions as to how this might be accomplished.

One of the participants said that words were not enough and asked for some indication of good faith by government. "Words are one thing," he said, "but trust is something else."

Levi's almost immediate response was: "How about it if we return 100 acres as a gesture of our sincerity?" That did it. A memorandum of understanding was reached involving a three-member committee which was to report to government before December 31, 1976 with government resolving the matter before June 24, 1977.

The important aspect of this decision was that Levi took it upon himself to make the commitment. He knew he would have difficulty if he asked Cabinet for approval. Some Ministers were lukewarm about the subject. Some were too busy with other matters. Some had no idea what was involved and I suspect a few were opposed.

The Union's cut-off-lands committee had created a lot of publicity and had continued to say they were ready to negotiate at any time. Following the cut-off-lands agreement, the Union's committee met with Levi.

They asked for government funds so they could research the matter. Levi, to his credit, refused to provide any money. He reminded them that they had stated many times they were ready.

While I was an M.P. many Aboriginal people contacted me about matters of concern to them. One such person, an elder from Kanesatake in Quebec, came to me with a problem similar to the cut-off lands question. He claimed that a portion of their reserve had been removed and given to the Roman Catholic Church's Seminary of St. Sulpice and they wanted it back again.

I got nowhere with the Indian Affairs Branch. They said it was a pre-confederation decision made by the Government of France. They wouldn't touch it. I contacted the Government of Quebec to try to resolve the matter at that level.

Rene Levesque was the minister in charge of such matters. I wrote to him in English. He replied in French. I got it translated. It needed a reply.

Through a friend of mine from Kahnawake, a Mohawk activist named Kahn-Tineta Horn, I got my reply translated into the Mohawk language and sent that to Levesque.

The next day I wrote to him again in English and attached a French translation. I said that it had occurred to me he might not be able to read the Mohawk language, so I'd enclosed a French and an English translation of it.

I got a reply written in the Inuit language, then a phone call from him. He was delightful. He said it was great fun to send such letters back and forth, and asked me how I thought he could solve the problem. I told him I had explained it fully in the first letter, but went on to tell him what was involved. It was another dead end. All he would say was that Indian Affairs was a subject that was federal in jurisdiction.

For a number of reasons, it was not possible to get any movement on land claims in B.C. One barrier was the federal government. It had the exclusive constitutional jurisdiction with respect to Native people and to reserve lands, but gave the province no indication of the mechanisms it would like to see established for tri-party negotiations. Premier Barrett kept saying, "Tell us your terms of reference and we'll be at the negotiating table."

I drafted a letter for Barrett to send to Trudeau. If crown lands were to be part of any settlement, asked Barrett, how was the federal government going to acquire those lands from the people of B.C.? The reply from Trudeau skirted the question.

In the fall of 1975, the federal government proposed that it meet with the provincial government and work out a bilateral agreement to present to Natives as a fait accompli. This was the top-down manner the federal government had always used in its dealings with Aboriginal people: "We know best what is good for you." The NDP government, rightly so, rejected that approach.

Another impediment was the escalating labour-management strife in the province which occupied the attention of government to a greater extent than did land claims.

A third matter of prime importance was that Calder, having had responsibility to get the federal government and Natives to the negotiating table with the province regarding land claims, had produced a blank sheet. I looked for documentation for the time he was a Cabinet Minister to find out what he'd presented to Cabinet. I found nothing in the way of strategy papers, analyses of the land claims, a public relations program, or plans to get the federal government to move.

One of the most important ventures he could have made was to present an "educational-type account" of land claims to cabinet so all of his colleagues would at least be informed. A number of Cabinet Ministers, especially those who had little, if any, contact with Natives, were not familiar with the land claims question beyond knowing that it existed.

I spoke with Cabinet Ministers about the land claims question and their need to take it more seriously. Within the Cabinet, I think Bob Williams was probably more of an obstacle than anyone else.

Williams was an M.L.A. for Vancouver East and Minister of Lands and Forests. He was an abrupt person who had sold himself on the idea that his way was the right way. Williams was the only one who was absolutely opposed to any negotiations to resolve land claims. As I recall it, he said, "They have no legitimate claim to the land; it's Crown land, not Indian land."

Barrett called an election for December 11, 1975. I took a leave of absence and worked on the campaign in the northwest part of the province. The NDP was defeated by the Social Credit Party which was led by Bill Bennett, W.A.C.'s son. Social Credit would get rid of me, so I beat them to the punch by resigning and going home to Aylmer.

The Social Credit Government elected in 1975 deserves to be applauded for honouring the cut-off lands agreement which Levi had produced and, over a period of time, that matter was resolved.

47

FAMILY

Julie was born on December 11. It's presumptuous for me to consider that I was a satisfactory birthday gift, but the defeat of Barrett's government on that day got me back home to live with my wife and Danielle in Aylmer.

I was forty-four years old when Julie and I met. At that time in my life I didn't have a sense of what a family was and, more importantly, what it could mean to one's self-esteem and personal well being.

Until I was about twenty, what family life I experienced was in houses or institutions occupied by people whom I can best describe as acquaintances. Even in Kimberley I always had the feeling that Dad didn't particularly like having me around. Mom was different. She was a warm, friendly person, but she still regularly cursed my reputed father and mother.

At twenty, and for some years after, I was more like a single person with no fixed address. I had married in my mid-twenties, but couldn't keep that marriage intact.

I liked Julie's mother from the moment we met. I felt that something "clicked" between us and got the impression that she liked me too, even though she knew nothing about me beyond what Julie may have told her.

I called her Mrs. Laberge, but Julie insisted I call her Mama. "After all," said Julie, "we're practising at being husband and wife."

Mama was a gracious person, at ease anytime I was in her presence. She was alert and bright, with a delightful sense of humour. Upon hearing something amusing one of her favourite expressions was "Mon Dieu", always said with a smile in her voice.

Mama was easily able to talk with Danielle and Anthony about matters which concerned them. They, too, could relate to her just as easily about her own interests. They proved time and again that opinions about a generation gap are bunkum.

Julie's three sisters and her brother also made me feel at home. Like all families, not everyone had the same opinion. There were strong differences. They were expressed, but the cement of the family didn't break.

When Julie and I married, her mother became Ma Belle Mama, such a loving and respectful French-language phrase, carrying much more impact than the stiff and distant "Mother-in-Law" of the English language.

Robert was eighteen or nineteen when he moved from Ottawa to live in the United States. He came to visit after Julie and I were married and immediately felt at home. He and Danielle would sit for what seemed like hours talking about their likes and dislikes, their hopes and fears, their wonderment about their future.

All of this made the family I'd recently entered more of a true and loving household than anything I'd ever experienced. Robert used to send us greeting cards to mark specific occasions such as Easter, usually addressed to "Julie and Dad." After one visit to us he sent a "Thank-you" card which I cherish and keep. The salutation said: "To Mom and Dad."

48

SUN TZU HELPED

I was 50 years old and retired; prematurely I thought. I wasn't happy with retirement. I had to work at something. I had to feel as if I was useful. Retirement wasn't acceptable; it was a drag.

I wrote a novel involving fictitious M.P.s and their exploits. It's still waiting for a publisher. I applied for a job with the Public Service Alliance of Canada, but at the interview concluded that the advertisement had been misleading. All they wanted was someone with a calculator to sit in the background at negotiations and feed them statistics. Richardson Securities of Canada wanted stock brokers. I told them the only thing I knew about selling related to ideas in the political arena. I was hired, contingent upon studying for, and passing, a supervised written test set by the Investment Dealers' Association. I got an honours mark.

I had no illusions about the nature of the investment business, but it was a job. I think I did reasonably well at it. At least I wasn't fired. I made some modest investments myself, getting a yield of about 30%. Generating a yield of 30% was not because I had any confidential or insider information. It was simply because I was on the scene and able to see the minute-by-minute transactions as they were relayed electronically into Richardson's office.

I knew the only criteria was money, but hadn't realized that it took precedence over ethics. If some company were to develop a new type of napalm bomb which would kill, say 100 people rather than 20, and the military showed interest, the recommendation would be to buy the stock.

If a client was absolutely opposed to alcohol we were advised not to pitch shares in any company which produced it. But, this was not an ethical matter, it was simply one of trying to keep that client in the fold. Being a stock broker wasn't totally satisfactory.

I got a leave of absence to return to B.C. and test the waters about running in the expected 1979 provincial election. Julie was supportive, even though it would mean a further absence from our home with no guarantee that I would be successful. At a nominating convention in Terrace, after more than a 20-year absence, I was once again our candidate in Provincial Skeena. Even though the bell hadn't rung this retired fire horse was ready to go.

What to do while waiting for the election to be called? Sun Tzu provided the answer. History is niggardly about this man, but it's known he was a Chinese military general in the Kingdom of Wu about 500 years before the birth of Christ. His clear and far-seeing thesis *The Art Of War* covers techniques, tactics, and stratagems about how to become victorious. His guidance regarding war applies to political and many other activities as well.

One of his dictums is: All warfare is based on deception; make the enemy believe that your situation is different from what it really is. If you are strong make the enemy believe you are weak, and vice versa.

So, when the media in Skeena asked what the NDP and I were doing to prepare for the expected election, my response was: "There isn't much one can do until the election is called; we are just sort of marking time until then."

What we were engaged in was a quiet, no-publicity type of membership drive. Also, out of sight of the media, I was doing an extensive and personal door-to-door campaign. If someone was home, I merely introduced myself as the NDP provincial candidate. I didn't ask for any commitment or how the person would vote at an election. Many knew me from my days as their M.P., which prompted discussions. I concentrated on the smaller communities and Native villages.

Cyril Shelford had been the Social Credit M.L.A. for the riding abutting Skeena to the east (Omineca) for about 20 years and had suffered defeat in 1972. He moved to Terrace and, at the election of 1975, defeated the NDP's Hartley Dent. Just prior to the 1979 election Shelford was appointed Minister of Agriculture.

Amusing twists are found along the campaign trail. In the community of South Hazelton I had a long talk with one friendly resident. He asked about the NDP's position on certain subjects and, by nodding his head and telling me he agreed with a number of our policies, gave me the impression that here was a vote. As we parted he stuck out his hand for a good-bye shake and said, "Good luck Mr. Shelford."

In the Kispiox Valley, a farming community, I met a person who declared that he was a socialist. Nice to hear. After a long interesting discussion I, having searched for his name in the voters' list, told him he wasn't registered and that I would get a voter registration card mailed to him. "Well," he said, "there's no need to do that. I'm an American citizen."

Anthony took time off from his job in Calgary and came to Terrace to help with the campaign. Julie remained in Quebec. She was teaching and Danielle was still going to school. It was a matter of some concern to me that my home was in Quebec. My chance of winning could have been injured considerably by not living in the riding. The Socreds, though, didn't know what to do about it. They tried a whisper campaign, but it didn't work. Having been the M.P. for seventeen years I was always considered a home-town boy.

I was guided by what happened to Claire Gillis, a long-time CCF M.P. from Cape Breton, Nova Scotia. Gillis bought a car in Ottawa and drove it back home bearing Ontario licence plates. That was a contributing factor to his subsequent defeat. In my years as M.P. I always had a B.C. driver's licence, kept B.C. licence plates on my car, and maintained a post office box in Terrace for a local address. Whenever I was in Skeena I lived in local hotels.

Our strategy, with thanks to Sun Tzu, paid off. We won nearly all the small communities, and a very large percentage of the First Nations vote. It was a two-way fight; the NDP versus Social Credit. We got 50.2% of the vote. Social Credit received 47.8%. Two independents got the rest.

On election night the Socreds in Skeena claimed that the election at a particular community (Moricetown) had been conducted improperly and ballots from there should not be counted. The Social Credit Party in Vancouver hired a lawyer to attend at the final count.

This lawyer was also hired to scrutinize at the final count for the constituency of Atlin, for it was a close race there. Atlin borders Provincial Skeena to the north. The Social Credit candidate in Atlin was Frank Calder who had deserted the NDP in 1975 and was elected as a Social Credit M.L.A. that year. In 1979 the NDP candidate was Al Passarell. On election night Passarell had a nine-vote lead over Calder.

On election day, at the polling station in Terrace, I saw Calder in the line-up to cast an absentee ballot for his home constituency. He then boarded an airplane and went back to Victoria.

The lawyer found the Moricetown vote above board and legal and proceeded on to Atlin. He returned and related to us Atlin's final count. Passarell had defeated Calder by one vote. The lawyer also told us that Calder's absentee ballot had not been counted because Calder had failed to sign the ballot envelope.

Now, with a one-vote lead the obvious move would have been to have a recount conducted by a judge. That's what happened in Skeena in 1953 when I won by thirteen votes.

The nagging question: Why didn't the Social Credit Party ask for a recount? Clearly Social Credit was content to get rid of Calder. Another question: Why didn't the Nishga'a Tribal Council apply for a recount? Obviously they didn't want him either. There are four Nishga'a villages on the Nass River. The people there voted for Passarell, giving him 241 votes to Calder's 171. Still another question: Why didn't Calder ask for a recount? Social Credit was re-elected as government and I suspect that Calder, having been rejected by the Nishga'a, was just as happy to escape into retirement.

We dubbed Passarell "Landslide Al." The irony is that he, like Calder, later defected to the Social Credit Party.

49

BARRETT BLEW IT

Julie, I, and our family of three cats moved from Aylmer to Terrace in 1980. It wasn't easy. Julie, born and raised in Ottawa, would be leaving her two sisters, a brother, and numerous other relatives to live in a small town devoid of the cultural and linguistic environment of the Ottawa area.

Julie often quoted her mother's advice about marriage: "You marry a man, you marry his country." It meant doing everything reasonable and respectful to keep the marriage intact. If Julie had been determined not to leave Ottawa and her family to come out west, I likely wouldn't have pursued the notion of being a provincial candidate in 1979. I'd have been unhappy, but would have said, "You marry a woman, you marry her country."

For the next couple of years I worked at being a good constituency representative; spent a lot of time dealing with individuals who had problems with government.

One night a resident came to our house and wanted me to accompany him to the police station to get his son out of jail. I, of course, asked what had happened. His father wasn't sure, but thought it might have something to do with drinking and driving.

I explained that there wasn't any way I could arrange for his son to be released. I suggested he hire a lawyer to see the boy first thing in the morning.

"What the hell use are you?" was his response,"We pay taxes to keep you in a cushy f... job and you won't lift a f... finger to help my son. Goddamn you anyway."

On another occasion a woman contacted me saying that the Greyhound Bus Company had lost her luggage and that they weren't working hard enough to find it. When I asked for details about dates and destination, etc., she said she couldn't remember. Eventually she admitted that the luggage had gone astray three years ago. Greyhound told me that they had compensated her for the loss, and she finally admitted that, too.

When the Legislature was sitting, I played a low-key role. I was a newcomer. I had to feel my way into a good relationship with M.L.A.s who had been there for many years; eleven were Cabinet Ministers when Barrett was Premier.

There was one striking difference between our federal caucus and the provincial caucus. In Ottawa we knew we weren't going to be government. In Victoria we could be again.

Another difference related to caucus meetings. In Ottawa caucus met once a week; if something urgent arose between meetings we were on our own most of the time. In Victoria caucus met every day, one hour before the House met. This daily event helped to keep us on track.

Caucus's social hours were also cohesive. The House didn't meet on Wednesday evenings so a card would be circulated among our M.L.A.s asking who would be available for Chinese food that night. Those of us who went had a great and convivial time. At times our uproarious laughter would attract the attention of other patrons who must have wondered about us.

The policy of the federal caucus regarding individual actions was easily understood. If Federal caucus members differed with a decision, the only request was that caucus be informed if that Member intended to vote contrary to the majority when the issue came to a vote in the

House.

In Victoria it was teamwork. We had differences about tactics and whether to support or oppose government-sponsored legislation, yes. But, when decisions were made, we were as one. I changed from being a so-called maverick to being a devout team player. So much so that Barrett, with caucus approval, had me take on the role of NDP House Leader.

I wasn't clear on what a House Leader was supposed to do, so I would be in my office at six or seven o'clock every morning trying to memorize the Standing Orders and other procedures and be able to use them to our advantage

I got a lot of help and sound advice from Lorne Nicolson, our M.L.A. for Nelson-Creston. He had pursued procedural matters on his own and for his own enjoyment. In my opinion, he knew more about procedure than anyone else in caucus.

My chore as House Leader was basically to see that our caucus pursued the decisions which we had made. It included presenting procedural arguments with the hope that our point of view would prevail with the Speaker. It involved working out timetables with the Government's House Leader.

The 1983 election was on May 5th. Both Danielle and Anthony took time out from their own activities and came to Terrace, again to help out in the campaign. I had the distinct pleasure of introducing them, and Julie, to a crowd of some 400 to 500 people who came to a rally to hear Dave Barrett. I did it with pride. I was more than happy to tell Danielle and Anthony that I was so pleased and so lucky that they adopted me. I was no longer an orphan.

The issue most prominent in people's mind during that election was the matter of restraint. Premier Bill Bennett was preaching a cutback on government expenditures and especially on public servants' wages. The economy was down and Bennett was presented by his handlers as the tough guy with tough measures to lift us out of the economic doldrums.

We entered that election without the government having introduced a budget. That was a plus for us and we played it as strongly as we could.

The public was responding favourably. In Skeena, I felt confident but hid that confidence from our workers. An election has to be an uphill fight from beginning to end. When a candidate starts to believe it's a sure thing, the only sure thing will be early retirement.

Barrett was great for thinking on his feet. He seldom, as far as I know, prepared speeches or had them prepared for him. His wit and quickness of mind were all he needed to make his points. He was a superb public orator. But, there was an instance during that 1983 campaign when his wit and sharpness failed.

Barrett, I believe during a television interview, blurted out that we would wipe out the restraint program if we became government. Then, he tried, unsuccessfully, to back out. In Cranbrook he told the media that he'd meant there would be a speedy review of the public servants' wage restraint part. At another time he stated he was only trying to goad Bennett into a public debate over restraint. Whatever he said after the television statement didn't matter. The damage was done.

Barrett arrived in Terrace shortly after that. I was able to walk out onto the tarmac and meet him as he came down the steps of the airplane. He asked me how it was going. I told him that we might not make it. He asked, "Because of my comments about restraint?" I nodded a "Yes." Then he admitted that it was a mistake, and that he wished he hadn't said what he did. "But," he continued, "we have to make the best of it."

Well, we did make the best of it, but Bennett made it better. Social Credit won with no trouble; 35 seats to our 22. In Skeena I got elected with over 50% of the vote.

There was no doubt that Barrett had to resign as leader. The only question about his departure was: When?

50

HIGH DRAMA FOR BARRETT

When legislators use filibuster they are accused of flaunting the mores of democracy. When they use closure the accusation is: dictatorship. But, the truth is that filibuster and closure are legitimate and necessary in a political democracy. Closure, though, can be used in such a way that it is dictatorship in disguise. That was the case during the 1956 pipe-line debate in the House of Commons.

A filibuster involves prolonged, repetitious, and extraneous debate. Points of order, appeals to the Speaker, motions for various purposes— all are used to take up time. Its function is to block or obstruct legislation considered objectionable, or which a political party thinks it can exploit.

Closure prevents any further debate and brings the motion under discussion to an immediate vote. Those who filibuster know that closure is in the works, but they also know it only becomes a reality when government so decides.

The trick is for government to sense when the general public is tired of a filibuster and will accept the curtailment of freedom of speech.

Another blunt tool used by government to hurry its agenda along is to have the legislative assembly sit continuously, all day and all night. Legislation by exhaustion. This practice is cruel from a health point of view. By contrast closure is humane.

The B.C. Legislature's first session following the 1983 election opened in the summer. Having been denied a budget prior to the election, the province clearly needed one. We got it, and got a lot more besides.

Along with the budget the government introduced a couple of dozen Bills designed to gut our public service and injure social programs. It wasn't only a surprise attack against the institution of government; it was an assault against society. Our caucus had no choice: filibuster. We decided right from the beginning to use every procedural tactic in the book to stop those Bills.

The trade union movement was up in arms against the legislative package. Art Kube, President of the B.C. Federation of Labour, asked if we could delay having the Bills come to a vote for a couple of weeks so the unions could organize a protest. No difficulty. Our caucus already had a much longer time table.

By mid-July, Kube and the trade union movement had spearheaded the formation of The Solidarity Coalition. The Coalition brought academics, religious leaders, trade unionists, and community groups together to fight the Socred's unwarranted infliction. There were mass demonstrations: 20,000 on the lawns of the Legislature, 50,000 at a march in Vancouver.

Sometime in September government decided it had had enough of our filibuster. To break our spirit it moved to have the hours of sitting extended, with no time set for it to adjourn—the all-day, all-night game. We weren't surprised and were ready to fight back. I'd developed a plan.

During my stint on the Loggers' Navy I had read how ships keep running safely twenty-four hours a day without wearing out the crew. We followed their technique, splitting our caucus up into three groups; in nautical terms, watches. Each watch would attend the Legislature for a four-hour period and then have the next eight hours off. My watch was 12 to 4, night and day. We could rest, but Socred M.L.A.s couldn't. They had to be available to defeat any motions we might put forward.

The first night was the worst. After working all day my watch had to be on the job at midnight. I slept a few hours that night on the floor in my office. So did others.

There are two methods of voting in the Legislature, one by voice and the other by what is called a division. A division requires each Member to stand and have his or her vote recorded. When a division is called, the Speaker pushes a button; bells ring throughout the legislative building alerting Members of the impending vote.

We used divisions as often as we could so that any Social Credit M.L.A. who might be snoozing in an office would be awakened. Our watch system allowed us to be fresh and alert, while the Socreds were the ones who became exhausted.

It was after midnight on October 5th. Chris D'arcy, our M.L.A. from Rossland-Trail, had moved a motion which would lead to a division. John Parks, Social Credit M.L.A. from Maillardville-Coquitlam, was in the chair substituting for Mr. Speaker Davidson. Parks wouldn't accept the motion, saying it was an abuse of the rules. Barrett appealed Parks' decision to the House. That wasn't accepted either because he didn't want the bells to ring and wake up his colleagues. Parks had clearly abandoned the requirement that the Speaker be neutral. He became an agent of government.

A procedural argument followed, lasting about an hour. It ended with Barrett refusing to obey the order from Parks to sit down. Barrett was then ordered to leave the House. He refused. Parks ordered the attendants to escort Barrett from the House.

My first thought was to have a number of our Members protectively surround Barrett. But, I quickly abandoned the idea because I suddenly realized that Barrett wanted to be removed. I didn't think Barrett needed to be urged, but I whispered to him, "Stay on your feet and force the issue."

Barrett was a scrapper. Being physically ejected from the House would dramatically emphasize that drastic measures had to be taken to stop the government's assault. He was not escorted from the House. He was dragged out on his ass and left lying on the floor of what is called the Speaker's corridor at the rear of the Chamber.

The Speaker is the ultimate power in the legislative buildings. About a week before the Barrett/Parks clash he had ordered the media not to gather news or interview M.L.A.s in the Speaker's corridor.

During the whole of the fuss with Parks, Mr. Speaker Davidson was in that corridor to enforce his order to the media. No interviews, no pictures. What did these champions of free speech do? They gave up on freedom and sucked up to the Speaker. The public never got the chance to see Barrett being dragged out of the Chamber and left lying on the floor of the corridor. It certainly would have made the front page of newspapers across Canada. It seemed to me that Mr. Speaker Davidson, like John Parks, had also decided to protect the Social Credit Government.

When a decision is made to filibuster there can be no backing off. It lasted some seven or eight weeks and had to be taken to the ultimate end of being forced out of the debate by closure.

Closure was invoked. Social Credit broke the filibuster. But, as far as the public was concerned, we didn't lose. We won.

51

STRIKE THREE

At a leadership convention in Vancouver in 1984 Bob Skelly, M.L.A. from Alberni, succeeded Barrett as Provincial Leader. Long before that convention I told Skelly that I'd support him. What attracted me was his concern about the environment.

Dennis Cocke, M.L.A. for New Westminster, heard of my support for Skelly and told me I was making a mistake. "Skelly," he said, "is a bankrupt." I asked him what he meant but didn't get a sensible reply, just a repetition of the accusation.

There were four other candidates, one of whom was Dave Vickers. Vickers was not an M.L.A. and had been a skilled and competent Deputy Attorney General when Barrett was Premier. His candidacy resulted in a serious split in caucus. It wasn't Vickers himself who was the cause of this split; it was one brought on by some of his supporters.

Rosemary Brown, an M.L.A. from Burnaby, and Cocke from New Westminster come to mind as being not only dedicated supporters of Vickers, but antagonistic towards Skelly.

Immediately following Skelly's election I had my first twinge of doubt about his ability as a leader. A meeting of caucus was arranged to be held in one of the rooms at the convention centre. As we were walking along the corridor I was beside Skelly, Brown a short distance behind us. I believe Cocke was close by also.

I urged Skelly to drop back and talk with them, to tell them they had put up a good campaign and to offer to work closely with them. To me, it's a newly-elected leader's responsibility to try to heal the wounds; to be gracious in victory and work to pull everything together. He didn't speak with them. He may have done so later, but the time to do the good deed was then so all could see. He missed a damn good chance.

Graham Lea, M.L.A. from Prince Rupert, was a leadership candidate also. Shortly after the convention he resigned from the NDP and sat in the Legislature as an independent.

There's a practice in the Legislature, outside the ordinary course of debating a motion, which allows a Member of the Official Opposition to comment upon any statement made by a Cabinet Minister. Lea, no longer in the Official Opposition, needed unanimous consent to comment. He asked for consent on one occasion and Skelly foolishly piped up and denied it.

As our House Leader I sat next to Skelly. I leaned over and told him he had made a mistake; that it was beneath the dignity of a leader to engage in such tactics. "If you ever want to do anything like that again," I said, "ask me. That's one of the reasons I'm here."

In the spring of '84 government moved to have the Standing Orders reviewed by a committee. Included within this committee's mandate were salaries and benefits for M.L.A.s.

Lorne Nicolson, Mark Rose from Coquitlam-Moody, and I were our Members on that committee. An important and influential Social Credit Member was Jim Nielson, Minister of Health.

When we got to discussing money, Nielson said that we had to look after our own interests; no one was going to do it for us. He was right on the mark. I agreed with him then and I do now.

Regardless, there is always a public uproar, often unjustified, when elected officials increase their own salaries or monetary perks. Upon reflection I think that any increase in the money paid to elected officials should be passed by one Parliament to come into effect in the following one. That way an elected official would escape some of the public's wrath. Dealing with the incomes for elected people is a delicate subject. There was a desire in that committee to be unanimous so that partisanship would not take advantage of the situation and lay blame and responsibility.

Neilson told the committee two or three times that our decisions would no doubt be acceptable to government and, while he couldn't speak for the Premier, he had every indication that Bennett would go along with what we finally decided to recommend.

I reported regularly to caucus what the committee was doing and what we were considering so far as money was concerned. It was at all times clear to caucus. No one raised any objections. We took Neilson at his word and made the report to the House a unanimous one. We got double-crossed; Bennett condemned the report and made political gains by so doing.

Either Nielson knew what was going to happen and lied to the committee, or he didn't know and Bennett had lied to him. I wasn't interested in trying to find out which one was the liar. We had a more compelling problem inside caucus. A few wanted to back off and dissociate themselves from the report. I reminded caucus that it knew clearly what we were doing and this was no time to show any caucus split or weakness.

Skelly, to put it politely, was apprehensive about going along with the report. He said a couple of times that he'd just received a wage increase because he was now Leader of the Opposition. He said that made it awkward for him to oppose the committee's report. Here was a time for him to be firm and precise, one way or the other, but all he did was flounder. It took agonizing effort, but caucus came out of it united in support and made the best of a bad situation. A lot of flack came my way because of my support of that report, most of it from our own Party members.

This was the third instance when I felt that Skelly's leadership fell short of the mark. But, like it nor not, he was our leader.

Skelly wasn't the only new leader of a political party. Bennett had resigned and, in 1986, was replaced by Bill Vander Zalm, a smiley, ebullient, charismatic guy. Skelly was no match for him. I doubt if anyone in the province's political scheme of things would have been.

There were a few in caucus who were after Skelly's head. Almost on the eve of the expected 1986 election they were eager for him to resign and for caucus to pick someone else. They even had a potential replacement in mind—Mike Harcourt. In the forefront of this cabal I identify Brown, Cocke, and Williams.

I consider the move to force Skelly's resignation subversive and destructive. It did nothing to bolster his self-esteem and it injured the Party.

I think I got along quite well with caucus members considering that I was charged with the task of pushing individuals to make speeches when they didn't particularly want to, or, worse still, convincing them not to speak when they wanted to. But, it didn't always work.

The debate on a particular Bill had been adjourned. It was our view that, when the Bill was called again, we should let it pass without further comment because our position on it was shaky and we could be put on the defensive by the government.

Eileen Dailly from Burnaby insisted on saying, as she put it, "a few words." I asked her not to, and told her why. She went ahead anyway and her few words progressed into a major attack against government. We took a verbal licking for the rest of that day. Afterwards she apologized and said, "You were right."

I found it difficult to work with two particular members of caucus: Brown and Williams. Both of them, I thought, were more concerned with their individual egos than with working co-operatively with caucus.

Differences of opinion are necessary for caucus to develop a consensus on issues. Those differences shouldn't result in animosity among members. I felt that both Brown and Williams had a shield which blocked them from being friendly and courteous. Exaggerated feelings of self-importance are often a mask covering up insecurity. I may be wrong making such an assessment of both Brown and Williams, but there it is.

My first dealings with Bob Williams were in 1975 when I was a consultant to the Provincial Government. In listening to him and to others who spoke of him I concluded there was something about him that was doubtful; something intangible; something which alerted me to be cautious about him. His rhetoric sounded phoney; his personality, poisonous. Many of his activities were disruptive to caucus unity.

The land-claims question had produced tense feelings between Natives and others in the Hazelton-Smithers area. Because the Social Credit Government had refused to enter into negotiations regarding these claims, Aboriginal people in the area had formed a federating organization, the Git'ksan-Wetsuweten Tribal Council, to co-ordinate their actions regarding land claims.

The Tribal Council had sued the provincial government. I had written to a number of people in the area stating what I thought were harmful consequences of the court action.

The Tribal Council maintained its court case only related to land and resources which were Crown owned. Legal advice given to me said otherwise; the court action, if successful, would have the effect of voiding every decision made by the Legislature of B.C. If that were the case individual ownership of one's land was in jeopardy.

I relied on that legal opinion, not on the Tribal Council's rhetoric. My letter pointed out that owners of private property would likely not be able to appear at any court hearing and that their interests might not be adequately represented.

The letter so angered a few First Nation leaders that they decided to run a Native as an independent candidate against me at the ensuing election. It was a punishment move because I had decided to speak up about a very serious aspect of their court action.

Vander Zalm, after conducting a media campaign, called a provincial election for October 22, 1986. We lost that election and Vander

Zalm became Premier. In Skeena the independant candidate got 4.6% of the vote, most of it from First Nations people who ordinarily had voted for the NDP. In addition the Liberals ran a candidate, something they hadn't done for years. Their vote was 4.9%. This, too, was from voters who had voted for us in the preceding two elections.

The Social Credit candidate was elected with 48.6%. Our vote was 41.7%. The strategy of the few dissident leaders worked. I lost, but so did they. They got an M.L.A. whose Party denied that they had any land claims.

Politics is not a baseball game, but I had now been defeated at three elections (1956, 1974, 1986). I was only sixty-one years of age, but had been in the political game for nearly 30 years. I accepted that three-strikes-and-you're-out should apply. I told the NDP Constituency Association that my political future was behind me.

52

ROBERT

A few days before the 1986 election Robert's friend, Allan, phoned and spoke with Julie. He told her that Robert had become seriously disoriented and unable to find his way back to their apartment. Allan knew where Robert had gone and was able to locate him and bring him home. Julie didn't tell me of this telephone conversation until we went to bed on election night. She said she didn't want to get me all worried and upset until the campaign was over.

When I first heard of AIDS (called GRIDS then) little was known about it. Robert was living in New York. Whenever we wrote or spoke on the phone we told him of our concern and the need for him to be careful. He was living in San Francisco in the mid-1980s when he told us he had contacted the AIDS virus.

I was devastated. All that we had been able to read about AIDS said that it was a terminal disease. Robert was going to die from it and there was not a single bloody thing we could do about it.

We could show love and affection, which we did. He came to Terrace to visit with us; we went to San Francisco to visit with him. We kept in constant touch.

I was on my way to San Francisco a day or two following the election. I met with Robert's doctor who said that his medical experience indicated that Robert had about six weeks of life ahead of him.

The only thing we could do to help, said the doctor, was to show Robert that we loved him.

Julie and Danielle drove to San Francisco, and Anthony flew from Toronto to be with Robert and me. During Robert's last couple of weeks he was not able to speak or give any indication that he recognized anyone. On November 20, at about 4:30 in the afternoon with all of us around, Robert died. We were thankful that he was not in pain; the virus, so said his doctor, had attacked Robert's central nervous system.

We brought Robert home to his place of birth and scattered his ashes in the waters around Siwash Rock at Stanley Park in Vancouver. Every year we go to Siwash Rock and cast white carnations onto the water. We watch them drift away and think of the pleasant moments we had with him, and how sad it is that he has missed so much of life.

Tennyson is so painfully eloquent with:

"I hold it true, whate'er befall;

I feel it, when I sorrow most;

'Tis better to have loved and lost

Than never to have loved at all."

53

RETIREMENT

It's only a matter of days before the phone stops ringing. A defeated politician is no longer of any use to a lot of people. What they want is a person who can fix things, someone in politics to serve them. In one sense it's a blessing not to be bothered with other people's personal troubles. In another sense it's a curse.

There was a guy in Skeena we called "The Witch Doctor" whose attitude about life was, to put it generously, a bit weird. He enjoyed showing people in positions of power or authority that he could make them do his bidding. Charged with causing a disturbance, he wanted me to have the police withdraw the charge. I told him there was nothing I could do; I wasn't a witness to what happened and didn't have the authority anyway. He reacted to that by having me subpoenaed as a witness. The "Witch Doctor" was his own counsel at his trial, but he didn't call me as a witness. Later he gloated to his friends that he'd "shown me" his power.

That kind of problem I was glad to be rid of. On the curse side was: What do I do now? How was I to satisfy the inner gnawing which demanded that I work at something? One activity from my IWA days came to mind, arbitration boards.

When the management of a company makes a decision which a union challenges, they can proceed to arbitration. An arbitration board sometimes consists of a union appointee, a company appointee, and an impartial chairperson. I'd sat on arbitration boards and could easily fit into the same role.

I wrote to a number of unions offering to sit as a union appointee if the occasion arose. I got a few nibbles, but nothing more. Most unions did such work in-house.

I worked a lot on our house, preparing it for sale. There was nothing to keep either Julie or me in Terrace and, for me, there was no attraction to stay there. Julie had a contract with the school board to teach until the end of the 1986-87 school year.

That September we relocated to the south part of Surrey in B.C.'s lower mainland. We bought a roomy house on a one-acre lot with alders, big-leafed maples, and some ground-cover which passed itself off as lawn.

Is it true that old men turn to gardening? If so, it's a decent sort of retirement activity and our Surrey lot was ripe for it. What I knew about gardening wouldn't fill a thimble. My familiarity with the subject involved picking dandelion blossoms for wine.

I'd also collected foxglove seeds on the Queen Charlotte Islands and taken them back to Quebec. I'd sowed them in late summer. The first year white and purple flowers pushed out from their poker-stiff stalks. The next year my confidence was injured. Quebec's cold winters had "done my foxgloves in." But, Surrey's library straightened me out. My Queen Charlotte seeds were probably from the Common Foxglove, a biennial which shows leaves the first year, blossoms the next, and then dies.

Over the next five or six years I dug into the grass with pick, shovel, and mattock to develop a dozen individual garden plots. I dislike organized and structured gardens. I think more in terms of assisting nature to produce some random array of plants, a kind of arranged chaos.

It consumed three summers, but finally I finished a pond garden. It's roughly forty feet long, ten feet wide, and up to three feet deep. Every spring dozens of frogs serenade with their courtship. Danielle teaches the kindergarten level in Vancouver. I pack the frog's gelatinous egg clusters and emerging tadpoles into her classroom so the city kids can see these wiggling animals and get what is probably their first lesson in biology. After a few days I return the tadpoles to the pond. Towards the end of the school year I give the children another look so they can see the bulbous start of the body and the emergence of tiny legs.

The encompassing atmosphere of this neighbourhood supports frog ponds, raccoons, coyotes, possums, and birds by the bushel. It also contains a 127-acre jewel called Redwood Park. The setting here is more agricultural than residential, more rural than suburban.

During one of my visits to City Hall I was shocked to find that two areas within our neighbourhood had been set down as Future Urban. No one could explain what this meant or how it came about.

I got maps and plotted the boundaries of these Future Urban sites. One cut through Redwood Park. Another not only sliced through the property of our neighbours just across the street, it put their living room in the Future Urban section and their bathrooms in some other designation. We had to do something about it.

Julie and I arranged a meeting of our neighbours, set up the maps, and suggested we form a ratepayer's association to make representations to City Hall. And thus was born the Redwood Park Neighbours' Association (RPNA). I became Chairperson.

We got nowhere with the bureaucracy at City Hall so we bombarded the Mayor and Council Members with letters and personal contact for about a year. It worked. City Council voted unanimously to eliminate any reference to Future Urban. I don't think we would have succeeded had I not kept my former political life and my party membership private.

I'll never forget a chance encounter at a nearby White Rock restaurant. We sat at one of the two side-walk tables and struck up a conversation with another couple at the adjoining table. They were good-humoured, smiley, friendly. So were we. Two retired couples enjoying the sunshine and each other's company. It got to the inevitable. "What did you do?" asked the man. "Well, I was in politics for many years." The next question was, "Oh, that's interesting. Uh… what party?" When I told him I was NDP the sunshine stopped—the ice was up our ankles. They abruptly removed themselves. Not even a courtesy nod of "good bye."

When we arrived in Surrey we discovered that the provincial NDP had established a municipal branch in Surrey called Surrey Civic Electors (SCE). You had to be an NDP member to be a municipal SCE candidate; if you ran as an independent you could be drummed out of the Party. When the Redwood Park Neighbours' Association was formed there were three members of Surrey's nine-member council who were NDP/SCE members. The other six were anti-NDP. That kind of atmosphere demanded that RPNA not only be non-partisan, but that no hint of partisanship appear.

When my political background was revealed by the anti-NDP group on City Council two of RPNA'a active members told me they likely would not have participated had they known of it at the beginning. They appreciated that I had kept party politics out of the way.

In 1995 the City of Surrey undertook a complete review of land use (i. e. what could be built and where). The document which gave legal sanction to all this was called the Official Community Plan (OCP). Having been bitten by municipal politics I envisaged that we might get some neighbourhood benefit from this review.

For about a year and a half our association wrote letters, presented briefs, badgered councillors, pleaded with bureaucrats, and met until we were almost sick of seeing one another in a formal way. Our objective was to protect our neighbourhood's tranquil ambience. To achieve this we proposed that the OCP include a new category (officially a designation) called Rural. Within this Rural Designation we proposed that the land be used exclusively for single-family detached houses built on lots of not less than one acre. No gas stations, convenience stores, used-car lots, hamburger joints, or cemeteries.

We succeeded and, as far as I know, Surrey is the only municipality in B.C.'s lower mainland with such a land-use designation. We brought this off because members of the RPNA worked co-operatively and unstintingly for a common goal and the common good. We kept our neighbourhood a peaceful place for living, for raising a family, for retirement, for gardening, for whatever helps make life pleasant.

54

JULIENNE

Julie enjoyed gardening, especially in the spring of the year when life again shows its form and desire. In 1996, when daffodils were poking their life forms to the surface, Julie was diagnosed as having pancreatic cancer. The daffodils and all their cousins had to fend for themselves. For three years Julie fought and used her powerful determination to beat cancer into the ground. May 14, 1999 was twenty-five years and two months to the day from the day we were married. At about 10:25 in the evening Julie's life ended. She was at home with Danielle, Anthony, and me.

Her last words to me that evening were, "I think I'm going to die." I said, "Yes, I think so, my darling, but you'll always be alive in my heart and my head and in Danielle's and Tony's heads as well. We love you so much."

Danielle had brought her mother a candle holder made by Bill Rennie, a Vancouver artist. It's a unique sculpture. Danielle had put a candle in it, placed it on the mantlepiece in our bedroom and called it "The Candle of Hope." We replaced it when necessary and kept it lit all the time that Julie was alive. At her death, I snuffed it out. It will never again be lit.

Julie had a lovely little battery operated clock at her side of our bed. I removed the batteries at the same time that I had snuffed out the candle. It, too, will never be operative again.

Julie, when a young girl, would end her bed-time prayers asking that all animals in the world have good and comfortable lives. She always had that feeling about animals and respected them just as she respected humans. She disliked mosquitoes, but couldn't bring herself to swat one if it landed on her. She would just shoo it away.

Julie was cremated. In her will she asked that our three cats, when they died, be cremated and mixed with her cremated remains. These cats, a part of our family, received the same respect and affection which we extended to one another.

Yes, I cried over the fact that she is no longer here. I cried over the fact that she, like Robert, will miss so much of life, its glory, its magic, and its mysteries. I'm glad I feel about Robert and Julie the way I do. They will never be forgotten. Let me paraphrase Shakespeare:

And when I think of you, dear friends,

All losses are restored and sorrow ends.

55

IT JUST HAD TO BE

A few years of grieving and I had exhausted my need for seclusion. Aloneness degenerated into loneliness and I began to feel dissatisfied with my existence and my life. I had spurned all offers to console and assist me through the sorrowful period following Julie's death. The pressures in the orphanage and other institutions taught me not to rely on others for solace. I did not and could not look to anyone else for comfort. I had to do it myself; to be in charge of me and my adjustment. But, there was one exception.

Danielle, who had her own grief to handle, kept in touch. She phoned every night to ask if I was O.K. or if there was anything she could do. We often had dinner together. I hope I was of help to her as she was to me.

Some activities became almost ritualistic. I had three cats, one named Perky. In the evening before supper I would sit by the fireplace and work on that day's crossword puzzle. Perky would snuggle beside me, purring and dozing. I would have a glass of wine while struggling to find a six-letter word for cat. When the crossword had defeated me, or I it, I would make supper and eat in front of the television set watching junk and drinking more wine.

Each night I'd go through a bottle of wine. After a while I concluded this wasn't the way to go, especially when I awakened the next morning with a fuzzy head and a sour mouth. So, I limited myself to half a bottle and put the other half in the fridge for the next night. When the next night arrived I'd drink the remaining half and often gulp down another bottle. I was becoming an alcoholic and didn't like it a damned bit.

In White Rock there's a senior citizen's facility. I joined, thinking that I could strike up a friendship with some fellow widowers; yes, widowers, not widows. I had no interest in seeking a relationship with some strange woman simply for the purpose of companionship. Maybe some of these other lonely guys would enjoy digging around in the soil with me. Give them something to do.

I visited the senior's headquarters one day to see what was what. There was a well-stocked library. Good. Lots of books. But no people. A billiard room had two or three tables, all of them in use. When you have a cue in your hand you don't want to enter into idle chit chat with some stranger. I watched the players, thinking that, because of my misspent youth, I could easily beat any one of them.

Upstairs was a coffee shop and a large hall with a stage at one end. It was filled with elderly people playing bingo. Did I want to spend my years playing bingo? No! I left the building and never went back. I'd sooner do crossword puzzles with Perky than sit with a bunch of seniors numbed into silence while searching for numbers. At least Perky and I could communicate with each other.

I can't pin down why I'm attracted to one person rather than another. It may be that no one can sort that out and it may also be that no one should be able to. To me, it's much more romantic to have the mystery.

For a few months it was touch and go about trying to contact a woman whom I'd met many years ago. The feeling I had about her, which had lasted over the years, was not explainable; it just existed. If I tried to find her I would probably only be intruding into someone else's life. She could be a grandmother. Her husband, if he existed, would at least say, "What's going on here? Who is this guy?"

I saw her first in Masset on the Queen Charlotte Islands during one of the many federal and provincial election campaigns (I don't remember which one). She was standing in front of a hotel seemingly just taking in the sights.

It was impossible not to notice her. She had striking, vibrant features and a stance that exuded self-assurance. She was wearing a red sweater. She wore other clothing, but I don't recall what. The sight of her triggered what I consider the normal reaction of a male to a beautiful-looking woman.

Later that day I was in Port Clements (another community on the Islands). Most of that morning I'd been door-to-door canvassing and had stopped at the local cafe for a coffee and a snack. She was there, the only customer, sitting at a table with a notebook and a tape recorder in front of her. My immediate thought was: she's a reporter. That, to me, meant publicity.

I asked if I could join her. She agreed. We exchanged names. Hers was Joane Humphrey. Gesturing towards her accessories I asked something like, "You must be a reporter?"

"Not exactly," she said. "I do free-lance interviews and documentaries for the Canadian Broadcasting Corporation. My professional name is J.J. McColl."

While my head was mainly on publicity it also embraced the fact that she was sunny and easy to talk with. I enjoyed being with her. I asked if she had ever heard of the Queen Charlotte's "Golden Spruce." She hadn't.

The "Golden Spruce" is (or was until some idiot cut it down) an anomaly in the plant world—a Sitka Spruce whose needle-like leaves were golden or faintly yellowish rather than the normal green of such trees.

Access to the "Golden Spruce" was through what appeared to be an old-growth forest. It was a mystic and magical stroll, almost a journey through time. Thousand-year old trees reaching for sun and sky shaded the moss-covered and moldering heaps of those spruce which had lived their life and fallen. Helping her over logs and other forest debris was romantic. I felt at ease. I fantasized, but didn't flirt.

In our separate cars we drove southwards towards Queen Charlotte City, she to interview at Skidegate and I to continue with the campaign work. We stopped beside a bridge to say good bye. While there she noticed a tiny and delicate frog. I picked it up, put it in her hand and said something inane like, "Because of him you will always want to come back to the Charlottes."

By coincidence we were both going to be in Terrace at the same time. From there she was headed for Smithers. I offered to drive her from Terrace to Smithers and show her the Git'ksan village of 'Ksan at Hazelton. During the drive we talked about a diverse range of subjects. She was a joyous person, humorous and articulate. It was an enjoyable trip with neither of us offering any romantic hints.

Finally, in the fall of 2001, I screwed up my courage and tried to locate Joane by telephone. Success. The concerns I had about intruding into her life were unfounded. She was not a "granny" and, in fact, had never married. She'd travelled extensively and pursued a career in broadcasting and writing plays. Her most recent venture was writing and composing a musical, "Menopositive! The Musical", which was playing in theatres across the country.

We met again on October 27th, 2001 and she revealed that she had also often thought about me.

Two months later, on New Year's day of 2002, we became engaged. Neither of us could explain why we so quickly moved from friendship to marriage. We were amazed and warmed by the music of love. It was like an article of faith—it just had to be.

On June 22nd we were married at a wonderful out-of-doors ceremony on a beach at Hornby Island. In addition to the usual vows about loving, honouring, and cherishing each other we wanted something more, something unique, something exquisitely ours. We recited, in unison, what we had harvested from a Jewish marriage-ceremony vow located on the Internet.

Two brief extracts: We vowed "… *to establish a home open to all of life's potentials, a home filled with respect for all people, a home based on love, trust, respect, and understanding.* " and "*May we live each day as the first, the last, the only day we will have with each other.* "

We didn't exchange rings at the ceremony, we exchanged necklaces. Now, each morning we offer the other a necklace and ask, "Will you marry me?" Then, we place a necklace around the other's neck, hold the pendant and repeat the affirmation about this being *"the first, the last, the only day we will have with each other.* " At night we hold the necklaces clasped in both our hands and silently wish or pray for happiness and good health for the other. Then we place them on a little bronze frog, the first gift she gave when we met again.

EPILOGUE

While writing this autobiography a few important subjects were touched upon. But, they led to opinions and analyses more appropriately expressed outside of the chronological order of events and experiences. Hence, my following opinions.

THE JUSTICE SYSTEM

What to do about criminal behaviour? A couple of qualifiers need to be put in place first. Those who commit criminal acts but, because of mental disorders, are unable to distinguish between right and wrong need to be to be dealt with as mental patients and not as criminals per se. Drug addicts should not be classified as criminals either.

A number of people argue, figuratively, for a return of the rope, the lash, and the paddle. They say that the more intense the punishment, the more likelihood the criminal will cease and desist. This is a kind of conservative revenge, often put forward as being on behalf of victims. To those who hold this view it is sweet; almost an addiction. Law enforcement officers tend to support the conservative view, partly because they see the same faces again and again. One estimate is that 10% of criminals commit 60% of the crimes.

On the other side are those who say: let the punishment fit the individual. Their opinion is that human behaviour can be adjusted. It is this liberal view which has permeated our criminal justice system. Under it, judges have generally been free to punish a person convicted of a criminal offence by imposing a sentence ranging from probation to whatever the law says is the maximum penalty for the crime in question.

However, political decisions have placed certain restrictions on this ability of judges to sentence as they see fit.

For example, Chief Justice Allan McEachern of the B.C. Court of Appeal, quoted in the Vancouver Sun of October 6, 1999, referred to Canada's Criminal Code. The law of Canada, he said, demands that: "… all available sanctions other than imprisonment that are reasonable in the circumstances should be considered for all offenders…"

B.C.'s Supreme Court Justice Ross Colliver, quoted in the Vancouver Sun of January 4, 2001 cites a section of Canada's Criminal Code which says: "… a sentence should be similar to sentences imposed on similar offenders for similar offences committed in similar circumstances."

Judges are biased. They are, after all, only human and have had many environmental forces pushing them this way or that. They have opinions about matters like social justice which may vary from the norm. I guess the trick is for each judge to recognize what has happened to them and try to be objective.

This leads me to the opinion that additional limits should be placed upon the degree to which judges have freedom to sentence.

Attempts to manipulate the minds and attitudes of those who have committed criminal offences is a valuable pursuit, but it should be confined to first offenders. Give each person who commits a crime one chance to change. If there is a second offence, the sentence should not be adjustable by a judge. It should be severe for each type of crime and set down in law as an absolute.

Those who commit criminal offences should understand that the first time is the only time that leniency and counselling will be offered. At this stage there should be one objective in psychological treatment. That should be to have the person admit, and accept as fact, that he, and he alone, is responsible for his own behaviour.

Allowing the person to place the blame on some outside factor is merely supporting what that person already believes. Accepting the myth that aberrant behaviour is inherited or environmentally produced gives the criminal a way out. It provides an escape from reality; it shifts the burden of responsibility. Having no responsibility to self prevents any expectation that the criminal can be responsible to, or for, anyone or anything else.

Many who have engaged in criminal activities are indeed unstable, selfish, and self-centred. Any compassionate feelings about others are minimal at best. They have little or no regard for authority. They don't respect or appreciate the values of society.

RELIGION

I am not committed to believing that there is or is not some spiritual being called God. To declare for or against requires simply a firm belief about something which cannot be proven. As far as such beliefs are concerned, I lump the devout and the atheist in the same category: one believes there is, the other that there is not. Both claim their belief is actual knowledge. They "know." Such claims are, to me, the ultimate arrogance. The fact is they don't know. They only believe and, with respect to the devout, they hope.

Classify me as an agnostic if you wish. I don't put myself in that, or any other similar, category. Maybe it's intellectual laziness, but I don't think it matters. The purpose of human life surely should be to correct injustices. We are here and what counts is how we treat our fellow human beings and all other living organisms.

In the dim past, when our forebears were crouched in the wilderness, they must have been frightened by the cataclysmic convulsions of their world. There would be no rational or scientific explanations for phenomena such as lightning, thunder, hurricanes, floods, volcanic eruptions, or droughts.

Our ancestors must have gazed at the millions of tiny lights in the sky and wondered about them. They looked at the silvery and glowing moon and wondered about its changing shape and its face. At times this untouchable, iridescent display would disappear and be replaced by intense streaks of crackling lightning and the rumblings of thunder. Some of the more imaginative would have attributed an ultra-human dimension to these wondrous and out-of-reach marvels.

Some who pondered over these mysteries would, using their own existence and that of animals as guides, conclude that some unknown and invisible being was causing what is generally accepted now as nature's events. Gods were created in the minds of those with the greatest imagination. These gods, different ones for different purposes, were eventually replaced by one. I believe the voices which Abraham, Moses, and guys like John Smith are reputed to have heard were more likely the voices of their own imagination.

Religion, when it has concentrated on moral values, has done some good. Its concerns about the homeless and the poor and the disadvantaged are commendable. Some of its activities, such as the inhuman cruelties which took place during the Inquisition, are repulsive.

In my view, those who believe that God exists must surely conclude, during moments of sober and private contemplation, that He doesn't give a good goddamn what people do. The rascals get away with their villainous actions more often than they should; honest, law-abiding people get screwed. Humans, having created injustices, are the only ones able to correct them.

At my death, the 75% of my body which is water will evaporate into our atmosphere. It will mix with other molecules of water and pour down upon the world, assisting in giving nourishment to living organisms. The other 25% will see its molecules and atoms merge with other molecules and atoms, and will also assist in giving nourishment to living organisms.

My eyes no longer will behold the rose; my ears no longer catch the music of birds; the perfume of lilac and hyacinth will no longer enchant me; my heart will no longer beat. My time on earth will expire and the atoms of my body will join again with the atoms of all pre-existing life forms, moving together with them along that grand space called time. This after-death vision is much more attractive and sensible to me than the one which pictures us living forever either in idleness alongside some imagined presence or as shovelers of coal alongside some other imagined presence.

NISGA'A TREATY

Europeans who came to what is now Canada entered into treaties with the Aboriginal people who lived here. These, to me, were clearly agreements between governments; they acknowledge that Native sovereignty existed. One treaty extended from Alberta into the Peace River District of B.C. In the mid-1800s about a dozen agreements were reached transferring land from some Aboriginals on lower Vancouver Island to the Hudson's Bay Company. The Supreme Court of Canada subsequently decided that these transfers were treaties and were binding on the Government of Canada. There were no other treaties signed with Indigenous people in B.C.

The Nisga'a is a nation of Aboriginals living along the Nass River Valley in B.C. In the late 1800s the Nisga'a complained to the Provincial Government that their land was being arbitrarily taken from them. They pursued this matter relentlessly for over a hundred years.

In 1999 a treaty with the Nisga'a was reached and approved by the Legislature of B.C. and the Parliament of Canada.

Some critics of the Nisga'a Treaty object to setting up another level of government. We must remember that the Nisga'a had complete control of their government before the European came. Even though it wasn't in writing they had a constitution; they had government. England didn't have a written constitution either, but it had government.

Canada has part of its constitution in written form and part of it unwritten.

The Nisga'a Treaty gives the Nisga'a control over their own lives, their own potential, their own destiny.

Those who object that the Nisga'a Treaty is unconstitutional because it creates another level of government are blind to the fact that the Nisga'a originally had complete self-government. That complete self-government was taken from them. What the Treaty does is simply give part of it back.

The Nisga'a Treaty is racist and should be cancelled; so say others. My response? It has to be based on race. When Europeans came they brought racism with them. Racism was written into the BNA Act of 1867 and has been there ever since. Based on our constitution, Parliament enacted racist legislation—The Indian Act.

Europeans told the Aboriginal people that the land and all its resources were henceforth "to be ours, not yours." The resolution of conflicting demands for European control resulted in these lands becoming Crown land, a European concept.

As far as society was concerned racism was O.K. because it continued to dispossess Aboriginal people of their land. Racism was O.K. because it shunted them off onto concentration camps (euphemistically called reserves). Racism was O.K. because it kept Aboriginal people out of sight.

Because of this legalized racism, Aboriginal people have been placed on the defensive. At every stage they have had to prove they were here before the Europeans came. They have had to prove that they are human like the rest of us are human. Those who object to the treaty with the Nisga'a are still demanding that Aboriginal people prove their rights.

The Nisga'a Treaty and others which must follow have to be based on the fundamental rights of Aboriginal people. Only in that way will the societal pendulum be brought back to some mutually acceptable position which will attract and allow us to live together in harmony and respect.

Those who, for whatever reason, advocate scrapping the Nisga'a Treaty want society to return to the days when colonialism prevailed and Aboriginal people were kept on the sidelines of society.

Natives were "invisible", discriminated against and ignored for years. The Nisga'a Treaty and others will give them the chance to reclaim the dignity which was stolen from them.

INDEX

ISBN 1553690045-1